Death Space

The true story of a deaf serial killer at Gallaudet University

by

Dr. Teresa Crowe

©2022 Dr. Teresa Crowe
All rights reserved.

No part of this book may be reproduced in any form whatsoever, whether by graphic, visual, electronic, film, microfilm, tape recording, or any other means, without prior written permission of the author, except in the case of brief passages embodied in critical reviews and articles.

This is a work of fiction. The characters, names, incidents, places, and dialogue are products of the author's imagination, and are not to be construed as real. The views expressed within this work are the sole responsibility of the author and do not necessarily reflect the position of the publisher or any other entity.

ISBN# 979-8-218-01000-3

Cover design ©2022 by Mary Budnitz
Edited by Alena Orrison, alena.orrison@gmail.com

Printed in the United States of America.

In memory of James Mason (1954 - 2010) who gave me the support I needed to complete the book and the confidence to publish it

Table of Contents

Part 1: 2000

Chapter 1: A Campus Murder.......................... 1
Chapter 2: Coming to Gallaudet...................... 11
Chapter 3: The Young Man with the Big Smile....... 19
Chapter 4: A Long Way from Home................... 27
Chapter 5: Friends 37
Chapter 6: The Investigation 50
Chapter 7: A Frightened Campus Community......... 60
Chapter 8: A Break in the Case....................... 69
Chapter 9: A New Normal.............................. 81
Chapter 10: Coming Together…...…................... 91
Chapter 11: Cracks in the Group...................... 100
Chapter 12: A Much-Needed Break................... 106
Chapter 13: A New Beginning......................... 112
Chapter 14: Another Murder........................... 118
Chapter 15: Another Investigation.................... 126
Chapter 16: Here We Go Again....................... 133
Chapter 17: Connecting the Dots..................... 142
Chapter 18: The Confession........................... 150
Chapter 19: The Interrogation........................ 157
Chapter 20: A Surprise that was not a Surprise...... 167
Chapter 21: The Announcement...................... 179

Part Two: 2002

Chapter 22: Letters to Melani.......................... 187
Chapter 23: A Shadow Life 196
Chapter 24: A Serial Killer............................ 207
Chapter 25: Funny Feelings........................... 217
Chapter 26: A Continuum of Behavior................. 228
Chapter 27: Motion to Suppress Evidence............ 236
Chapter 28: Trial Day One............................ 241
Chapter 29: Trial Day Two, Morning.................. 252
Chapter 30: Trial Day Two, Afternoon................ 262
Chapter 31: Trial Day Three......................... 273
Chapter 32: Trial Day Four........................... 281
Chapter 33: Trial Day Five........................... 292
Chapter 34: Trial Day Six............................. 309
Chapter 35: Trial Days Seven and Eight............... 338
Chapter 36: Closing Argument........................ 351
Chapter 37: The Sentencing.......................... 361

Part Three: 2009

Chapter 38: Atwater Federal Penitentiary.............. 364
Chapter 39: My Life is Good.......................... 372
Chapter 40: Too Quick to be Believed................. 382
Chapter 41: My Prison World......................... 393
Chapter 42: A Stable Future.......................... 401
Chapter 43: An Unfolding, Continuous Loop of Time 411
Epilogue.. 419

Author's Note

In the fall of 2000 and after 13 years of professional practice as a social worker in the deaf community, I returned to my alma mater as a professor in the social work department at Gallaudet University. A few weeks into the semester, I arrived on campus to learn that a deaf freshman, named Eric Plunkett, had been found murdered in his dorm room. In February of the spring semester, Benjamin Varner's body had been found. After the investigation had concluded and the murderer arrested, I learned that one of my former social work students had been friends with the murderer. This raised many questions for me. Why didn't the murderer's friends know what he was doing? How were these attacks carried out in the small, insular, on-campus community at Gallaudet University? What did the killer's group of friends think once he had been arrested? What happened at the trial? Where were the killer and his friends now?

This book is the culmination of the answers to my questions. I had unique access to interviews with the group of deaf friends and the killer because I communicate fluently in American Sign Language (ASL). However, ASL is a visual, non-written form of communication. Thus, direct quotations from those interviews were transcribed and translated by me. Similarly, the 1000+ pages of court transcripts included court transcriptions recorded by a courtroom transcriber who typed what an interpreter translated into speech from the deaf individuals' ASL testimonies on the stand. In cases where court transcripts yielded stilted, grammatically incorrect language, I polished the sentence structure while maintaining the substantive content and context. In interviews with people who were hearing, I audio-recorded our sessions and transcribed them.

The deaf community is very small in comparison to the hearing community. The national and international deaf communities offer connections that are unique and have very few degrees of separation between deaf people. Because of this, individuals who had been friends with the killer preferred that I only use their first names, which I respected in this book.

I cannot imagine the pain that the families of Eric Plunkett and Benjamin Varner endured. Through the course of the investigations and trial, the families not only had to undergo the devastation of the losses of their loved ones but also the relentless pursuit by the media in this high-profile case. Therefore, I tread gently with the families. I reached out to both Eric's and Ben's family members to participate in interviews. Some family members of Eric Plunkett's family agreed to participate, while others preferred not. The family of Benjamin Varner did not respond to requests for interviews. My interviews with Joseph Mesa occurred while he was imprisoned in Atwater Federal Penitentiary in California.

I interviewed Dr. Jane Fernandes, the former provost of Gallaudet University. I met with Jennifer Collins, the former prosecutor on this case. I interviewed Dr. Robert Poallard, the forensic deaf expert after obtaining written consent from Joseph Mesa. I attempted to interview police detective, Pamela Reed, but the Varner family had not given her permission to talk with me. I met with a Baltimore County homicide detective to understand how homicide investigations were processed. I interviewed the former public relations director at Gallaudet University, Mercy Coogan, who provided me with internal PR documents, such as press releases and speeches for the university president and provost, from the time of the murders and investigations.

I accessed video recordings of the vigils and student gatherings through an archived video collection at Gallaudet University. I watched recordings and read articles from news outlets. What could not be obtained through direct interviews, was accessed from court transcripts, court reports, police reports and affidavits, arrest reports, appeals court records, transcripts of depositions, autopsy reports, crime scene sketches, and crime scene photographs.

Part One: 2000

Chapter 1
A Campus Murder

On Thursday night, September 28, 2000, 9-1-1 dispatchers received a report from an officer at the Department of Safety and Security (DOSS) at Gallaudet University that one of its students lay injured in his dormitory room. They dispatched officers from the fifth precinct of Washington, D. C. Metropolitan Police Department (MPD), only two miles away. Police cars flashing red and blue lights entered the campus through the front gate on Florida Avenue. The DOSS officer standing at the campus security gatehouse directed them around the campus loop toward the opposite end to Cogswell Hall. They needed to get to the west wing men's hall, specifically to room number 101, as fast as possible.

By the time students, faculty, and staff arrived on

campus on Friday morning, September 29, police officers, detectives, campus police, and news reporters inundated Gallaudet University. While personnel from the coroner's office and police detectives processed the crime scene, excited reporters on campus scrambled to conduct interviews. The reporters circled the large group of Gallaudet students, faculty, and staff gathered in front of Cogswell Hall in search of prey. However, they soon realized that they were unprepared for the capture.

They climbed atop concrete posts to shout at the large crowd. "Can anyone hear me?" one yelled. "Hey! Can someone hear me?" asked another. No response.

The reporters, microphones in hand, and camera crews swam among the crowd searching for someone, anyone who would give an interview. They stared, transfixed by the flicking hand-shapes and the exaggerated facial expressions of the surrounding people. Everyone around the news reporters used American Sign Language. They surely had realized that Gallaudet University was a college for deaf people. After all, the university is a historical landmark. Yet, they came unprepared. Without sign language interpreters, the reporters were unlikely to capture the reactions and perspectives of the campus community. They would most certainly not record direct quotes, at least not at that particular moment. Inevitably, after realizing their mistake, they arranged for interpreters to meet them on campus. Later that day, the police released the name of the victim, Eric Plunkett, a freshman at Gallaudet. The police planned to investigate the case as a homicide.

The administrators at Gallaudet University made their staff ASL interpreters available for investigators, campus town hall meetings, and media interviews. Within two days of Eric Plunkett's death, newspaper reporters and television media interviewers from twenty-three different outlets descended upon the campus en masse. However, that was only the beginning. News of Eric Plunkett's murder instantaneously circled the globe and reached the eyes of deaf individuals and communities everywhere. The general public took interest as well. The homicide of a deaf freshman on the grounds of Gallaudet University made national and international headlines.

The discovery of Eric's body caused fear and unrest throughout the campus. The attack seemed brazen. Not much happened without the scrutiny of others in the small, close-knit campus community. Everyone knew everyone else's business, or they thought they did, until now. The media bombarded anyone and everyone for interviews, which exacerbated the anxiety and fear on campus. Police officers, DOSS officers, and other investigators called for investigative interviews. Chaos ensued as all the outsiders demanded more information about the homicide.

While reporters and investigators scoured the campus community, the administrators at Gallaudet University set up a crisis management team to work with police, manage the public relations nightmare, and host community meetings. Dr. Jane Fernandes, Gallaudet's Provost, led the group along with staff from Gallaudet's Mental Health Center, Student Life, Public Relations, DOSS, and the Commander from the Metropolitan Police Department (MPD) Fifth District, Commander Jennifer Greene of the MPD fifth district. This coordinated team would work together to manage the crisis, keep fears and unrest at bay, and, hopefully, lead to the successful arrest of the killer.

Students were tired of the swarming media presence on campus. They feared the killer would murder another student. In the midst of all this, students were still taking classes. After all, students, staff, and faculty expected Gallaudet University to continue with daily operations. Dr. Fernandes added community campus meetings to offer students updates for information and opportunities for questions.

During a campus meeting early in October, one student stood in the audience and signed to Commander Greene, "Why has the media had open access to the campus? How can this be stopped? They interview any student. They pursue every student. How can this be controlled?"

She responded, "The media has a job to do. We understand that their role is to report information. Nobody at this university will force you to stand before a television camera or talk to a reporter and discuss this situation."

Fear gave rise to different theories about the murder. One popular idea was that a person outside the campus, obviously a hearing person, had come inside the campus fence, sneaked into the dormitory, and killed Eric. The administrators and DOSS seemingly agreed because they soon enhanced security measures. Officers worked double shifts and restricted access to dorms. Gates leading onto campus were closed, leaving access only through a guarded front gate. No one was going to breach the campus without someone knowing.

Another student asked about the campus lockdown. The director of DOSS, Bernie Holt, responded, "We know students have a lot of concerns about accessibility to dorms, about the dorms being locked, and limited hours. We're doing this because we're trying to take precautions to make it harder for people to go into the dorms who shouldn't be there. Students on campus don't feel comfortable right now. The MPD doesn't share their information with me or any other administrator. We know what you all know. What we know is that it's a homicide investigation."

Another theory about the underlying reasons for the murder surfaced among students. The student body had elected Eric Plunkett as a new student officer to Gallaudet's Lambda Society, an organization for gay and lesbian students. After the police announcement of Eric's murder, many gay and lesbian students awoke horrified to find threatening notes indicating "you are next" taped onto their dormitory doors and hung in random places around campus. They feared that Eric's murder was a hate crime committed by someone or some group with a homophobic vendetta.

However, detectives found this theory unlikely. They decided to investigate the case as a homicide rather than a hate crime. In response, the National Gay and Lesbian Activists Alliance attended a meeting hosted by the Human Rights Campaign to discuss the Gallaudet students' concerns. Gay and lesbian students told those in attendance that they were fearful in the aftermath of Eric Plunkett's murder. They complained that Gallaudet historically did not forward gay-related harassment complaints to the MPD, fifth district. Though MPD had a Gay and Lesbian Liaison Unit (GLLU) at their headquarters, there was no way for deaf students to complain directly to police because there was no telecommunication device for the deaf (TTY). As a result of the discussion, the Gay and Lesbian Activists Alliance purchased two TTY machines and delivered them to the fifth district.

    The local and national gay community organizations voiced upset with the administrators at Gallaudet. They claimed the university was not protecting its LGBT members. Their concerns were justified. Gallaudet's first deaf president, I. King Jordan, later addressed the concerns publicly. In a letter written to the editor of The Washington Post titled "At Gallaudet, We're Facing Up to Our Failings," Dr. Jordan acknowledged that gay and lesbian students on campus were continuing to experience discrimination and ostracization. He described the experiences of discrimination that many deaf and hard-of-hearing people face. In recognizing the diversity and richness within the deaf community, it must reject bigotry and hate. Dr. Jordan wrote, "If we allow some people to be treated unfairly because of who they are, on what ground do we stand when we defend our rights and our position?"

***

On Friday, September 29, 2000, Eric's mother, stepfather, and sisters flew from Minnesota to Reagan National Airport, the closest one to Gallaudet. The distraught family's first stop was at MPD's fifth district for questioning. They then rode two miles to the on-campus Kellogg Hotel, where they met with administrators from Gallaudet. Chris Cornils, Eric's stepfather, went to the D.C. morgue to identify Eric's body. That evening, two students, Joseph Mesa and Melani DeGuzman, said they were friends of Eric and asked family members to sign a poster created as a tribute to him. The study body was planning an informal student vigil for another evening. That night and into the early hours of the following day, Mrs. Cornils, Eric's mother, had written a letter to the campus community on letterhead from the Mental Health Center. She hand-delivered it to Gallaudet's president. I. King Jordan read the letter to the campus community later that day.

Back on campus, mayhem, misinformation, and

speculation fueled rumors and fear. Mental Health Services offered counseling sessions to students to help manage the distress, distrust, and grief of the murder and the frustration and fear of an uncaught killer. They offered walk-in services, support groups, and individual sessions to students in their dormitories. Specially trained counselors reached out to those closest to Eric and those who identified as gay and lesbian.

At one campus community meeting, a news reporter asked, "Did witnesses indicate that they heard a struggle?"

Chief Ramsey responded, "You have to remember that this is a school for the hearing impaired. That adds to the complexity of the case. Maybe some felt vibrations or saw something, or even heard something. We're trying to determine that. We have to reconstruct the victim's movement."

The director of the Mental Health Center described Gallaudet as the "Mecca of the Deaf Community," but now it was a place of unrest and trepidation. The murder of a deaf student thrust this place of comfort and belonging into a different light, and the killer remained at large. Reporters flooded the campus. Police investigators worked the crime scene and set up a command post. Detectives called students, faculty, administrators, and staff for interviews.

Eric's family and friends were grieving while simultaneously battling news-hungry press. Students, especially those living in the dormitories, wanted to know if they were safe. Everyone wanted answers. Who would want to kill a deaf college student, and why?

Chapter 2
Coming To Gallaudet

Gallaudet University is a historic landmark on ninety-nine acres of land in the northeast quadrant of Washington, D.C. Abraham Lincoln penned it into existence in 1864 as an educational institution for twelve deaf and six blind students. In 1856, Gallaudet was a small school and dormitory on only two acres of land donated by Amos Kendall, the postmaster general. Originally called the Columbia Institution for the Instruction of Deaf and Dumb and Blind, its name changed in 1894 to Gallaudet College in honor of Thomas Hopkins Gallaudet.

After traveling to Europe and learning about a form of manually signed communication from the French Royal Institute for the Deaf director, Abbe Sicard, in Paris, France, Thomas Hopkins Gallaudet returned to the United

States. In 1817, he and Laurent Clerc founded the American Asylum for Deaf-Mutes in Connecticut, the first American school for the deaf. Laurent Clerc became the first deaf teacher of deaf students in the United States. Thomas Hopkins Gallaudet's son, Edward Miner Gallaudet, later became the new Columbia Institution for the Instruction of Deaf and Dumb and Blind's first superintendent.

When Abraham Lincoln signed the legislation that created Gallaudet College in 1864, he appointed Edward Miner Gallaudet president. The first commencement ceremony for three deaf students occurred in June 1869, their diplomas signed by President Ulysses S. Grant.

In 1954, Gallaudet College integrated the educational centers for deaf children as part of the institutional structure. In 1986, Gallaudet was granted university status and was known as Gallaudet University ever since. The grounds expanded to ninety-nine acres, which are now home to Gallaudet University, the Kendall Demonstration Elementary School, and the Model Secondary School for the Deaf.

Gallaudet University offers deaf, hard of hearing, and hearing students opportunities to obtain bachelor's, master's, and doctoral degrees in a wide range of majors.

Gallaudet University is now known as the only higher educational institution for deaf and hard-of-hearing students globally. It is considered a cultural and social hub for Deaf communities, both nationally and internationally.

On August 27, 2000, Eric Plunkett joined 344 other deaf first-year students and 976 deaf upperclassmen to pursue their dreams of obtaining college degrees en route to their lifetime careers. Like many who came before, their cohort included deaf students from all over the world. All came to Gallaudet to study, socialize, and live in an environment where sign language is the norm. The vast majority of deaf students were born to hearing families, meaning that their relatives could hear and speak. Gallaudet's world was the inverse of what many had experienced until the point of arrival. This world was designed specifically for deaf people. Here, students could reject stereotypes that labeled them disabled and, therefore, unlikely to achieve success. This world welcomed them to participate in any activity as much or as little as they desired.

Gallaudet University is where hands, faces, and bodies express language rather than ears and mouths. Everyone in the campus community, from professors to campus police to librarians to cafeteria workers, uses

American Sign Language (ASL). Residential advisers, counselors, administrators, even the university's president, and many others use ASL. ASL and other variations of sign languages convert the tones and cadences of speech into facial expressions. Whispers of secrets translate into a forward lean of the shoulders, a duck of the head, a fast sweep of the eyes to make sure no one is watching, and then the flick of fingers and facial expressions to convey its message. Bursts of anger or frustration spring forth in the flash of the eyes, a scrunching of facial features, and the abrupt, rhythmic speed of the signs. All emotions, from disgust to joy to excitement to sadness to contentment, reveal themselves on the body. Cues can be subtle or overt. The curled lips, widened eyelids, toe bouncing, shoulder rolls, or face stillness convey important messages. Eavesdropping can be achieved from yards away, simply by having your eyes scroll across the visual space and lock onto a signed conversation. Full-out staring is considered rude, so the subtle visual pass-over is essential to snoop successfully. You should delay telling secrets until you are in an enclosed and private space where no one can see.

    Coming to Gallaudet is like jumping into a cool swimming pool on a stifling, hot day. The larger world is one where daily living is stuffed with hearing people who take the privilege and accessibility that their speech and auditory ability offers for granted. Most deaf people live in this world, where only a fraction of the English language can be understandable on the lips. The lips, those crafty tools, make it hard to understand whether the coworker says, "You have talent" or "You have a salad." Does the waiter ask, "Do you want peas?" or "Do you want beets?" Does the hiring employer say, "You get paid $15 an hour" or "You get paid $50 an hour."

It is exhausting to study and stare at a person's lips and guess at understanding what they say. There is no need for this at Gallaudet. You get your identification card, dormitory assignment, class lectures, library books, and meals from people who can sign to you. There is no more guessing or feeling left out of conversations. There is no more explaining that you are better qualified for a job than another hearing applicant. No. Gallaudet is like no other place in the world. The community is a world designed for deaf people. It is a place where deaf people, no matter their countries or states of origin, become threads woven into a vibrant, textured fabric. In the outside world, many share experiences of exclusion, inaccessibility, and invisibility. In Gallaudet's world, they can become who they were born to be.

Gallaudet University recognizes that Deaf spaces, architectural spaces that support and empower visual learners, are essential to creating an inclusive and accessible environment. Deaf spaces include clear sightlines so everyone can participate in conversations. They have adjustments to lighting and seating so that watching visual conversations is less cumbersome. It optimizes the sensory impact of physical structure often overlooked by the larger hearing society. Deaf-centered designs include careful consideration of spatial features and physical proximity, allowing deaf people to optimize the distance needed to see and interpret facial expressions. It helps a deaf person to maintain an appropriate signing space for an easy flow of communication.

Deaf students, faculty, and staff who come to Gallaudet may look different, sign different, and come from different familial and cultural backgrounds. They may have different life experiences and cultural customs. However, when they come to campus, they enter a world created for them. There, they can feel like they are genuinely part of a community that recognizes and embraces their experiences, needs, and values.

Friendships at Gallaudet form fast and are often lifelong. From the moment they enter its world, they see what a deaf world looks like in physical form. Deaf people live, study, socialize, and work together in one geographic space. They are not likely not to experience this unique environment outside of the university. They are on equal footing, a level playing field, for competitive on-campus jobs, scholarships, opportunities, and choices. In this world, they have access to signing individuals in all of their life domains, including education, housing, employment, health care, religious services, campus security, social events, and meal gatherings. Though the Victorian Gothic buildings that dot the campus remind them of a painful past when deaf people were labeled not only as deaf but also dumb, contemporary Gallaudet opens its arms and whispers, *I see you*, and then brings them into the fold.

This is why Eric Plunkett came to Gallaudet. He wanted to be a part of a new world, one that would not only accept him as a deaf person but would elevate him as an equal with others around him. When Eric first arrived at Gallaudet, he found immediate friendships. Though his friends were deaf like him, they came from different parts of the world and brought new ideas, perspectives, and beliefs. Like him, they had plans for their lives. They would become teachers, writers, biologists, social workers, business managers, and anything else they desired.

One of Eric's first friendships began when he met Joseph Mesa, JJ, as his friends called him, and his girlfriend, Melani, at the new student orientation. They shared stories of where they came from, what they liked to do, and plans for their future careers. Then later, to their surprise and pleasure, Eric and JJ learned they lived across the hall from each other in Cogswell Hall.

Chapter 3
The Young Man With The Big Smile

I felt there was something very inspiring about him (Eric). He would smile and seemed very down to earth. When I saw him go to class every day, I'd feel sparkles. Other friends said the same thing.

—a fellow student at an informal gathering outside of Cogswell Hall, 2000.

"Eric was born a happy baby. He came out smiling," said his father, Craig Plunkett. In the many tributes and memories shared about Eric by his family, childhood friends, and college friends, Eric's big smile was one of his many beloved attributes. Eric exuded warmth and welcome to everyone he met. His gregarious nature extended to not only family and friends but also strangers. Indeed, Eric was a happy child and a happy young man. Despite the challenges in his life, Eric found a way to keep a positive attitude and openness about life. Cerebral palsy has marked Eric's life since birth. Even as a young child, he was burdened with multiple doctors' visits, but that did not slow Eric down.

"Eric used leg braces to walk until he was about five years old," Eric's father recalled. "I remember carrying him on my shoulders. After two operations when he was six and fourteen, Eric could finally walk on his own."

Eric's mother had contracted rubella while pregnant. As a result, infants born to mothers with rubella can manifest many syndromic symptoms. Babies can be born deaf and/or blind and may have additional physical conditions, developmental delays, and mental health issues. Doctors designate these constellations of symptoms as congenital rubella syndrome.

When Eric's parents learned he was deaf, they learned to use sign language to communicate with their son. His parents' willingness to learn sign language separated Eric from most parents with deaf children who never do. Their ability to communicate with Eric as an early child most likely shaped Eric's positive outlook on life. It provided stability and grounding that would enable him to dream of a successful future.

"Eric was very independent. He was always like that. He'd literally wear you out just being so curious," Craig Plunkett recalled. "He was probably four or five when we first got him into school. I don't know if we were doing an IEP (individualized education plan), but we were talking with the teacher. He was roaming around. Eric went to the drinking fountain; he had that thing pulled apart. I told her this kid would take everything apart. He was curious to see how everything worked." Mr. Plunkett's face softened at the memory. Suddenly, he formed a smile.

"One day, I couldn't find Eric. He had walked five blocks to the mall to go to the movies. He went to the movies a lot. One afternoon, I went to the theater to find him. The man who worked there told me that he was in theater number five. I walked in and told Eric, 'You're not going to the movie. We're going back home!' Eric said, 'Dad! Dad! I want to watch the movie!' If Eric wanted to do something, poof! He was gone."

Eric's independent and curious nature was a source of pride and achievement and caused worry for his father. "I would tell him that there are some very bad people in the world, but Eric said he wasn't worried. He said he could fight them. I tried to tell him that someone could get to him. One time I was about thirty or forty feet behind Eric as we were walking home from the mall. There was this guy following him. I ran up to Eric, which made the other guy veer off. I asked Eric if he realized that someone was following him. He said, 'Oh no, Dad. No one was following me.' This was when Eric was about sixteen or seventeen years old. That was really scary. He was so trusting of everyone."

To Eric's childhood friends and family in Oregon and Minnesota, Eric was the boy who loved coffee, theme parks, Chip and Dale Disney characters, horror movies, Benihana-style Japanese restaurants, and traveling. Eric owned an extensive DVD collection that included 300-plus titles, which he brought to Gallaudet.

From a young age, Eric traveled all over the United States. Mr. Plunkett recalled, "Eric loved to spend time with his cousins in the Los Angeles area. He traveled all over the country when he was a teenager because Chris Cornils' father was an executive for the radio industry. They would have conventions all over the United States. So, Eric would go with Chris or he would travel by himself. [Eric's mother and stepfather] would put him on a plane, and he'd go to a city. Chris' father would pick him up and take him to the convention center. Eric would greet people at the conference registration. He would have on his red jacket. He had no problem getting on a plane and going to Atlanta by himself."

Even in unexpected circumstances, Eric seemed to adapt and thrive. His father explained, "One of the times he traveled, the plane he was on was diverted to Seattle instead of Portland. Eric didn't realize that he was going somewhere else. Yet, he knew that the timing of the flight was off. There was a lady across the aisle who could fingerspell. So, the lady signed to him what was going on. In the meantime, my wife and I got word that the flight was going to Seattle instead of coming home. The lady's husband was a pastor from Vancouver. They said they offered to rent a car and drive Eric down with them. They brought him to the airport here in Portland."

Eric seemed to bring out the good in people around him. He elicited friendliness and assistance when he most needed it. Though hearing people sometimes view deaf people with pity, Eric and his family did not see it the same way. For Eric, his physical challenges and deafness were a part of him. He found ways to overcome limitations and barriers. His smile and happy spirit brought people toward him. His slight build coupled with the physical challenges from cerebral palsy only served to strengthen his resolve. He learned to face his trials with fortitude, courage, and resilience.

His father remembered a time when Eric was about four years old. "The doctor gave us a handicapped placard because Eric had so many doctor appointments. I thought it was great. Eric started asking questions about the handicapped card. Eric said, 'I'm not handicapped! I'm not handicapped!' He wanted to be normal. He wanted to be thought of as just a normal kid. He ripped off the card and wouldn't let us use it. He wouldn't be labeled."

Eric's family fostered his sense of adventure, independence, and confidence from an early age. Eric learned he was capable of achieving his dreams. When Eric was four, he wore a tiny helmet, leather jacket, boots, and sunglasses purchased by his father. Bungeed to his father's chest, he motorcycled through the mountains and along the coast of Oregon. The father/son pair felt the swoosh of air on their faces, the expansiveness of the open road, and the exhilaration of being alive.

Eric's love of Chip and Dale began with a childhood trip to Disneyland in Los Angeles, California, with his mother and father. There, in front of the Haunted

House, Chip and Dale stood greeting visitors. When Eric ran to greet them, they used sign language with him despite their mittened hands. Eric, Chip, and Dale communicated with each other in sign language as onlookers gathered around them. When other children tried to approach the characters, their parents held them back so the young deaf boy could have his moment with them. From that moment, Eric, thinking that all Chip and Dale characters could sign, amassed an extensive memorabilia collection.

"The world was his," Mr. Plunkett whispered.

Eric grew into a handsome young man. In pictures with his friends and family, Eric's happiness and joy radiated through the smile on his face. He was not one to smile small. In photos, the twinkle reached his eyes; his lips parted to reveal perfectly aligned white teeth. Eric's smile was contagious. It was as if all that was good in life became a portrait upon Eric's happy face. In his high school graduation picture from the Minnesota State Academy for the Deaf in 2000, his eyes sparkled with delight. He wore a royal blue graduation robe, his father's arm wrapped tightly around his shoulders. His smile revealed it all; there was no stopping him now. To see Eric's smiles in pictures, one cannot help but smile too.

He had received his acceptance letter to Gallaudet

University by the time he graduated from high school. One of Eric's friends recalled, "He was VERY happy to be there. I was with him when he graduated from the Minnesota State Academy. Eric said to me on graduation day, 'You know what? I was just accepted to Gallaudet University!' I congratulated him big time. He was a wonderful person. There was never anyone like him."

    Once Eric arrived at Gallaudet in August 2000, he moved into his dorm room number 101 at Cogswell Hall. New student orientation started the week before classes began. It was there he met many friends, all deaf freshmen like himself. Eric's adult life was just beginning. He had left the comfort of the familiar to embark on a new journey into a world not yet known to him. However, this world was one with hundreds of other deaf students like him, a place where he would develop his own deaf identity and live among people like him, his own deaf community. He would see that the deaf world had a place reserved especially for him. His deaf friends and experiences in the culture of the deaf would catapult him into a new adventure, one that would be life-altering. At the start, he made two new friends, JJ and Melani.

Chapter 4
A Long Way From Home

When I'd fly home from MSSD (high school) to see my parents, I'd only fly first class. I used a platinum credit card with unlimited spending. I've never flown coach in my life.

—JJ

JJ and his girlfriend, Melani, both grew up on the U.S. territory island of Guam. "I was raised on a ranch on a mountain top called Yago. We liked to eat fresh meat, which is a part of Chamorro culture. So, I used to kill the chickens; my father killed wild pigs," JJ said.

JJ and his family consider themselves both Chamorro and Catholic, not an unusual blend of cultures for the home area. Chamorro is the indigenous culture of people from the Mariana Islands, which includes Guam. Chamorro people believe in the power of ancient ancestors, spirits, called Tao-Tao, and cultural healers. JJ integrated the religious beliefs of the Catholic church into the indigenous Chamorro culture as the center point of his childhood. JJ's parents were the most influential people in his life.

    JJ is the third oldest out of four children from Joseph Mesa, Sr., and his wife, Grace. Josephine is the oldest, followed by Joella, then JJ. Patrick is the youngest sibling. Mr. and Mrs. Mesa, Sr. suspected something was wrong with their third child when he was about four months old. Unlike his siblings, JJ did not respond to sound cues. They took him to multiple doctors' appointments to find out the problem, which led to hearing tests. A little over a year later, doctors diagnosed JJ as being profoundly deaf. He wore hearing aids, but his deafness was so extreme they did not help. His parents later brought him to Los Angeles, California, for an evaluation for cochlear implantation, a surgical procedure to implant a mechanical device deep in the inner ear. However, the physicians warned of additional potential risks if JJ underwent surgery. They decided to wait until JJ was old enough to make that decision on his own.

JJ grew up under the strict family rules of his father, a career U.S. Army military supply systems analyst.

Mr. Mesa explained, "[As a child], JJ didn't go out. I didn't allow any of my kids to go out [alone]. When they go out, we all go out as a family. There are chores for the kids when they get home from school. When they misbehave or get out of line, I talk to them first and tell them what I am going to do. I spank them, whip them. Then after that, we sit down and talk again. We talk about what just happened and if they understand. That's the way we were brought up back on the island."

JJ was not a perfect child, but he showed deference and respect to his family, especially his father. Still, there were communication difficulties. Neither of JJ's parents signed fluently. The lack of communication sometimes led to misunderstandings. Mr. Mesa explained, "I'd ask him to do things, you know, before I got home. If when I got home from work, it wasn't the way I wanted it done, I got upset. He would come back and ask me why I was upset. I would tell him that I didn't like how he did things. Then he'd say, 'Please, please. You need to look at me. Face me. Sign. Tell me what you want so that I can understand you. You know you tell me things, but as you tell me things, you turn your face, and I can't see what you're saying. So, I'm sorry that I didn't do what you asked me to do. Let me go ahead and do it again.'"

Mr. Mesa was a stern disciplinarian to all his children. "There were a lot of times JJ was whipped. If a stick was right there, that's what he'd get whipped with. If we used a belt, we'd bring him inside the house [to get it]. If we're outside, it would be a piece of wood. It could be a garden hose. If we were in the jungle, I'd break a branch and then whip them out there. That's the way we were brought up back on the island."

Yet despite the rigidity with which Mr. Mesa oversaw his family, all the members felt close and connected. They ate meals together and conversed for hours. They enjoyed spending time together and learning about each other's days. Family conversations often left JJ out, JJ, though; no one signed fluently. The lack of communication frustrated JJ. He perceived their unwillingness to learn to sign as a cue that he was unimportant. JJ lacked full involvement in the family's conversations and activities. He caught bits and pieces of information and read the body language of his family members. He scrutinized the facial expressions and mannerisms for understanding and clarity. His comprehension frequently fell short.

Mr. Mesa explained, "Coming home from work, sometimes we'd all find ourselves sitting down talking. We'd talk about what happened at work, what happened at school. Well, JJ was totally different. For him, those things never occurred. Sometimes the family would play basketball or volleyball, laughing and joking with each other, patting each other on the backs. JJ wouldn't understand. All of a sudden, he would just punch the ball in a different direction, like it wasn't a game. Sometimes he would leave and look for a quiet space at home. Sometimes he would just sit right underneath the coconut tree and watch the animals."

As JJ got older, his behavioral problems at home and school escalated. Teachers and classmates reported thefts. JJ started to perform poorly in school. Mr. Mesa was also unhappy with the educational system. The educational system for deaf children in Guam was vastly different than those in the mainland United States.

"We don't have deaf schools back home [in Guam]. There are only two places on the island where we can send our kids. One is the elementary/middle school, and the other is the high school. The hearing-impaired kids are mainstreamed with hearing children in regular classrooms," said Mr. Mesa.

JJ's father worried that JJ's academics lagged behind the other hearing children at school. Because the school was ill-equipped to educate deaf children effectively, Mr. Mesa was concerned that his son would fall increasingly behind. As a result, JJ's parents went to the United States to explore other educational options. They knew that other schools for deaf children used different methods than those used in Guam. They wondered if they placed JJ in a school that specialized in deaf education, he would succeed. It made sense to them. If JJ could interact with his teachers and classmates fully because everyone would use sign language, he might have a better quality of life. He might feel more connected to people. JJ might have a chance for a full and happy life as an adult.

Mr. and Mrs. Mesa thought about deaf schools in California and Hawaii, much closer to home. Dr. Jane Fernandes and an educational team from Gallaudet flew to Hawaii and then to Guam to train families and educators about the deaf community. JJ attended one of those sessions.

Dr. Fernandes recalled, "JJ was a cute deaf kid who signed. Guam's [school system] couldn't give JJ enough support. JJ's parents wanted to do good for him, but they didn't have the resources in Guam."

In the fall of 1995, when JJ was sixteen years old, Mr. and Mrs. Mesa transferred JJ to the Model Secondary School for the Deaf. MSSD is one of the premier high schools for deaf and hard-of-hearing students in Washington, D.C. JJ's parents anticipated that he would blossom in this deaf environment. JJ would finally have access to a good education and a social life with his peers, something he lacked in Guam. At MSSD, JJ's grade point average was mediocre, around 2.5. However, considering his low starting point, he was improving academically. Unfortunately, behavioral problems manifested shortly after he arrived.

Dr. Madsen, a psychologist, said, "There were reports [from MSSD] that something was happening there. For example, he was disciplined for having punched his hand into the wall and caused damage. That was in October of his first year. He was also disciplined for having an altercation with another student. He was disciplined for having caused another student to get angry. JJ said to me that he didn't feel like he was fitting in very well."

The psychologist's assessment was accurate; JJ missed his home. He missed his family, the food, and being around others in the Chamorro culture. Mr. and Mrs. Mesa struggled with the decision of whether JJ should remain at MSSD. JJ was homesick, but he was also improving academically. He had friends. He functioned well in the deaf environment. They decided to keep their son in school there with frequent flights home to visit. JJ persevered and graduated from MSSD.

He then applied for admission to Gallaudet University, located on the same campus as MSSD. Though he performed well in other subjects, such as math and science, his reading level tested at Grade 2.7, which did not qualify him for admission to the university. Instead, the admissions team recommended he enroll in the English Language Institute (ELI) on campus to improve his academic skills for preparation for Gallaudet University. There, JJ would focus on English and reading mastery. Once achieved, his chances of success would be better.

As in MSSD, JJ struggled at ELI; his anger and destructive behaviors escalated. He stole money, credit cards, and a computer from his classmates. When administrators caught JJ stealing money from a classmate, Carl Pramuk, the dean of ELI, suspended him for two years and required him to pay a restitution of $3000. JJ returned to Guam and got a job to save money.

Dr. Madsen explained, "When JJ was frustrated,

when he was angry, when he was upset, when things weren't going the way he wants, he started acting out, started doing things. JJ was a boy growing up developmentally and socially backward, dramatically so... not a little, a lot. Developmentally not reaching milestones, socially not reaching milestones. His academic deficiencies may not be atypical for those who are deaf, but they distressed him and knocked him out of what he wanted to do his whole life. The period of remedial efforts, not wanting to be where he was, fantasizing about going home, he gets involved in all of this property crime."

After the first year of suspension, JJ wrote a letter of apology to the administrators at Gallaudet. Dr. Fernandes recalled when Carl Pramuk asked for JJ's reinstatement, "Carl said that JJ had worked in Guam and earned the money to pay back the Gallaudet student. He wrote that he was ready to resume his education. At Gallaudet, this is what we do. Carl told him to come back [to ELI]."

JJ returned to ELI and completed his courses, then reapplied for admission to Gallaudet University. This time, he was accepted. His college admission coincided with the admission of his childhood friend and romantic partner, Melani DeGuzman. JJ had planned to start his time at

Gallaudet differently. With Melani by his side, he would feel confident and avoid the problems that plagued him at MSSD. Together, JJ and Melani would achieve their dreams along with a whole community of other deaf students.

By all measures, the beginning of the semester was going as expected. Classes, social time, campus activities, and new experiences filled their lives. A group of friends formed, each member coming from different parts of the world. The group found comfort from one another as they faced exciting and uncertain times.

Chapter 5
Friends

We would all go to the mall and have fun. JJ and Melani came home with me for Thanksgiving. They met my family and had a good time. One time we had a party in the lobby at the dorm. It was a private party. We played some train game; if someone stood up, then someone sat down. It was JJ's idea, and it was fun. It was a small party. We had food and joked around. JJ made funny faces and we couldn't laugh. It was a lot of fun games.

—Manda

Melani and JJ first met in Guam when they attended the

Mulujan elementary school in the southern region. From that point on, they both went to the same schools until JJ left for MSSD. JJ's and Melani's families knew each other well and shared the same values and island culture. JJ was the one person in Melani's life upon whom she could depend.

Like JJ, Melani was raised in a traditional home that valued hard work and mutuality. She was friendly and shy, qualities that endeared her to her friends. She looked at JJ as a protector in childhood and now, as a young adult, going into a college far from home. JJ was Melani's first love and felt like they fit together like a hand in a glove. JJ offered Melani comfort and security in this new deaf world. He would help her navigate the enormous city and the big deaf world at Gallaudet.

On August 27, 2000, JJ's parents accompanied JJ and Melani to campus to move them in for their freshman year. They first went to JJ's dorm room 102 in Cogswell Hall to put away his belongings. Then they went to Melani's room 332 in Krug Hall to help her. When they arrived, Manda, Melani's roommate, was there to greet them.

As is characteristic of Deaf Culture, Melani, JJ, and Manda began to share information about their experiences and hometowns. Melani introduced JJ and his parents and explained that they were all from Guam. Manda said she was from Middletown, Ohio, a rural area of the state. Manda seemed shy and quiet. Her only best friend, another deaf girl, lived down the street from her parents. Before coming to Gallaudet, she and her friend spent most of their time together. Manda was close to her mother, stepfather, and brother. She felt nervous moving to Washington, D.C., an urban area that was the exact opposite of her hometown. Like Melani and JJ, Manda felt reticent yet exhilarated about this new college environment in a new city. They all hoped that they would be successful and happy.

Melani, JJ, and Manda said their goodbyes to the parents and walked across the campus. Their first workshop of the new student orientation would begin shortly. The Kellogg Auditorium, equipped with state-of-the-art technology, is designed for visual signed communication. The deaf presenters for the new student orientation stood at a podium on the left of the stage. Close-view cameras projected their faces and hands onto a large monitor against the back wall of the stage so attendees could easily see the presenters' signs and fingerspelling. The interpreters sat in the front row, speaking into the microphones for attendees who could hear. Live closed-captioners, who typed the interpreters' voices word-for-word, projected sentences across the screen as well.

    JJ, Melani, and Manda found their seats near the front of the auditorium. Here they could have a better view of the presenters. JJ and Melani noticed a young Asian girl sitting a few seats over and invited her to sit with them. They introduced themselves and explained that they were from Guam. Sara said she was born in South Korea, but her family lived in Chicago.

    Sara's family spoke Korean, a language that Sara felt was too hard to use when signing in American Sign Language. She spent her youth in a deaf program in Chicago, where she learned to use ASL fluently. Like Michelle Obama years before her, Sara attended the Whitney Young High School. At Whitney Young, she attended sign language-interpreted classes with hearing children; an educational programming model called mainstreaming.

    As the new student orientation week ended and classes began, JJ, Melani, Manda, and Sara strengthened their friendships. They added new members to their group. Manda discovered that she and Chad were both from small rural towns in Ohio but, surprisingly, had never met each other in the small deaf community. Manda and Chad shared the friendly and cordial mannerisms that come from growing up in small, close-knit farming communities.

Chad grew up in Zanesville, Ohio, about an hour east of Columbus. Like JJ, Melani, Manda, and Sara, he attended a mainstream program where he used Signed Exact English to communicate. Signed Exact English is a sign language that utilizes an English structure with individual signs for each word. In Chad's senior year, he discovered that one of his teachers used American Sign Language. The teacher showed Chad the beautiful fluidity of the pictorial language that did not depend upon English structure. Chad wanted to know more. He applied to Gallaudet after attending an on-campus open house before his high school graduation.

Anna also joined the group of friends. She told them she left her native Philippines when she was sixteen years old to attend the last two years of high school at the Florida School for the Deaf and Blind in St. Augustine. Like Melani and JJ, Anna had a gentle manner and a traditional island upbringing. She was close to her family but longed for a deeper connection with other deaf people. Anna's mother was fully blind and brought Anna to the United States, hoping to start a new life for her and her daughter. The United States offered many more opportunities for deaf children than did the Philippines. When Anna first arrived at Gallaudet, the diversity and independent nature of deaf Americans shocked her. It seemed to her that they were very different from the quiet, humble characteristics of Pacific Islanders. Anna was relieved to meet JJ and Melani, who shared similar cultural beliefs, food, and norms. With new friends with similar backgrounds as she, it felt like everything would be fine. Like Chad, Manda, JJ, and Melani, Anna attended mainstream schools without accessibility to American Sign Language. Like many of her new friends, Anna's parents didn't use ASL fluently.

    Another friend, Cappy, first approached Melani and Anna in the cafeteria. Cappy's friendly, energetic, and enthusiastic style gave her the confidence to ask them if they could guess her age. Melani and Anna estimated about twenty years old, which made Cappy's face alight. Cappy informed them that though she looked very young, she was thirty years old. Cappy, an African American woman born and raised in Brooklyn, New York, came to Gallaudet after having difficulty getting interpreters for classes at Long Island University. After her father died in 1999, Cappy left the home she shared with her mother and transferred into Gallaudet as a junior. Cappy's happy and upbeat personality prompted quick and easy friendships with other members of the group. Soon after meeting each other, Cappy and Anna became roommates.

    The diverse group of friends became closer as the semester began. Chad moved in with JJ. Melani and Manda continued to share their dorm room. Cappy and Anna became roommates. Sara had another roommate but continued to hang out with the group. The friends visited each other's rooms often. They ate dinners together in the cafeteria. As a group, they often went off campus for adventures to the Smithsonian museums, the zoo, Union Station, restaurants, and other well-known places in Washington, D.C. They enjoyed watching movies, especially horror movies, when they had sleepovers. Because of the antiquated educational systems in their home territories, JJ, Melani, and Anna attended remedial English classes together.

    Despite the different cultures, backgrounds, and hometowns, they all shared the same dream: to go to Gallaudet University, immerse themselves in the deaf world, and get their college degrees so they could begin their professional lives. At Gallaudet, they were just like any other college students in the country, but now they did not need to struggle to understand lectures that professors taught or friends who tried to speak with them. They felt a part of a community of deaf people who, like them, used sign language. They were connected as a group by their shared experiences as deaf people. They shared struggles in communicating with their hearing family members. Each battled with inclusion in a broader society where spoken language was expected and taken for granted. Even deeper, they were each connected by solid and invisible threads of shared cultures, small communities, and desires to be accepted and respected. They had each left their home communities to join a larger community where their belonging and experiences mattered.

The laughter, camaraderie, and newfound freedom in their group of friends soothed any anxiety or worries they each may have had at the beginning. The entirety of metropolitan Washington, D.C. awaited their arrival. To venture off campus into the city, they just needed to hop on a shuttle bus and ride to Union Station, where boutiques and restaurants abounded.

Gallaudet University offered a shuttle bus from the dormitories to the Washington, D.C., metro. A few blocks away, Union Station was the common starting point for other metro stops that connected grocery stores, shops, and tourist sites. A rider can scan a map of colored, intersecting lines from the underground metro station to determine what stop is nearest to the desired destination. Twists of orange, blue, green, yellow, and red lines look like the tentacles of an octopus with an intersection of all the lines at the center. Gallaudet students rode the metro often. Sometimes their final destination was Union Station itself because of the unique stores, restaurants, and food court. The shops there offered various goods and styles, including clothes, souvenirs, luggage, perfume, and books. Other times, the group needed to go to Safeway, close to the waterfront, for groceries to keep in their dorm rooms.

The group of friends spent many days and evenings together. JJ spent most of his time with Melani, often sleeping in the dorm room that Manda and Melani shared. The group met for group activities, parties, dinners, and games. They formed a surrogate family that would help them get through the struggles of college life.

JJ and Melani became friends with Eric Plunkett during the first week of the new student orientation after discovering that Eric lived across the hall from JJ. Melani and JJ knew from the way Eric walked he had cerebral palsy. They sometimes offered to help him, especially carrying groceries or books. Early in their friendship, Eric described to JJ and Melani some of his physical challenges.

He told them he could not ride a bike but was very independent anyway. JJ said he was lucky to have a large dorm room without a roommate. Most of the other freshmen had to share rooms.

Gradually, JJ and Eric got to know each other better. JJ knew Eric was gay. He had seen another freshman, Thomas Minch, often visit Eric in his room. That did not seem to bother JJ. He continued to visit Eric, borrow some DVD movies, and help him with grocery shopping at Safeway. When classes started, JJ offered to help Eric with his math homework.

On Wednesday evening, September 27, 2000, JJ told Melani that he and Eric were taking the metro to the waterfront to go to Safeway and shop for groceries. He asked if Melani wanted to join them, but she declined, having homework to finish before the next class. JJ handed Melani the key to his room and told her she could study there while they were shopping.

Eric and JJ took the Gallaudet shuttle bus to Union Station, where they caught the green line to Fourth Street, SW, near the waterfront. They browsed the aisles of Safeway, filling the cart with the groceries they would need in their dorms. JJ helped Eric with the grocery bags on the metro and the shuttle bus back to campus. When they arrived back at Cogswell Hall, JJ noticed that the door to his room was closed. JJ figured Melani must have been studying somewhere else.

JJ asked Eric if it was okay to leave his bags in his room while he went to find Melani. He explained she had his dorm key; he could not get back into his room until he found her first. Eric was happy to accommodate JJ's request.

JJ walked to nearby Krug Hall and found Melani studying in her room. He asked if she would come back to Cogswell with him so they could make dinner. When they returned to Cogswell, JJ and Melani saw Eric's door open and told him they had come to pick up the groceries.

The next morning, JJ awoke and headed to class. Later in the day, he met Melani to discuss their courses. They decided they would make spaghetti in JJ's room that evening for dinner.

During dinner, Melani said to JJ, "I wonder if there is something wrong with Eric. I haven't seen him all day, and his door is closed."

JJ shrugged, but Melani continued, "Really, I think something's strange going on. I think you better tell the R.A. to check on him."

JJ asked, "Really? You think I should?"

"Yeah. It isn't like Eric to have his door closed."

JJ told Melani that he would first go down the hall to the bathroom and then go to his room to flash Eric's door light. When he came back, he confirmed Melani's suspicions.

"Wait a minute. I think I smell something funny. I think I saw something black underneath Eric's door."

Melani and JJ went to Eric's door and pressed the button to flash the light inside. Eric did not answer. Melani told JJ to find the resident adviser on duty, Lauren Buchko, to see if she could help.

JJ told Lauren, "I smell something funny in Eric's room." JJ signed Eric's name by forming the letters E and P on his left shoulder.

"What do you mean?" asked Lauren. "Something related to drugs or alcohol?"

"No. Something else. Something smells funny."

Lauren agreed to check Eric's room, but she thought it best to find the other R.A., Thomas Koch, who was responsible for the male side of the dorm.

JJ said, "Please check because I was supposed to meet Eric around eight o'clock this evening."

It was now 8:45 p.m.

Lauren asked Tom to come to the hall outside Eric's

room to see if he could smell something strange. JJ, Melani, Lauren, and Tom pressed the door light again, but there was no answer. Tom said he did not smell anything unusual but asked Lauren to go back to the R.A. office and grab the master key. When she returned, she handed the key to Tom.

With Lauren, JJ, and Melani standing around him, Tom inserted the thick key into the door lock on Eric's door. When he opened the door, the four saw a lot of blood on the floor. The body of Eric Plunkett, clothed in blue jeans and a long-sleeve white semi-button-down shirt, was lying on the floor with his torso partially exposed, surrounded by a lot of blood.

Tom quickly closed the door. Lauren rushed back to the R.A.'s office to call a security officer from DOSS. She told them to call an ambulance because it looked like someone was severely injured.

In the meantime, Lauren, Tom, and the DOSS security officers moved all the first-floor residents to other halls and dorms. Students expressed confusion about what was happening and why they had to move to other rooms. Officers called for an ambulance. A short time later, police detectives arrived from the Fifth District of Washington, D.C., to begin the investigation.

Chapter 6
The Investigation

I had just started as Provost, then the murder happened. During the chaos and ups and downs, it was such a mess. It was terrible to face Eric's parents. How do you prepare for that?

—Dr. Jane Fernandes

At 8:52 p.m. on Thursday, September 28, 2000, campus security called 9-1-1 to respond to an incident at Gallaudet University in Cogswell Hall, room 101. Officers from the Fifth District Violent Crimes unit arrived at the scene. They scanned the room to ensure that there were no potential threats, like an individual in hiding or firearms lying around. They blocked access to the room and instructed Gallaudet security to remove students from the wing until a supervisor or evidence technician arrived. DOSS officers and Metropolitan Police Department officers blocked off access to the dormitory, minimizing any possibility of disturbing the crime scene. They blocked the only two entryways through the front lobby and a third near the back stairwell. An officer carefully entered the scene. Officers called the Mobile Crime Lab to send technicians to help assist in the investigation.

For fear of the crime scene contamination, officers cordoned the doorway to Eric Plunkett's room and the hallway leading to it. Anyone who walked into the area could potentially leave body hairs, skin cells, fibers from clothing, fingerprints, and other types of trace evidence. Only trace evidence of those who had immediate access, including the victim and the perpetrator, would be theoretically left at the crime scene. Preserving the crime scene meant preserving the evidence. A physician from the D.C. Medical Examiner's Office arrived at the dormitory room and pronounced Eric Plunket dead. They then transported him to the M.E.'s office for an autopsy.

Homicide Detective Kyle Cimiotti arrived on the scene. He observed the victim appeared to have died as the result of a violent exchange in the dorm room. A crime scene photographer took two rolls of colored pictures of Eric's body. The detective noted the placement and condition of the body and the condition of the room. The forensic team documented as many aspects of the scene as they could before allowing the M.E.'s office to transport Eric Plunkett to D. C. General Hospital.

Meanwhile, at the campus crime scene around 10:15 p.m., senior ranking detective James LaFranchise contacted Officer Grant Greenwalt from the MPD's Forensic Services Division to come to a crime scene. By now, all the students' rooms sat vacated. No one other than MPD was allowed to enter the area.

By 10:35 p.m., the Mobile Crime Lab crime scene investigator had arrived. Officer Greenwalt had worked in the MPD for thirteen years, nine of which had been with the Mobile Crime Lab in the Forensic Services Section. Mobile Crime Lab officers respond to severe crimes like murder, rape, arson, and suspicious deaths. Their roles are to document the crime scene, preserve evidence, take photographs, sketch diagrams, and then disseminate the evidence to different laboratories for analysis. For an indoor crime scene, there can be a lot of evidence. Officers look for trace evidence, such as hairs, fibers, and bodily fluids. They collect evidence from every part of the room. By the time Officer Greenwalt arrived at this crime scene, he had already investigated over 900 crime scenes in his career. Officer Greenwalt was considered a veteran forensic investigator by the time Eric Plunkett's case came to him.

When Detective Greenwalt arrived to document the crime scene in room 101, he started by stepping into the room alone and closing the door. He held his notepad and sketched the layout of the room. Eric's room, he noted, was a little larger than the standard size. The room was a single, meaning that Eric lived alone in this room. Eric's room measured fourteen feet wide by sixteen feet ten inches long, with a window along the wall opposite the door.

Eric's room looked like a typical college student's room: messy. Pizza boxes, Oodles of Noodles, Diet Coke cans littered the room. A computer sat upon a wooden desk; his stacked clothes lay on the floor. He positioned his bed against the back wall. His desk was perpendicular to the head of the bed. Across the room from the bed and desk was a closet with double doors. An oak desk chair lay broken in pieces near the entrance.

Eric's body lay face down with his head near the doorway. Officer Greenwalt noted that Eric's body appeared battered and bruised, but his head and lower torso appeared especially so. As Officer Greenwalt continued to sketch, another officer, Kemper Agey, joined him to photograph the room. He took seven rolls of color photographs.

Officer Greenwalt tested the dark spots on the walls and carpet with a chemical agent. The test indicated that the stains contained hemoglobin, which is a compound found in blood. He collected more samples from pieces of the desk chair. He swabbed Eric's green terry cloth bathrobe that lay nearby and tested a stain on parts of hearing aids. Officer Greenwalt tested stains splattered on the walls that appeared to be blood. The tests indicated the presence of a mixture of blood and bile. Finally, he swabbed material on Eric's body and then slipped pieces of the hearing aid into evidence bags.

The extreme violence of the crime was evident to the officers in the room. Arcs of blood and bile had cascaded three-quarters of the way up from the floor to the ceiling. A broad sweep of splatter painted the entire end of the room. Officer Greenwalt wrote in his notebook that the pattern of mixed fluids appeared as though the decedent had vomited, breathed it into his lungs, then expelled it out into the room.

The officer drew symbols in the sketch, indicating

blood marks from dragging Eric's body. The killer had moved Eric from an area close to the door toward the center of the room. Blood spots saturated the floor from Eric being dragged, his head picking up more blood on his face. The trail was one continuous path from where he first fell to where the killer left him.

The desk chair with blue cloth seat, its legs separated and loosened, lay toppled nearby. Blood covered the underside of the chair and had dripped between the separated joints. Officer Greenwalt noted the details of the loosened legs. The murderer had nearly severed the chair's legs from its frame. To the officer, it appeared the killer had used the chair multiple times to batter Eric during the murder.

Officer Greenwalt bagged twenty-two pieces of evidence, including a bloody sweatshirt, a TTY machine used as a text-type telephone by deaf people, a copy of a bloody footprint found on Eric's chest, bloodstained jeans, the broken chair, pieces of hearing aids, his backpack, and a pullover shirt that appeared to be larger than Eric himself. The forensic photographer had taken seven rolls of colored photographs of the scene.

Technicians "printed" the entire room by dusting every surface with black magnetic powder. Technicians took more than one hundred photographs and sealed the rolls of film. Fingerprints were lifted and recorded. They cut areas of drywall from the walls. He sent the collection of evidence to the Forensic Science Laboratory Division in D.C. They removed Eric's Gateway computer from his desk to bag as evidence. The officers called the United States Secret Service Electronic Communications Office to send someone to transport the computer safely and preserve it for the subsequent investigation. Officer Greenwalt stayed at the crime scene until 4:30 a.m. on Friday, September 30th, when his documentation and data collection was complete.

At the medical examiner's office, Dr. Getrude Juste-Hjardemaal was on duty when Eric's body arrived. Dr. Juste-Hjardemaal had worked in the M.E.'s office for about five years. The Medical Examiner's Office investigates violent deaths, such as those that occur due to blunt impact trauma, gunshot wounds, deaths from accidental or intentional ingestion of substances, some deaths that occur in the hospitals, and deaths that occur in police custody. By the time Eric arrived at her office, she was well-experienced for the task and had performed over 2000 autopsies.

When Eric arrived, the M.E. sought to determine

the cause of death by examining Eric's body, documenting external injuries or lesions, photographing the body, and sometimes x-raying the body. Then she conducted an internal examination of his organs and tissues for injuries or disease processes that led to his death. Once she had examined Eric's body both inside and out, she would file a report.

Her first step was taking photographs of Eric's body. She then weighed Eric and recorded his weight as 134 pounds. She collected biological evidence for a sex kit to see if there were traces of saliva, blood, semen, urine, skin cells, or hair that the killer had left. She swabbed his skin, genitalia, anus, and mouth for evidence, scraped under his fingernails and combed through his hair.

The M.E. noted Eric had two superficial abrasions and redness running down the length of his neck toward his torso. There were deeper hemorrhages inside his neck. The larynx, comprised of the small cartilage bones in the neck and allows one to speak and breathe, was broken. The M.E. ascertained that a lot of pressure must have been applied because, generally, the larynx does not break easily. She determined that this injury alone could have resulted in death because, once this cartilaginous skeleton was broken, Eric would have been unable to breathe.

Dr. Juste-Hjardemaal also noted a peculiar injury under Eric's neck. There was a large patch of abraded or scraped skin under his chin. She wrote that this pattern of damage to the neck was consistent with the act of someone applying compression by the crook of an arm. It appeared someone tried to put Eric into a chokehold.

Eric's head had multiple injuries. Many abrasions and lacerations were evident. A blunt object had injured his head rather than a sharp object, like a knife. Numerous injuries to the right side of Eric's face indicated he was hit repeatedly with the same object that had injured his neck. The individual responsible for the attack had damaged the left and right sides of Eric's ears. The bridge of his nose was broken, and his eyelids had cuts. The brain had swelled as a result of the beating. The M.E. concluded that the broken chair found in Eric's room inflicted a lot of his injuries. Some of the head injuries appeared to have been caused by being kicked in the head. She considered all the head injuries inflicted as fatal wounds.

The M.E. report also documented injuries to Eric's torso on the front hip, chest, back, and buttocks. She concluded that he had sustained abrasions from being dragged across the floor in his dorm room. The autopsy report indicated that Eric Plunkett had died as a result of blunt impact trauma to the head and neck with subdural hemorrhage, subarachnoid hemorrhage, and fractures of the larynx. Dr. Juste-Hjardemaal ruled the death a homicide.

At the direction of Commander Jennifer Green of the Fifth District MPD, Detective Cimiotti and his team set up a command post in the dormitory to coordinate the investigation strategy, organize interviews of potential witnesses and suspects, and establish a timeline leading up to Eric's death. He had a copy of Greenwalt's report from the crime scene and the M.E. report. He would need to consider how he would investigate when most witnesses and potential suspects were deaf.

Chapter 7
A Frightened Campus Community

When you're interviewing people, you treat them as witnesses, per se. What have you heard? Did you see anything? Has anybody come to you to tell you anything? Things of that nature.

—Detective Kyle Cimiotti

On October 3, 2000, the campus community and Dr. Jane Fernandes and Commander Jennifer Greene of the Fifth District, MPD, gathered in the Elstad Auditorium for the first community update. Students, faculty, and staff clamored into the auditorium to get news of the murder and its investigation. Dr. Fernandes and the police commander took the stage with interpreters ready.

Commander Greene started, "The Metropolitan

Police Department, specifically the Fifth District, is vigorously investigating this crime. As we go through our day-to-day operations, we have been receiving a lot of information about this crime as far west as California and Oregon to where we are now. It takes time to follow up on all of the leads. One of the issues we're dealing with is working with the hearing impaired. So, it takes time to get the interpreters. I can't go into specifics of the investigation itself; I mean the crime scene and what we found. What I will try to do is dispel any myths or rumors about it. But I will not go through the specifics of the crime scene, so we do not taint the investigation."

Fear permeated the entire campus community. For many deaf students, there had always been a separation between the deaf world and the hearing world. Communication between deaf and hearing folks had often been truncated, glossed over, or absent. The ironed perimeter of Gallaudet's safe haven that had once helped them feel protected and safe seemed to have a gaping hole, one through which a murderer could crawl. Suspicions about a dangerous outsider grew. For those who had always held a deep distrust of the hearing world, the murder of one of their own by a hearing outsider was fast becoming a distinct possibility. It was as if deep wounds had been festering all along, exacerbated by all of the missed dinner conversations, the lost jobs, the lousy service, the incidents of disregard, the mockeries, insults, and affronts perpetrated on them simply for being deaf. This wound that began with the realization that they were different, whether it came at five years old, ten years old, or eighteen years old, was now at the forefront of many minds. It was as if Eric's murder had scratched open the infected wound, and now the pus could not be contained. The murder showed them just how untrustworthy outsiders could be. Yet could one be certain that it was an outsider who murdered Eric? Perhaps the perpetrator was closer to home.

In the busyness and rigors of daily college life, with classes, projects, and homework, everyone now had to cope with the knowledge that a killer was close to home. The important question was, how close? The small, close-knit community that had felt so insulated and safe was now at the center of a burgeoning rumor mill. Students now looked at their friends with new questions and suspicions. How well did they really know their roommate? Was there a secret side to a deaf classmate, one about which no one knew?

The media and news outlets continued to inundate the campus with increased fervor. By now, they had learned that interpreters were the key to securing interviews, asking questions, and planting hypotheses. It was not only the killer who was inside the campus community but also groups of reporters and camera crews.

Underneath all the chaos, like a faint thrum in the background, police officers and detectives and DOSS officers scurried with purpose and presence. Uniformed officers stood outside and inside Cogswell Hall. Other men and women not part of the deaf community spoke to one another without signing. Students and faculty assumed they were either members of the press or of the police force. Their constant presence, more than anything, conveyed the message that someone dangerous was close by, someone who could potentially kill again.

Police set up a tip line hoping to get some type of lead on the case. They, along with the Gallaudet administration, implored students, faculty, and staff to come forward with anything, even it was insignificant. Perhaps the police were unaware of the door they were opening in such a small community. Perhaps it did not matter that one assumption would fuel the next, then the next. In any case, there were plenty of rumors about who killed Eric and why. Someone who knew details of Eric's love life left an anonymous tip for MPD. The tipster indicated that Eric was involved with a man named Thomas Minch. However, Thomas had another lover; his relationship with Eric meant he was two-timing. This scorned lover could be the murderer, the person indicated. Another male caller corroborated the scorned-lover motif. He alleged that a scorned lover had become so enraged at Eric's involvement with other lovers that he beat him with a chair. Detectives followed up only to discover that the scorned lover story was false, and the individual named had not been in the area for at least two years.

Another rumor circulated that Eric's computer camera had been recording the murder the entire time. Police had sent Eric's computer for analysis. Again, this allegation was false. There was no video recording of the murder on his computer.

A student alleged Thomas had a history of violence in his past. According to the interviewee, Thomas had murdered Eric because of his extreme moodiness. Violence between the couple had erupted and resulted in Eric's death. Police found no evidence of this tip and ruled this out. Another student reported that a friend engaged in an online chat with someone who claimed to be the murderer. The student gave a copy of the conversation to the police, but this tip was also a dead end.

Students laid all sorts of allegations on their classmates for Eric's murder. Some said they observed other students acting strange. Another saw someone with a bruise. Another noticed a change in someone's demeanor, a student behaving withdrawn and quiet. Police tried to sift through the reports and tips to rule out legitimate information from the rumor mill.

At the community meeting, one student asked Commander Greene, "The student body would like to know why this campus is still open when the murderer could possibly still be on campus? Do you feel we should close the campus?"

Commander Greene said that campus closure was under Gallaudet's administrators' authority, not the police department. Gallaudet's administrators would decide the best way to keep the campus secure.

Another student asked, "We understand that the murder weapon has been found, but no arrest made. Are their fingerprints on the weapon? Are they matched to any known criminals? Will Gallaudet DOSS officers begin taking fingerprints of the students?"

"We have the murder weapon. It is under forensic investigation at the FBI lab. The FBI always examines the forensic evidence for crimes in the District of Columbia.

We have no suspect and no motive. It is imperative that if anyone has any information, please give us a call," responded Commander Greene.

The commander explained that police investigators were not pursuing the case as a hate crime, but if they were, they would consider it a motive but would not change the investigation process. She explained the media had been reporting a lot of misinformation. In combination with the student rumors on campus, the police felt it best to be involved with the community town halls to receive accurate and up-to-date facts.

Several students complained they were not receiving enough information from Gallaudet's administrators and MPD. They wanted to know more about the communication process and how MPD was communicating with members of their community during the investigation. What would MPD do to prevent communication barriers from happening now and in the future? They wanted MPD officers to learn American Sign Language to communicate directly with students without interpreters. Students reported that some of the gay students were still receiving threatening messages. Commander Greene instructed them to report these threats to DOSS first. Then DOSS would forward them to the MPD.

Dr. Fernandes thanked the commander for answering questions about the investigation with the campus community. She signed to the campus community, "Gallaudet has a crisis management team. I meet with them every day, sometimes twice a day. We review new information and things we need to take steps to improve the situation. We have been trying to meet every day with King Jordan. He is aware of everything about the situation. We had some serious safety concerns that the community expressed. We continue to work with the D.C. police and DOSS to resolve this. DOSS and Student Affairs have taken several steps to increase security."

Dr. Fernandes listed the concrete steps taken by administrators to allay the campus community's fears. The chief of DOSS increased the number and frequency of campus officers on patrol. They limited the number of students going into the residence halls. Off-duty police officers assisted DOSS in patrolling. They restricted entrance to the dorms, allowing only students residing in each building to go inside. Both DOSS and police officers would monitor entry to and exit from campus. In the evenings, from 6:00 p.m. to 6:00 a.m., the only access to campus was through the front gate. Everyone would have their IDs checked and recorded. All individuals would be subject to a series of questions about their purposes of being on campus.

Dr. Fernandes also addressed several concerns about students' behaviors that placed others at risk. She said, "We are increasing the number of patrols and security. We need all of you to cooperate in this effort to help each other make this a safe place. You must not invite strangers into the dorm building. It is important that you only let people that you know into the dorm. It is important if you see a stranger or suspicious person, immediately call DOSS. It is very important that you call them right away. If there are any threats, you must immediately call security. Any threats to the Gallaudet community will not be tolerated."

Gallaudet's administration and many campus community members suspected the murderer was an outsider to the deaf campus. Many felt confident that it was a stranger who was killing deaf people.

Chapter 8

A Break In The Case

I felt so sorry that Eric had cerebral palsy. He was always a very happy boy, always smiling. He never seemed to have any troubles. I'm glad I had my friends, Eric, Ben, Manda, Cappy, Anna, and Chad. I remember hugging Eric's parents at his memorial service. I could see his spirit around me.

—JJ

Dr. Jane Fernandes and other Gallaudet administrators stayed long hours on campus. The crisis management team frequently met to discuss the latest updates and decide what steps to take next. Police tape still cordoned the first floor of Cogswell Hall. One afternoon, Dr. Fernandes walked to the back of Cogswell Hall to join a private meeting with Dr. King Jordan, Gallaudet's president, Fred Kendrick, the director of facilities, and the chief of campus security. After the meeting, Dr. Fernandes walked toward the front of the building and passed JJ, heading into the police interview room. She remembered JJ from an educational consultation in Hawaii when he was only fifteen years old. A friendly kid from a lovely family, she recalled. Because of that first meeting in Hawaii, JJ came to MSSD the next academic year. As she passed him, JJ smiled and waved.

Police escorted JJ into the interview room to meet with officers. Because JJ made the initial report to staff that something was wrong, police were anxious to meet with him. While in the interview room, the officer asked JJ if he knew of anyone who might want to hurt Eric. JJ told the officer no, but he knew Eric was gay. The officer asked him why that was an essential factor. JJ responded that earlier in the day, on Thursday, September 27, JJ had witnessed an argument between Eric and another freshman named Thomas Minch.

"I saw Eric and Tommy arguing. Not like a big fight, but arguing," JJ said.

"What were they arguing about?"

"They were arguing something about 'my home state is better than yours. No, mine is better.' That kind of argument. They weren't arguing about a relationship," JJ responded.

JJ told the officer that Eric seemed very upset after Thomas Minch's visit. He suspected there was a romantic relationship but could not be sure. To JJ, Thomas seemed nice, but he did not know him well.

Detectives continued to interview other students and kept detailed logs of each interview. They met with Jamon Freemon, who had been with Eric in his dorm room a couple of days earlier, on Tuesday, September 26. Jamon asked Eric if he could borrow his computer. Eric had said sure. Curtis Bush had last seen Eric in the hallway shower at 8:00 a.m. in Cogswell Hall on Wednesday, September 27. Travis Hayes had just met Eric at a gay party in the early part of the semester, two or three weeks prior. An acquaintance of Eric's, Ryan Zarembka, said that he had not known Eric well but remembered seeing him around midnight on Wednesday, September 27.

Childhood friend Kelli Beechy knew Eric from Oregon. She had last seen him on September 24 but had instant-messaged him on the computer between 11:00 p.m.

and 2:00 a.m. on September 27. During their conversation, Eric told her he had met an older man, a thirty-year-old teacher, he found attractive. Kelli told detectives that Eric liked talking to his friends through the computer and kept in touch frequently.

Police asked Benjamin Varner if he had known Eric. Ben met Eric at the beginning of the semester and only knew him superficially. Other acquaintances, Christopher Harris and Brad Dale, first met Eric during new student orientation but did not know him well. Christopher Beyer met Eric at the beginning of the semester and had last seen him in the dorm at 1:00 a.m. on Thursday, September 28. Eric had always kept open his door when he was home as a sign of welcome for anyone to stop by and chat.

Another friend of Eric's, Stephanie, told detectives she last saw Eric at 11:00 p.m. on September 27. She said Eric disclosed to her he was gay and was looking at pictures of gay men on the internet. Travis Hayes stopped by to see the two in Eric's room. She said Eric typically left his dorm room door open until he went to sleep. Around 11:30 p.m. or 12:00 a.m. that night, she stopped by again to check on him; Eric was sitting at his computer desk.

A timeline of Eric's murder began to form.

Christopher had seen Eric in the early hours on September 28. Before that, there were multiple sightings and interactions, but nothing after 1:00 a.m. It seemed Christopher was the last person to see Eric alive. Information poured into the police command center about suspicious people and potential motives. Though many students were fearful the killer was not yet caught, the suspense and drama of it all also captivated them. Many donned their sleuth caps and flooded the police with information.

One such piece of information was an anonymous call to the command center. The caller said Thomas Minch had a secret lover and named the man. The caller disclosed that this lover became jealous when he discovered Thomas and Eric were sexually involved. Another student, Timothy Neil, reported to detectives that Thomas and Eric were in a relationship. Detectives interviewed Brett Budzinski, Thomas Minch's roommate, to corroborate the information. The roommate described Thomas as an angry man who could not handle criticism and was prone to temper tantrums. Brett knew Thomas was gay even though he emphatically and angrily denied it. Brett had found two computer discs with nude photos of Thomas and Eric. He handed the disk to the detectives.

The theater manager later confirmed with detectives that Thomas had been at a theater rehearsal on the evening of September 27. Jerry confided that Thomas seemed down and distracted that evening. He described Thomas as "a moody loner" who did not ordinarily show much emotion. Melissa, a childhood friend of Thomas's, said he had a good relationship with his family. She had known Eric and Thomas were good friends. She described him as friendly but "moody." Melissa's roommate, Rayven, disagreed. Rayven told detectives Thomas "was weird and immature."

Milena, a friend of Thomas's, had seen Eric in Thomas' room on one occasion. She said Thomas seemed like a friendly and happy person. She had heard rumors they were a couple but did not know if this was true. She told detectives Thomas had told her that he had last seen Eric at 6:00 p.m. on Wednesday.

The information JJ revealed about witnessing an argument between Thomas and Eric, along with interviews with many of their friends, and the corroborating evidence seemed to indicate there was indeed a romantic relationship between the two. This caused Thomas Minch to become a prime suspect in the case.

One thing was clear to Detective Cimiotti. It was time to bring Thomas Minch into the station for official questioning. The detective suspected that Thomas might know more about the murder than he admitted. On the afternoon of October 2, 2000, he approached Thomas in the cafeteria with two interpreters and several DOSS officers. The detective told Thomas that he needed to ask him some questions. He asked Thomas if he was willing to ride downtown to the MPD station with him. Thomas agreed. After they arrived, the detective, Thomas, and an interpreter went into the questioning room.

Thomas William Minch came to Gallaudet University in fall 2000 from Greenland, New Hampshire.

Detective Cimiotti asked Thomas, "Where were you on the evening of Wednesday, September 27?"

"I was at theater rehearsals," answered Thomas.

"When was the last time you saw Eric?"

"The last time I saw him was about two weeks prior," said Thomas.

"I think you're lying," said Detective Cimiotti. "We have witness statements that they saw you and Eric together on Wednesday evening, September 27. What is your relationship to Eric Plunkett?"

"We were friends," replied Thomas.

"Have you ever had sexual relations with Eric?"

"No."

"You're lying. I have gathered evidence and talked to over a hundred individuals, all of whom said that you knew Eric Plunkett and had a sexual relationship at least once with him," said Detective Cimiotti. "I didn't pull your name out of the air. There were several pieces of evidence and facts that led me to you." The detective paused. "I'm going to go outside for a moment with the interpreters and give you an opportunity to think about what you just said."

After a while, Detective Cimiotti and the interpreters returned to the room to resume the questioning.

"Did you know that Eric was gay? Did you know what his sexual preferences were?" asked the detective.

"Yes, I know he was gay, but I am not."

"Have you ever had any desire or was ever attracted to another man?"

"Never," Thomas responded.

"I think you're lying. There are people who know about at least one sexual encounter between you and Eric."

"We had only touched each other. That was all," said Thomas.

"Are you sure that was all that happened?"

"Yes. I last saw Eric two weeks ago."

"You're lying," said the detective. "There are people who told me that there was at least one sexual encounter."

"Okay. I was curious and had one sexual encounter that involved a blow job with Eric. But afterward, I realized that this encounter was stupid. I don't like men that way. I'm straight, not gay."

Detective Cimiotti continued the pursuit. "So, when was the last time you saw Eric?"

"I saw him outside the dorm."

"When was that?"

"Several days before."

"You're lying," said the detective, not taking his eyes off Thomas.

"I was the stage manager for a theater production. I was at the theater that night."

Thomas became nervous. He started shaking and covering his face.

"If I told you what happened that night, what would happen to me?" Thomas asked Detective Cimiotti.

"You will be right in the eyes of the Lord. You will feel better once you admit this. Would you like to say the Lord's Prayer together?"

The detective and Thomas held hands.

Thomas said yes, and they proceeded to recite the prayer.

"Our Father, who art in heaven, hallowed be thy name; thy kingdom come; thy will be done on earth as it is in heaven. Give us this day our daily bread, and forgive us our trespasses as we forgive those who trespass against us; and lead us not into temptation, but deliver us from evil. Amen."

After a moment, Thomas said, "Okay, I was in Eric's room that Wednesday night. I was looking at a poster that I had given Eric for his birthday. Eric came behind me and touched me. I pulled away and said, 'I'm not gay. I'm straight. I want a wife. I want children. I've told you a million times that I'm not gay.'

"Eric said he could change my mind. I told him he couldn't. Eric tried to touch my arm, but I pulled away and went to leave. Eric grabbed me again, and I pushed him. Eric fell, and I left immediately," Thomas explained.

Roughly six hours after the initial interview, Detective Cimiotti said, "I'm going to have to arrest you. I'm going to read you your rights. You have the right to remain silent. Anything you say can and will be used against you in a court of law. You have the right to an attorney. If you cannot afford an attorney, one will be provided for you. Do you understand the rights I have just read to you? With these rights in mind, do you wish to speak to me?"

Thomas said he did not want to say anything further without an attorney. Detective Kyle Cimiotti charged him with Murder II and had Thomas processed into jail. At last, the community and the MPD could rest; they had caught the killer.

Later, on the evening of October 3, 2000, the MPD released a statement to the press:

UPDATE: At approximately 5:38 p.m., an arrest was made at the fifth district. Arrested was eighteen-year-old Thomas Minch, a freshman at Gallaudet University from Greenland, New Hampshire. He is charged with murder II in the death of Eric Plunkett and will be arraigned tomorrow at D.C. Superior Court. A subsequent investigation revealed that Mr. Minch and Mr. Plunkett were apparently involved in a physical altercation over a personal dispute when Mr. Plunkett was killed. Commander Greene wants to thank the Gallaudet University staff for their cooperation in this investigation.

She also wished to commend all those who worked so hard on the case, including lead detective, Detective Kyle Cimiotti.

Chapter 9

A New Normal

Q: At what point did you decide whether there was probable cause to arrest and charge Minch with homicide?

A: There was a review of the crime scene. It seemed like there was a lot of passion in the killing, which with the detective's experience as well as my own experience, can have to do with a passion killing between people who are involved. The fact that Plunkett and Minch were involved in a sexual relationship—that came into play that this could be a domestic violence type of situation. The fact that Minch had lied previously about his alibi where he was during the time that we suspected the murder took place, as *well as his denials of seeing the decedent on the night in question, coupled with Minch's statements about going to [Plunkett's] room with him. Plunkett came on to him sexually, and seeing Minch's state when he talked about his sexuality, Minch became almost enraged in the interview room. He started pounding his fists on the table, and stood up. I mean, he practically became violent in the interview room. So, that, Minch's statements and just the totality of the information that we had at the time, led us to believe that Mr. Minch had murdered Eric Plunkett in a fit of rage over sexuality.*

—Detective Cimiotti's supervisor, Lt. Pavlik, during a deposition.

The next day, Dr. Fernandes called a press conference to share the news of the arrest. She told reporters, "King Jordan and his wife are in Minnesota attending the funeral service for Eric Plunkett. Last night the police arrested a person for the murder of Eric Plunkett. We're relieved that the case is solved for Eric's family and friends. Our thoughts and prayers are with Eric's family today. Our heart is broken that the person arrested is a Gallaudet freshman and a part of our community. It hurts us. The students, faculty, and staff are provided counseling and spiritual support to help them deal with this tragic occurrence."

With the murderer caught, students resumed their classes, parties, and activities. Those who had initially lived in Cogswell Hall relocated and settled into their newly assigned rooms. Anna, Manda, Chad, JJ, Melani, and Cappy were relieved with Thomas Minch behind bars. They continued their social activities, hanging out in each other's rooms and going places together. They reminisced about the birthday party Melani and JJ had thrown Anna just a few days before, on September 29.

Anna and her friends had felt sad about Eric's murder. The atmosphere at the birthday party was heavy because of Eric's death. The friends tried to support one another.

"Melani and JJ threw me a surprise party and invited all of our friends. The party was held on the second floor in Peet Hall. I guess there were maybe thirty people there. At the beginning of the party, we prayed for Eric. Everyone took turns talking about him. After some time, we continued with the party. They ate cake and enjoyed being together. JJ, Melani, and I partied all night," Anna said.

"We had all of these fun games at the birthday party," Manda explained. "We played some train game; it was JJ's idea. The party was pretty small, but we had good food and joked around. There was a game where you weren't supposed to laugh no matter what. JJ made all of these funny faces and tried to get everyone to laugh."

Though the semester seemed to progress slowly, the friends had each other to lean on. They could get through this. There were two people lost in their small deaf community, one deaf man at the hands of another deaf man. It was unimaginable that there could be such violence and violation within the deaf community. Deaf people were already often marginalized in the outside hearing world. There was always a level of uncertainty and distrust there, but this new experience was inside their community. It was almost too much to handle. The group tried to continue on as before now that Thomas Minch was under arrest. They were sad, yes, but at least they were no longer afraid. Relief replaced fear; safety replaced danger.

Anna said, "One night in Krug Hall, we got together for a slumber party in Chad's room. He slept in his bed; the rest of us slept on the floor. Melani, JJ, Cappy, Sara, Manda, and I watched movies and ate popcorn. We played games. We asked each other silly questions like, 'Who will be the first to get married?' or 'Who will have their baby first?' It was all just fun."

It was as if they wanted to sweep the past few weeks away and pick up where they left off. The absence of their classmates always sat in their minds, but somehow, they needed to resume their lives. With their primary group of friends intact, they banded together. They wanted connection and security again. They wanted to scrub away the residue of the murders from their mind. They thought they could go back to the beginning of the semester and start again.

The friends could not un-know what they learned after Eric's murder and Thomas's arrest. On the surface, they tried to behave as they once did toward each other, but cracks in the unit surfaced. Change rippled through the group, though none would fully understand the catalyst. The once outgoing, boisterous energy of the group slowly faded. The group's foundation began to rumble, and the murder and arrest profoundly affected each member.

As if bolstered and emboldened by the murders, JJ, who had initially appeared humble and helpful, started to brag to his friends about having nice things. He boasted about his new bike. He gloated about the gifts he bought for his girlfriend. His presence in the group became more pronounced, as if he finally had the opportunity to show them he could protect them. He now followed Melani around, keeping a watchful eye. While JJ may have felt he was exerting his masculinity, his behavior began to affect Manda and Melani's relationship.

As if safeguarding Melani, he spent most of his nights sleeping in Manda's and Melani's dorm room. JJ's and Melani's coupling increased in frequency and intensity. The motion of their bodies banging against the wall and the tables. The desperation of their need for connection and rebalancing outweighed Manda's need for sleep. Manda was not going to put up with their behavior. Frustrated at the changes in the behavior of her roommate, she confided to Anna one night after classes.

"How would you feel if two of your roommates had sex? How would you feel?" Manda asked.

"I don't know how I'd feel," responded Anna. "I'd tell them to stop. I'm not sure how I'd respond."

"Well, my roommate is having sex. Her bed is against a table, so when they have sex, the table bumps against my bed. They wake me up."

"Melani told me that JJ was her first sexual partner. I know JJ had many other partners," confided Anna. "Melani told me that JJ wanted to have sex too much. JJ told her he needed it often, but Melani was sore from having too much. JJ didn't care. He'd keep bugging her for more. Melani and I talk openly about their sex life. She told me, 'I'm so sick of sex.'"

Though they knew Gallaudet offered counseling and support at the on-campus counseling center, most of them never went for help. Like many small, closely connected communities, the group of friends mainly relied on each other to help them through the strains of their lives. They shared intimate details, their most guarded secrets only with one another. Yet sometimes, it felt like there was still a chasm preventing them from totally trusting one another. After all, the lens through which they had seen Gallaudet and the deaf community when they first arrived at the campus now felt distorted. Separately, they each struggled with feelings of a sensation of unrest.

Anna recalled, "Our group of friends talked about our feelings. We only talked with each other and only to the ones with whom we felt most close. I, personally, didn't feel it was safe for me to talk to anyone outside our group. It isn't a part of Filipino culture to discuss problems with outsiders."

About a week after the announcement of Thomas's arrest, Chad decided to move in with JJ to share the dorm room. Chad felt close to JJ. He was helpful, considerate, and easy-going. The first few weeks of school had been stressful. Now that Chad knew more about his friends, he thought living with JJ would be the answer to a bad relationship with his current roommate.

"JJ was a humble guy. He was very, very helpful. When JJ asked me to move in with him, he helped me move my things. He was always involved in helping other people. He was a very good man, laid back. We had fun hanging out with all of our friends," recalled Chad.

JJ had the national flag of his home territory, Guam, hanging on the wall. JJ showed Chad pictures of his large family and was especially proud of his niece, nephew, and father. Chad felt happy that he was now living with his friend.

Melani became involved with a student Bible study group. Following her religious upbringing in Guam, she found the study group supportive and nurturing. Although a conservative Christian, she was outgoing and loved having fun with her friends even though they were not as religious. Strain crept into JJ and Melani's relationship, though. JJ had become increasingly more controlling toward Melani. He made his demands clear to her numerous times, many of which Manda observed when they all were together.

"JJ told Melani that she could no longer go out with anyone except him or me," said Manda. "He said that he would protect Melani and me. One time JJ saw that I left $100 on my dresser. He told me, 'You need to hide that money, so no one steals it.'"

JJ explained to his friends that they, especially Melani, grew up on an island and were very sheltered from the misdeeds of others. When Melani was ready to leave for Gallaudet, her father had asked JJ to watch over his daughter and take care of her. JJ promised to protect her; his demands to narrow her group of friends were one way to do this. Because Manda lived with Melani, JJ would now watch out for her, too.

Melani's friend, Sara, explained, "Melani was a very, awkward, but sweet girl. He was an easy person to get along with. She was friendly and very much in love with JJ."

One night, the group went to JJ's room to make dinner but ended up staying until the early hours the following day.

"JJ said he was going on a job interview," said Sara.

"He needed help picking out interview clothes. I helped him pick out an outfit and some shoes."

Though changes were happening underneath their relationships, they continued to depend on each other for help and advice.

After the arrest of Thomas Minch, the group of friends felt relief that the whole ordeal was over. For Thomas, however, this was just the beginning.

Chapter 10
Coming Together

Reporter Question: Did witnesses indicate that they heard a struggle?

Chief Ramsey: You have to remember that this is a school for the hearing impaired. That adds to the complexity of the case. Maybe some felt vibrations or saw something, or even heard something. We're trying to determine that. We have to reconstruct the victim's movement.

Now that Thomas was in custody, detectives obtained search warrants for Thomas's room and belongings. They retrieved computer disks in his dorm room. Thomas's roommate told police those disks would reveal the relationship between Eric and Thomas. They seized Thomas's computer. Detectives pulled information from his AOL account. They took his diaries. They collected samples of Thomas's head hair, pubic hair, saliva, and fingerprints to compare with samples taken from Eric's body. They drew blood for DNA analysis. Detectives took his shoes to compare prints and fibers found at the murder scene. They got a search warrant for Thomas's home address in New Hampshire. They talked to Thomas's friends and family. They thought they had their man.

Later that evening, the MPD commander threw a party at the precinct to celebrate the arrest. Champagne bottles were popped. Relief and merriment ensued. However, Detective Cimiotti was not in a festive mood. Commander Greene encouraged the detective to join the party.

"Why aren't you partaking in the celebration?" she asked the detective.

"Well, commander, nothing for nothing. You know,

I closed a murder last month, and nobody threw a party. I don't see the necessity for this one here."

"You've got an issue," the commander told the detective.

"Well, clearly, it's the whole posture because it was a high-profile case. That was why it warranted a party. I don't think it does." Then the detective walked away.

Neither the commander nor the detective realized that there were problems with the case. By 10:00 a.m. the following day, a lieutenant told Cimiotti to get over to Assistant Chief Gainer's office now to block a potential "no-paper" for the case. There did not seem to be enough evidence to keep Thomas in jail. Detective Cimiotti talked with the assistant chief to make his case, but his attempt failed. The prosecutor decided not to proceed with the case, hence the "no-paper." He decided there was no probable cause. Thomas Minch would be released.

After Thomas's release, Detective Cimiotti asked someone else to take the case. They needed fresh eyes to reanalyze the evidence. Commander Greene brought in Detective James LaFranchise to continue with the investigation. Still, the police had no concrete leads. Though Thomas Minch had been released from custody, this did not mean that he was no longer a suspect. The release was due to a lack of evidence. The detective team followed leads, conducted interviews, and solicited tips, but the case was getting cold.

Two days later, on October 6, Gallaudet University held a vigil for Eric Franklin Plunkett. On the cover of the memorial service pamphlet, Eric's face and his trademark smile greeted the attendees. Below his picture, an Irish blessing:

May the road rise up to meet you,

May the wind always be at your back,

May the sun shine warm upon your face,

The rains fall softly upon your field,

And, until we meet again,

May God hold you in the palm of His hand.

Chris Soukup, the Student Body Government president, introduced himself and asked people in attendance to hold hands and raise them, reminding the community of its sense of unity. Father Gerard Trancone, the deaf chaplain for the Deaf Ministry in the Archdiocese of Washington, D.C., offered prayers. Dr. MJ Bienvenu said a Taos Pueblo Prayer. A long list of family, friends, and faculty present, along with Dr. Fernandes and Dr. Jordan, gathered to remember the young freshman whose dreams had vanished.

Across campus, students held informal vigils. These informal gatherings reinforced the importance of Eric's sense of community and belonging at Gallaudet with his peers. In one meeting outside of Cogswell Hall, students stepped forward one by one to share their experiences with him. Some held candles. Others allowed their tears to roll down their cheeks. They held hands and hugged one another.

A slender young man approached the front of the group and signed, "I used to be the R.A. on the first floor [of Cogswell Hall]. When the incoming freshmen arrived this semester, we had put Eric's name on the bulletin board, welcoming him to Gallaudet University. What does Eric Plunkett's name mean to us? It means that he was a good man. He was very assertive. He accepted his challenges. I will never forget his name on the bulletin board. I will never forget him."

Another young woman stepped forward. "I met Eric and his family at the new student orientation. He has a really nice family. They are really shocked. Their hearts are broken. From my first meeting at the table with his family, they were really warm and welcoming. This is so unbelievable."

Another young woman said, "He is innocent. When I first met him, he was a warm person, friendly. He had a nice smile and a great personality. He always smiled. One day I will see his soul. I see his soul in everything around me. His soul is screaming, 'I am still here! I am still alive!'"

JJ stepped forward next. "It's hard for me to say something. I remember when Melani and I first met Eric at the Edward Miner Gallaudet building. We talked. After that, I learned that he lived across the hall from my room. He left his door open; I left mine open. We'd visit each other and talk. I remember he asked me to tutor him in math. He had a lot of difficulty with math; I'm good at it. So, one day he had a math quiz. After he got a good grade, he came to me and thanked me for helping him pass the quiz."

Melani stepped forward next to JJ. "I will never forget Eric. I enjoyed talking with him. He was friendly and had such a great personality. I'm shocked and feel so bad. Why did he have such a short life?"

Another man stepped forward. "The first time I met

him, he was full of energy, so full of life. He was inspiring and enthusiastic. He joined our student organization and became secretary; he was the best. I really enjoyed working with him. We will miss him and keep him in our memories forever."

A man placed a flower near a memorial poster the students created. "We are all so shocked and sad about the loss of Eric. We have a big community here, 2000 of us. The loss of Eric is a rip in our fabric. Out in the world, we are discriminated against and oppressed. Here at Gallaudet, communication is accessible. But now Eric's disappearance makes me wonder. Are we safe? A month ago, when Eric came to the new student orientation, he became a very important person in our community. He was a successful student. One of his teachers told me, 'He was a very serious student. He was motivated and a good role model for others. But it wasn't only for other students. Eric motivated many people. He got involved with our community in many ways. He had emailed me and said he wanted to join the Lambda Society of Gallaudet University, even as a freshman. He impressed so many people, not only his teachers and fellow students, but friends, family, and many more. He was so young. This is hard on us. We were in the process of welcoming Eric to Gallaudet. Our community is hurting because of the loss of this student.

"Many people go through life. Do they understand what it means? No. They're half asleep and go about their work, their business. They have the wrong goals, the wrong vision. There are three important things: One: Love yourself and love others; two: Give to your community; and three: Make something purposeful of your life. Eric was a good example of that. He loved his community and gave back to others."

A woman with whom Eric attended the Minnesota State Academy signed, "I was a senior when Eric came into the high school as a new student. I don't know if anyone knew him, but he inspired people. My only regret is that I was very busy. I didn't have a lot of time to talk to him, but I know that he was very happy to be here. On his graduation day, he came up to me and said, 'You know what? I was just accepted to Gallaudet University.' I congratulated him big time. I was always like a big sister. Eric was a wonderful person. There was never anyone like him. I will miss him."

"Eric was a student in my class with other freshman, sophomores, juniors, and seniors. Eric was inspiring. He would smile and be very down to earth. Then two weeks ago at the Lambda Society at Gallaudet, I saw him come in, and then I realized he was one of us. I would see him go to class every day and exude sparkles."

"One time, I went into a building on campus to buy a soda but was short on change. I asked Eric if he had a quarter; he gave me a dollar. I put the money into the slot, but the kind of soda I wanted was empty. So, Eric and I walked to another building and found another machine with the soda. Eric and I sat and chatted for over an hour," another student said.

After each student had a chance to share their memories, they lit their candles, raised them into the air, and walked across campus. Eric's memory would live forever among them.

Chapter 11
Cracks In The Group

I guess JJ was about five feet, eight inches. I'm a little taller, six feet, two inches. He has a thin mustache, a goatee, and sometimes short hair. He is physically solid and strong; he could lift heavy things. He wore shorts all the time. I've never seen him in pants. He didn't have strong ASL skills like a native signer, but he signed okay. When he was mad, he'd sign very fast. If he were angry with someone, he'd sign to himself. But most of the time, he was easygoing. —Chad

Detectives continued their investigation, but no new leads surfaced. Students grew accustomed to the presence of officers on campus and resumed attendance at their classes. Gallaudet administrators took even more measures to increase security on campus. There were permanent escorts set up for students who had night classes. There were off-campus escorts. DOSS officers had increased foot security patrols throughout the entire campus. The university installed blue emergency lamp posts with buttons people could push in cases of emergency. Added lights illuminated darker areas around campus. Each dormitory hall now had video surveillance on each floor. The front gate guards continued to check and record the identification of every individual arriving on campus. For most everyone on campus, life slowly returned to normal.

    The group of friends continued to hang out, albeit more vigilant than at the beginning of the semester. JJ and Chad were doing well living together. The situation was ideal for Chad; JJ hardly slept in the dorm room, instead preferring to sleep in Melani's room. Manda's frustration with her roommate and boyfriend continued to grow. Still, Manda and Melani were close friends. They would figure out how to make things better.

    The end of the semester approached. Chad's mother

called to inquire about numerous credit card charges a week before Thanksgiving break.

"Chad, you know your credit card is in your dad's name now. The bill is up to $700," said his mother.

Chad opened his desk drawer and saw that his Federal Union Mastercard lay right where he always left it. Chad had only used the credit card to fly home and emergency purchases. No, his mother told him, the credit card was now maxed out. She listed the purchases made: November 1, 2000: $47.53 from Watch World for a watch and watchband, and $211.48 from Staples in Georgetown for a scanner; November 3, 2000: $81.42 from Bon Voyage for a Jansport backpack, $32.45 toys from Flights of Fancy, $280.24, two other watches from Watchworld, and $8.46 from a novelty store in Union Station.

Chad had not made these charges, but he knew someone who may have. He started his own informal investigation to find out who among his friends had done this. Recently, JJ had boasted about new purchases. JJ explained that his vocational rehabilitation counselor had paid for them. Chad knew that Vocational Rehabilitation Services often paid for items that deaf students needed for college, like computers and books. JJ's explanation made sense.

Chad thought about other friends. He knew Manda spent a lot of time in his room playing games. Chad let her stay in his room, even if he wasn't there. Chad approached Manda about the charges.

"Hey, did you use my credit card to charge some things?"

"No! I don't have a computer. Why would I need to do that?" she said, angry that her friend would accuse her of such a thing.

Chad and Manda walked back to his dorm room. A new scanner sat on a table in their dorm room. Did V.R. pay for JJ's new scanner? Manda and Chad talked about what to do. They would confront JJ when he and Melani were together in his room. That way, there was less chance that he would get out of control. JJ sat on his bed and watched the two friends.

Manda began the conversation. "Now, JJ, don't get mad or explode. We want to ask you something. Did you use Chad's credit card to buy things?"

JJ replied, "No. Why would I do that?"

"Chad always left his credit card in the desk drawer."

JJ's face clouded with anger.

"I'm just asking you, that's all," said Manda.

JJ jumped up. Chad glanced at the watches on JJ's and Melani's wrists.

Chad said, "JJ, you told me that you hated watches. I see that you have a new watch on your wrist. You, too, Melani. When did you get the watches?"

"A long time ago," signed JJ.

"Recently," signed Melani at the same time.

"Show me the receipts so you can prove that it was your money that bought the scanner and watches," said Chad.

Melani started to cry and ran to the bathroom. Rage bloomed on JJ's face.

Chad asked JJ, "Why did she go to the bathroom? I was only asking if she took the credit card."

JJ stomped to the nearby desk. He yanked open the desk drawers, tossed papers around, and looked for the receipts. He slammed the drawer shut.

"I can't find them right now. No! I did not take your credit card," JJ signed.

JJ took a step toward Chad, anger and aggression in his body posture. Manda feared JJ would hit Chad. They stared each other down. JJ tensed his body, preparing to fight.

JJ asked, "Do you want to move out then?"

"Yes, I don't trust you," responded Chad.

Shortly after that, Chad went to the DOSS office and filed a theft report. He wanted out of his dorm room as soon as possible. Chad found another roommate quickly. This one lived across the hall from JJ.

Chapter 12

A Much-Needed Break

I don't know what was inside JJ's mind. He was cool, though. He was like my brother.

—Manda

Relationships among the group of friends showed signs of strain. Rather than celebrate the brief holiday break together, they went in separate directions. The Thanksgiving holiday would provide them a reprieve from the semester's stresses and allow a reset. It seemed to the group of friends that Gallaudet was not exactly when they had envisioned during their senior year of high school. They had each anticipated a world of connection and community, something so different than what they had experienced up to that point. The attraction of Gallaudet was the deaf world. Not only was the university a physical, secured, and perimetered place, an actual location, it was also a deaf utopia designed exclusively for them. The fall semester had tarnished their perception. Yes, it was still a community of other deaf people like themselves. It was also a place with unexpected tragedies and savage cruelty.

The Thanksgiving break would act as a moratorium of sorts. The group of friends would spend some time doing things apart. Anna decided to stay with other friends rather than spend time with Melani. She would stay on campus with other international students whose homes were too far away to travel for the short break. JJ and Melani soon had plans of their own.

Manda thought that a road trip to her family's home would help and invited JJ and Melani to accompany her. On the Tuesday before the holiday, they borrowed a car from a mutual friend. JJ insisted he drive most of the way and taught Manda how to navigate using a map. Close to eight hours later, they arrived in Middletown, Ohio.

On Thanksgiving Day, the trio rode with Manda's

father to visit her grandmother. After riding with Manda's father to visit her grandmother, Melani, JJ, Manda, and her family went back to the house for a meal. Thanksgiving dinner was bountiful. They feasted on turkey, dressing, mashed potatoes, corn, and macaroni and cheese. They topped off the meal with slices of pumpkin and pecan pies.

After dinner, Manda's mother told the friends to leave the kitchen so she could clean the dishes.

JJ said, "No, I will help you with the dishes."

Manda's mother said, "No, no. I invited you here."

JJ was insistent. "No, I will help you."

"No, no. Go away."

JJ's face blushed with frustration.

Later that evening, Manda's mother confided to her husband that she thought JJ had a bad temper. She described how upset he was when she told him to leave the kitchen. Manda's mother shared her concern about JJ's temper with Manda. She told her daughter she thought he could be explosive. Manda did not seem concerned at first. After all, she knew JJ and Melani very well.

Yet, Manda knew that things between the group were changing. JJ and Melani were seemingly never apart. She knew all too well their sex life had reached a crescendo. If they continued to thrust sleepless nights upon her, she would need to reconsider her living arrangements. Manda had hoped the holiday break with her family would help the three of them strengthen their friendships, but now she had doubts. Now her family was concerned for her wellbeing as well.

The group of friends returned to campus for the final push to the end of the semester. The killer was still at large. JJ and Melani hung out together almost all the time. The bonds between the friends seemed to be weakening. The end of the semester assignments and exams wore on them. Christmas break could not come fast enough.

Before the semester came to a close, the friends decided to host a Christmas party in another dormitory building, Carlin Hall. They planned to have a gift exchange of ten dollars or less. One student, Tom, had drawn Anna's name for the exchange but disclosed to JJ that he did not have enough money for a gift. JJ gave Tom the money. At their holiday party, the friends played games and ate snacks. JJ handed Anna a Christmas card: *Anna, make sure you work hard and study hard before you go out with friends.*

Anna, Manda, Melani, JJ, and Cappy talked about their hopes for a better spring semester. They wished each other a nice break. When the university closed for the semester, they packed up their dorm rooms and returned home for their well-earned holiday breaks. The new year would usher in better relationships and a return to their ideal community.

Mid-January 2001 marked the beginning of a new semester, a new year, and a new path forward. They each unpacked their belongings and prepared for another step toward their life goals. On January 26, Manda and a couple of friends first went out to dinner to celebrate Manda's birthday. Meanwhile, JJ and Melani planned for a surprise party. Melani received a text that Manda was on her way back to campus. When Manda and her friends walked into the lounge in Hall Clerc, they jumped and signed, "Surprise!" Each friend told a story about how they met Manda. At the party, the group of friends felt renewed and hopeful. Maybe they could all start afresh.

However, it soon became apparent that things were not going as well as they had planned. JJ and Melani resumed their sexual activities in the bed next to Manda. Manda became increasingly frustrated with the pair. Manda asked them to stop and go somewhere else. JJ and Melani refused. Manda thought maybe she could appeal to Melani if they went somewhere to hang out. Manda invited Melani, just the two of them, to the mall. Melani declined, saying that JJ forbids her to go out without him.

Melani confided, "Something is strange with JJ. The other night I awoke to find JJ gone. When he came back, I noticed he was all wet. I asked him where he had been. He said that he had just gone to take a shower. Very strange."

Manda told Melani, "I don't feel comfortable with you guys anymore. You don't socialize with anyone anymore."

"I know. I feel stressed about school and the new semester," said Melani.

Manda had reached her limit with JJ and Melani. She decided to look for a new roommate immediately.

It seemed each group member began the semester living with different people. Manda found a new roommate named Michelle; Melani moved in with Andrea; Chad lived with someone else as well. Already the bonds between the friends seemed to change.

Chapter 13

A New Beginning

Joseph and I got along well even before we became roommates, often watching movies together with a group of friends, going out around D.C., and spending many hours chatting around the tables at the cafeteria enjoying meals and good conversation. I felt that Joseph and I got along well, and he was a natural choice for a new roommate.

—Chris

The start of the new semester in 2001 ushered in feelings of hope and new beginnings among the campus community. Faculty, students, and staff were ready to resume their routines. Dr. I. King Jordan, Gallaudet's president, welcomed back the campus community on January 12, 2001. He highlighted the university's efforts in the wake of the loss of Eric Plunkett. He said the tragedy had highlighted several problems with conduct against the LGBT community on-campus. King Jordan implored students to respect one another and embrace the differences of others. He appointed a special assistant, Mr. Lindsay Dunn, to focus on the university's diversity effort. Mr. Dunn developed immersive and intensive activities for students, faculty, and staff designed to address diversity, especially sexual orientation.

The university hosted several workshops during Enrichment Day, an event for students that precedes classes beginning. King noted the focus of the Board of Trustees meeting in early February would be on the issue of diversity. There would be reports from various on-campus committees and councils to the Board. In March, they planned for a "Stand Down" day for the entire community to focus on diversity and move forward with an inclusive environment. Gallaudet University took complaints by the LGBT community seriously and would do its best to squash continued harassment.

The university had planned to upgrade its technology systems, including upgrading its email provider. In addition, King Jordan said the university had purchased an information management software package called PeopleSoft, which would help integrate aspects of university life. A two-day retreat was scheduled for the President's Council to develop a strategic plan and announce institutional objectives. A large event, called Deaf Way II, was in the planning stages. The event would host thousands of deaf people worldwide to focus on issues relevant to the deaf community. The president's speech was to bring hope and renewal, in essence, a new beginning, to the campus. Indeed, students returned with an optimistic attitude.

The investigation team for Eric's murder continued to follow tips and leads. Students who moved from the first floor of Cogswell Hall into new dormitory rooms settled into their new spaces. The alliances between the group of friends had irrevocably changed last semester, but they hoped their friendships would strengthen once again. Everyone was ready to move on and leave the past in the past. Since Chad had a different roommate, JJ knew he could easily find another friend.

JJ knew two other freshmen, Christopher Beyer and Benjamin Varner, who, like him, had changed rooms after the murder. Chris, a transfer student from another university, moved in with JJ in Krug Hall. JJ and Chris got along well. The two seemed a natural fit. JJ felt optimistic that he would have a better relationship with his roommate this time. JJ and Chris hung out a lot. They often watched movies and ate dinner in the cafeteria. Chris, JJ, and Melani took a running course together.

Ben had wanted a roommate too, but instead he was assigned a single occupancy room on the fourth floor of Cogswell Hall. JJ continued to develop his friendship with him. JJ would visit Ben in his room to socialize. Sometimes JJ borrowed money but made sure to pay him back. Occasionally, he would ask Ben for help with his computer.

Diane and Willie Varner had sent their son, Ben, to Gallaudet from San Antonio, Texas. Ben had been born profoundly deaf and was the tenth generation of deaf relatives on his father's side of the family. Like his peers, he came to Gallaudet to be among true peers and to learn in an environment immersed in sign language. Ben was interested in studying cultures, geography, and history. Because of Gallaudet's uniqueness as a global hub for deaf education, Ben chose there to begin his journey into adulthood.

When Ben first moved into the dorm during the fall semester, he decorated his room with items he and his mother had bought the previous summer at Linens and Things. He chose a wastebasket, backpacks, lamps, and other decorations for his room. Knowing Ben loved to eat apples, his mother purchased him a small paring knife that would be substantial enough to slice through the apples. This insignificant item was Ben's reminder of home.

Ben developed friendships with several deaf students from international countries. He and his friend, Sui, developed a close friendship and often met to eat together and hang out with other friends. On Thursday, February 1, 2001, at 6:00 p.m., Sui and Ben had made plans to have dinner together at Sui's house. She made a delicious meal of chicken, fish, and rice mixed with onions. Knowing Ben loved apples, she included them in the meal. After dinner, Ben went to Mohamed's, another friend, room. He brought the leftovers from dinner to share. Mohamed correctly guessed that Sui prepared the meal, whose food, he agreed, was delicious. Mohamed and Ben talked about homework and girls. Then Ben said he had to go back to his room but would be back later that evening.

On Friday, February 2, at 8:00 a.m., Ben was

supposed to have met Mohamed to go to class but never showed. At 2:00 p.m., Sui waited outside the field house, but Ben never showed. At 4:00 p.m., Sui went to the library to await Ben's arrival, but again, he never came. Both Mohamed and Sui were concerned because their friend was always punctual. He would never miss an appointment without letting them know. Something was very strange.

Chapter 14

Another Murder

Ben liked apples, and he liked them peeled at home. So, I knew he would need something to peel them with. I didn't think a plastic serrated knife would be good enough for him. So, I took him to Linens and Things, and while we were in there purchasing lamps and wastebaskets and bookbags, and that sort of thing, I said I would get him a kitchen knife also so that he could peel his apples. So he wouldn't worry about his diet. I didn't want one too long. I chose one that was sturdy, so he wouldn't accidentally cut himself.
—Diane Varner

On Saturday, February 3, at 4:15 a.m., the fire alarm in Krug Hall emitted piercing sounds and blinking lights. Following dormitory protocol, the residential advisors checked every student's room to ensure they had left to meet outside the building at a designated spot. Scott Pfaff, the R.A. assigned to the fourth floor, first went to the first floor to get the master key, then climbed the stairs to the students' rooms. He first checked the women's wing on the left side. Some students were still asleep. He woke them and asked them to go outside. After about ten minutes, the fire alarm stopped. Scott's boss, Carl Ewan, wanted him to check all the rooms on both wings anyway.

    Oblivious to the small droplets of liquid on the floor, the resident advisor hurried to complete his task. Scott checked the first door on the left, then the right in the men's wing. The next door on the left was Ben Varner's room. When Scott opened the door, a blast of cold air accosted him; Ben's window had been left open. Ben's room was a mess. Scott wondered if Ben had come home drunk from a sorority party that had occurred the night before. Ben's mattress toppled on its side just inside the door. A plastic bottle of some type of red-colored drink sat on the desk, the mattress leaning against the desk chair. A blanket looked like someone had thrown it to the floor. A copy of *The Macmillan World Atlas* lay on the blue-carpeted floor, a wristwatch next to it. Ben must have been really drunk from the party, but Ben was not like that, at least not that Scott had seen.

Wait. Scott saw Ben's feet protruding from under the bed mattress. Scott looked closer at Ben's room. The atlas and wristwatch had some type of deep red stains on them. There were stains on the carpet and on his penny loafer shoes. Scott realized that something was very wrong. Puddles of red liquid soaked through the carpet in multiple areas. An empty bottle of Big Red and blood-spattered paper towels filled the metal-wired trashcan. Scott saw splattered blood and bloody handprints. It was as if someone had wiped off their hands across different areas of the room. He immediately contacted his boss and campus security, who contacted 9-1-1.

The medical examiner and homicide officer, Detective David Murray, were called to the scene. The M.E. pronounced Ben as dead, then transported Ben's body for autopsy. Detective Murray, a seasoned thirteen-year veteran of the police department working in the forensic science division, started to investigate the crime scene.

"When I first arrived on the scene, prior to entering the room, I opened the door and realized that the crime committed that morning was a crime of great violence; there was blood splatter all over the walls in there," said Detective Murray. "I observed the victim lying on the floor entangled with the sheets, a clothing rack, and a chair. The room was in disarray."

Ben's closet door was open with the light on inside. His desk drawers were left open. Someone had strewn clothing about the room. Detective Murray noted that Ben's room appeared to have been ransacked. The mattress of Ben's bed was pulled off and laid across his upper torso.

Ben lay in the middle of the floor with the fitted sheet and top sheet on top of him. A clothes rack balanced on top of him as well. A comforter lay discarded near the front entrance. The mattress sat on its side between the edge of the bed and Ben's body. Ben was on his back in a large pool of blood. Blood spatter covered all four walls and his chest of drawers. Thin rivers of blood dripped from the sides of the oak bed. Someone had strewn books across the mattress-less frame, apparently searching for something.

The perpetrator had committed a vicious, frenzied attack. Blood droplets splashed across Ben's window, leaving a speckled view of the nearby parking garage. Blood had sprayed across the heater vent. Droplets landed on four of a six-pack of Tropicana orange juice bottles. Unlike Eric's murder, the desk chair sat neatly underneath the desk, a computer and keyboard perched on its top. Blood drops speckled all the walls in the room from floor to ceiling. A red basket of showering accouterments sat atop the desk.

To Detective Murray's trained eye, it appeared that a terrible struggle had ensued with the perpetrator winning. The detective carefully retrieved Ben's broken eyeglasses from the radiator across the room. He searched deeper and found bits of broken glass that were part of the left lens. The detective picked up a hearing aid that had dislodged from Ben's ear during the apparent struggle. He placed the items in small plastic evidence bags. On top of Ben's oak dresser next to his razor lay a blood-swept swath.

Ben's closet door was open, revealing short-sleeved shirts of many colors. His flip-flops and sneakers spilled out. A folded red towel hung neatly from the towel bar affixed to the inside closet door. Behind the door sat a small white coffee pot and a small half-emptied plastic container of Palmolive dishwashing liquid.

The crime scene photographer snapped pictures of inside and outside the dorm room. The Crime Lab team printed the area with fingerprint powder and discovered a bloody footprint in the hallway. They placed small, numbered placards next to blood droplets leading from Ben's room down the hallway toward the exit door.

In the autopsy room in the early hours of February 4, 2001, Dr. Lee began photographing Ben's body, starting with his clothing.

She noted, "The clothing was pretty much soaked with blood, particularly his shirt. There were cuts in the clothing consistent with stab wounds.

"He had stab wounds to his head, neck, and body, as well as wounds on his left cheek and palm of his hand. There was also blunt trauma injury caused by an instrument. This blunt trauma can be caused by a fist, a foot, or falling on the floor. There was evidence of bruises and scrapes on the body."

It appeared to Dr. Lee that Ben's injuries were consistent with being hit or kicked. Ben had defensive wounds, slashes on his palms, evidence that he was trying to protect himself. A great fight ensued. Ben had not wanted to succumb to the savagery inflicted by his assailant. In the end, Ben suffered approximately seventeen stab wounds to his head, face, neck, chest, and abdomen, and ultimately lost his life.

Dr. Lee's autopsy revealed multiple wounds that

could have led to Ben's death. There was a stab wound on the right side of the head, above the hairline near the ear. One stab wound penetrated the skull and entered the brain's outer layer, resulting in bleeding around the brain. Another injury was just beneath the right eye, two slashes interconnected caused by the twisting of a knife. Others were in the lower right eyelid, on the left side of the nose, and yet another piercing the left eye. There was another on the left side of the upper lip. The right side of the neck indicated two wounds. The brutality of the attack was striking.

In an attempt to finally end the competition, the perpetrator had cut Ben's throat, revealing a three-inch gaping wound at the front base on the base of the neck that traversed from the front to the right side, thereby cutting the airway. As if fearful that Ben would somehow escape the deep wound to his neck, the intruder stabbed Ben in the top of the chest and cut the jugular vein along with the windpipe. Ben's stomach was stabbed twice, once to his right hip. Another two stab wounds came from the right side of the back into the right lung.

Ben's body sustained other, more minor injuries and abrasions. There was a bruise and an abrasion around his right eye. However, the more extensive stab wounds to the lung, eye, jugular vein, and skull could have each been fatal. The killer had acted in a frenzy that ended in overkill. Any one of the stab wounds would have resulted in his death, but the killer kept at it, ensuring that there would be hardly anything left intact when he finished.

Dr. Lee needed to determine the approximate time of death. She did this by examining the contents of Ben's stomach. The rice and onions from Sui's dinner helped to approximate the length of time from when he last ate to the time of death. It was up to eight hours, which meant that Ben was likely killed between the late hours of February 1 and the early hours of February 2. Dr. Lee wrote that the cause of death was a homicide due to the stab wounds inflicted to his head, neck, and chest.

Chapter 15

Another Investigation

As time went on, it was hard to admit that it was someone on campus who murdered them. I remember we were under high security, checking IDs. I kept thinking that we were lax in checking IDs. I can see myself at the time not realizing that it was someone on campus. In hindsight, I looked at Chief Ramsey's face. He knew it was someone on campus. Everyone was a suspect. Even I could have been the murderer.

—Dr. Jane Fernandes

Upon discovering Ben's body on February 3, police told students to vacate the fourth floor of Cogswell Hall and move to the second floor of another dorm for interviews with police officers. Students from other floors walked to the cafeteria to await further instructions. They moved about freely in the cafeteria, discussing the morning's events. Chief Ramsey and Detective Lorren Leadmon, a detective in the violent crimes branch of the MPD, addressed the students living in the dorm and those on campus. They told them a homicide had been committed and asked if anyone had any information to come forward to the police. Students could either go to DOSS or approach any officer they saw on campus.

Meanwhile, Detective LaFranchise continued to investigate Eric's murder separately. Though the two murders had similarities, both were freshmen, deaf, and both occurred at Gallaudet, there was no evidence that the two were related. In the course of Eric's investigation, Detective Franchise discovered that Eric's wallet had been stolen from his dorm room and used within twenty-four hours after his death. Someone had made a transaction at Riggs bank on September 28 at 1:27 p.m., then made five purchases at stores in Union Station. The first charge was made at Bon Voyage for a Jansport backpack; the second in the amount of $31.62 for two children's rompers with images of the Washington, D.C. capitol and monument. A third charge was attempted online for $4008.65 for two bikes, a Diamondback '00 XR-8 bike and an Intense Uzzi SL, and a bike accessory, a Marzocchi '00 Z2 Atom 80 Fork. The bike vendor later declined the purchases because the card had reached its maximum. Finally, toward the end of September, a charge was attempted one last time to pay for a membership on a pornography website. This time, the vendor declined the card immediately because of insufficient funds.

Unexpectedly, the detectives learned that Thomas Minch had been visiting Washington, D.C., to comply with a court order to provide DNA evidence. Urgently, they obtained search warrants for Thomas's home in New Hampshire. They also requested copies of purchase receipts from Made in America and Bon Voyage stores to analyze the forged signatures for Eric.

A comparison of Thomas's signature on the forged receipts revealed that the two styles differed. They searched Thomas's house for the toddler rompers and backpacks but found nothing. Finally, the DNA from the crime scene in Ben's room did not match Thomas's. Thus, police ruled out Thomas Minch as a suspect.

Back on campus, JJ and Melani approached Detective Leadmon in the cafeteria. An interpreter stood nearby to translate. "I have information about Ben Varner. He was gay," said JJ. The officer made a note but did not ask further questions.

Detectives Pamela Reed and Darryl Richmond, veteran homicide detectives, were transferred from other units and assigned as lead detectives on Ben's homicide. They set up a command center on the second floor in Carlin Hal, where, two floors down in the basement, DOSS offices were located. The detectives used dormitory rooms on the second floor to interview students.

The first step was to create a timeline of events. Based on the M.E.'s report, the detectives estimated that the murder took place between Thursday, February 1 at 9:00 p.m. to 9:00 a.m. Friday, February 2. The detectives knew that Gallaudet University issued each student had a key card to allow them entrance into their dormitory building and to buy meals in the cafeteria. So, they retrieved the records of who had used their key card to enter Cogswell Hall and obtain meals during the timeframe in which someone had killed Ben. The key card records showed that the last time Ben had used his meal card was on Thursday evening. On Friday, there was no record of

Ben using his key card to enter the building or his meal card in the cafeteria. Ben was also absent from his classes on Friday, something that he never did. He had missed his scheduled appointments with his friends. He also missed his medical appointment to follow up with treatment for his kidney stones.

On the morning of February 3, Detective Monica Coleman, with the K-9 patrol division, conducted a track with her police dog. Her goal was to see if the dog could pick up the scent of a suspect who had left the crime scene. She found blood droplets leading from outside Ben's room down into the basement of Cogswell Hall, where a door was open. She commanded the dog to track the scent from the basement door to the outside.

"The dog was put on the blood droplets down in the basement of the building. He immediately went outside, up the stairs, across the grassy area into the parking lot area in the back of the building. He immediately went over to the dumpster. There were two dumpsters in the back of the building. The dog went to the first dumpster and began to indicate, which means he began to sniff very hard on the dumpster," said Detective Coleman.

She opened the dumpster lid and saw toppled boxes inside. The dog continued to indicate on the dumpster. She told the K-9 the instruction word "up," which commanded the dog to jump into the dumpster. Once inside, the dog sniffed around and pushed aside boxes with its muzzle. As the dog moved the contents, Detective Coleman saw a jacket. The dog sniffed the coat and put it inside his mouth. The detective instructed the dog to leave it and jump out of the dumpster. She then told the officer on the scene that objects inside the dumpster needed to be recovered.

    Detective James Trainum asked Detective Darryl Richmond to move his pickup truck next to the dumpster so they could search for evidence and put items in the truck bed. Detective Trainum jumped into the dumpster and handed Detective Richmond items beginning at the top of the pile. He gave him the jacket that Detective Coleman found. He then found a knife under some trash bags in the front center part of the dumpster. Detectives sent the knife and jacket to Anthony Onorato of the FBI for DNA analysis. Sandra Wiersema, an FBI analyst in the shoe print and tire tread unit, was asked to come to the crime scene to investigate shoe prints found by the police.

    The FBI sent an analysis to Cogswell Hall to examine a latent shoe print found outside Ben's door. Analyst Wiersema found a print on the floor leading from Ben's doorway down the hallway.

"I had the impressions photographed first to be sure that we would have a record of what they looked like at the time I arrived at the crime scene. Then I decided to chemically enhance the bloody impressions. I did that using ametoe black, a chemical that reacts with the protein in the blood. It turns the blood from the reddish-brown color that you normally see to a deep blue/black color," explained the analyst.

The chemical processing increased the contrast of the footprints. Even faint impressions that are difficult to see with the eyes can be enhanced chemically. The analyst took pictures after the enhancement and printed them at the laboratory.

"We have a footwear database in the laboratory, which has a number of shoes in it that are coded by design. By that, I mean if there is a circle on the bottom of the shoe, then it would be coded into the database by circles. I can actually do a search of the shoes that are in the database."

The database search indicated that detectives needed to look for a Nike Air Sever Max model, size eleven.

Chapter 16

Here We Go Again

My orders from the president, Dr. Jordan, were to cooperate with the police in any way we could. And so, we held crisis team meetings. Every day we tried to make sure that the community heard the news before they read it in the paper. We were addicted to email. By then, pagers were becoming popular; that forced us all to use pagers a lot. We tried very hard to keep ahead, but things were happening. And there were rumors. You know, it was the pizza delivery guy. It was all kinds of craziness and then the unfortunate incident of Tom Minch. The investigation was going around in circles. It's easy to look back and say, well, could have, would have, should have, or I can't believe the D.C. police didn't think of that. There were so many of those.

—Mercy Coogan, Public Relations Office at
Gallaudet University

On Monday, February 5, 2001, Gallaudet administrators held another press conference for yet another murdered student. Chaos, fear, and anxiety again beset the campus community. The faculty, students, staff, and reporters watched the university president's speech. The atmosphere was heavy and somber, the campus community scared and insecure. President Jordan, Provost Fernandes, DOSS chief Bernard Holt, and police officials stood before the distraught crowd.

"I'm very sorry that we have to come together like this again," said King Jordan. "It's truly very, very sad that we have to come together to talk about the tragedy of another murder. We're shocked. We're angry. We're upset, but we're strong. Our community is strong.

"I've been involved in discussions and meetings since 5:00 a.m. on Saturday morning. I promise you I've never seen the Gallaudet community so strong. We continue to be strong. I don't know what to think about another murder. I know you don't know what to think about another murder. But we are a good community. Your friends are my friends, and we will continue to work together against violence on our campus.

"I want to take a minute to thank the community when this became known. People on campus right away started to volunteer to work together. Faculty, staff, and students who live off-campus came and offered their help to us.

"People have been a big help to me and to Gallaudet. I want to thank the mayor of D.C. The mayor came to me and offered his support in any way he could. In fact, his deputy mayor came on Saturday morning and stayed until midnight. She now pages me on my pager every day, often several times a day, offering to help in any way she or the mayor can. City Council Member Orange came on Saturday and offered his help and support. The chief of police came to Gallaudet several times and promised me that this case is a very high priority. They're working very hard to make progress.

"Some of you, like me, have been frustrated that we get information from the newspapers or television instead of getting information from me or the police. This morning I saw things in the newspaper that I had never seen or heard before. I called Chief Ramsey and told him my frustration. He said he felt equally frustrated because that information was not from the D.C. police department but leaked to the media. So what you see in the newspaper about the investigation and information about the grand jury, all of that is not coming from D.C. police or the US Attorney's office. It comes from leaks to the media.

"I met with Ben Varner's family. They are grieving. It's a very, very difficult time for them. They feel that the Gallaudet community is very supportive and helpful, but please understand they're going through an awful time. Also, the family of Eric Plunkett has contacted us and offered their help and support in any way they can.

"Let me say one more thing about information. Please, students who live on campus, please call your parents if you haven't yet. Let them know you're okay. Let them know that the university and police and Gallaudet security are working hard to ensure your safety."

King Jordan read a letter written by Eric's mother, Kathleen Cornils.

Dear Dr. Jordan,

This letter is from a mother whose heart is absolutely broken. The love I have now, and always had for my son Eric, knows no bounds. He has always been my pride and joy. His deafness was challenging, yes, but it gave us the opportunity to meet many people and learn about many things we never otherwise would have known.

Eric was a truly loving, caring, sensitive young man. He liked people, and the advancements in communications technology gave him the opportunity to meet many people. He was surrounded by people whose lives he touched. I don't think they will ever forget the good-looking young man with the big smile who usually had a kind word and made them laugh.

His greatest joy in recent months was his graduation from the high school and his acceptance letter to Gallaudet. When he received his acceptance letter, we framed it and put it on display next to his high school diploma. The acceptance letter would later be replaced by his diploma from Gallaudet!

Although receiving that diploma will now never happen for Eric, my strong hope is that this tragedy does not deter other students from pursuing their goals and dreams at this university. Attending this university was a long-time goal of Eric's, and he achieved that goal, if only briefly. I hope that every student who has the same goal is able to attend and become involved in the wonderful programs you have here.

While the depths of my personal sorrow are indescribable, I can still respect the tremendous job you will now have to reassure concerned students and parents. I am so sorry for that.

Please know that Eric's brief stay here was a wonderful part of his life – his first real step towards independence. Though it ended tragically, I know he was happy here and enjoyed all of the incredible support your staff and faculty provide.

My sincerest wishes for continuing success for Gallaudet,

Kathleen Cornils

King told the community that they could get mental health services and spiritual counseling from the on-campus units. He said that a memorial service was being planned for Ben.

He continued, "I made a decision that for the rest of this semester, we will close Cogswell Hall. The room where the murder happened will be a crime area for a long time. You can't go into that wing of Cogswell Hall. Instead of students going to their rooms and picking up things and seeing detectives, it would help all of us to close the dorm for this semester and move students to other rooms."

Provost Fernandes took the stage and offered her support. She assured the campus community that the administration and police were working closely. She recommitted resources to ensure student, faculty, and staff safety.

MPD Commander Greene addressed the gathering. "Good morning. This is a very unfortunate situation. The Fifth District wants to be partners with Gallaudet in a happy and safe environment. We want you to see us as being helpful and can come to us for information when you need us. It's so unfortunate that we're here again. Because it's happened again in a short period of time, we've committed many resources to try and resolve the issue. The Chief of Police, the Mayor, and the Deputy Mayor have given their complete support. We've received support from downtown."

The commander said that Detective Lieutenant Brian McAllister and Detective Lieutenant Michael Pavlik with the MPD Fifth District brought a new team of detectives and FBI agents to campus to help with the investigation. She explained that newspaper and television reports were obtained by leaks, possibly by someone in the police department. While police were investigating the crime and administrators were trying to calm the community, leaks to the press inflamed fears and worries. Parents feared their children were in danger. Gallaudet administrators tried to allay anxieties.

DOSS director, Bernie Holt, addressed concerns about the safety in Cogswell Hall. He explained, "When Eric Plunkett died, we took your suggestions. We've upgraded camera systems, adding alarms in November, December, and January. Then we have another death. I welcome your suggestions about what we need to do. We have officers working twelve-hour shifts. We have off-duty police officers working for us."

One of the lead investigators, Detective Pamela Reed, said, "I've interviewed many... more than 120 students already. Many students say they want this, or this, or this, but that's not always successful. For example, some students enter the dormitory from the back door. Others let other students who don't live there into the dorm. If students do that, then using the sign-in card is pointless. It means that students need to take care of themselves and tell others 'no.' You think, 'oh no, it's not a big deal,' but you don't know if the other students are doing the same thing. Do not leave the door open or allow other students to come in. I know you don't want to be tattletales, but at the same time, you need to inform someone if that's happening."

Students were convinced that the murderer had come from off-campus, gone into the dorm, and killed the two freshmen. They asked about having the fence around campus raised; even so, they reasoned, people could climb no matter how high. Others commented they saw students leaving dormitory doors propped open with trashcans and leaving their doors unlocked. Dr. Fernandes agreed that allowing doors to be propped open could enable strangers to get inside the dorm. The group had many more questions about the murders and how to protect themselves than they had answers. The killer was still hunting. Many wondered why the police could not catch the murderer, especially when both deaths occurred in the same dorm building. They had to trust the team of detectives tasked with finding the killer before someone died again. If anyone had any inkling of strange behavior, unusual comments, or known any rumors, they would go to the police. And run to detectives they did.

Chapter 17

Connecting The Dots

While another team continued investigating Eric's case, Detectives Reed and Richmond proceeded with Ben's. On February 12, 2001, Detectives Reed and Richmond learned that on February 1, someone had cashed a check from

Ben's account. They rushed to Riggs Bank near campus and asked security personnel for the video of the transaction. Detective Reed reviewed the footage of a man cashing a check at the teller window.

"There, I saw Mr. Mesa cashing that check. We confirmed that the check was cashed that morning when we assumed that Mr. Varner was dead. Riggs Bank was able to stop a truck that sends them to wherever they process them. I actually got the check off the truck," said Detective Reed.

"The bank also pulled the signature card when he opened up his account. They have a special machine for their tapes. They were able to give me still photos from every angle on which I could see Mr. Mesa on tape."

After Detective Reed had the check and photos, she called back to the command post. Detectives decided to check JJ's key card usage to see when he visited Ben to get the check.

"Mr. Mesa entered Cogswell Hall on the night of February 1 at 2032 hours, which is 8:32 p.m. He entered again at 2059 hours, which is 8:59 p.m. He entered again at 2113 hours, which is 9:13 p.m. He last entered at 2207, which is 10:07 p.m.," said Detective Reed.

On February 12, 2001, Detective Reed asked officers to

find JJ and invite him to interview downtown at police headquarters. Police found JJ and drove him and Melani to the police station. JJ asked if Melani could accompany him inside for the interview. Detective Reed responded no, they never let other people inside other than the person doing the interview. Once seated, she started right in to ask JJ about the check she had just retrieved from the bank truck.

"Have you ever gotten any money from Benjamin Varner?" asked Detective Reed.

"No," JJ answered.

"Has Ben ever written you a check? Has he ever charged anything from you?"

"No."

Detective Reed asked him for DNA samples. JJ agreed and allowed them to swab his cheek. The detectives took JJ to the cell block for fingerprinting. When they finished, the detectives offered to take JJ back to campus. They asked JJ if he wanted them to stop somewhere and get something to eat from Wendy's.

"Yes. Can I get a number six? I'd like two orders, one for my girlfriend."

The detectives brought JJ back to meet Melani in the lounge area of Krug Hall. Detective Reed told them they could take a break and eat. They asked an officer to stand by the door near JJ and Melani. She then went back to the command post in Carlin Hall to complete the paperwork for a search warrant for JJ's room and get a judge's signature.

Detective Michael Murphy stood at watch at the dorm when JJ, Melani, and an interpreter approached him.

JJ told him, "I remember that Ben Varner had given me a check. I also remember seeing Ben at the bookstore. He purchased a part for a computer for me."

"What kind of part?" asked Detective Murphy.

"Oh, I don't know the name of it, but it's something that destroys viruses."

"I don't know what the detectives asked you in your interview, but you need to tell them," responded the detective.

At 2:00 a.m. on Tuesday, February 13, Detectives Reed and Richmond had their search warrant. Crime scene technicians, Detectives Jeter and Lancaster, went to JJ's Krug Hall dorm to execute the warrant. Detective Lancaster entered the room and opened the closet door on his immediate left. He took a photograph of the closet inside room 301. He saw there were two pairs of shoes, both Nike Sever Maxes, size eleven. One shoe was lying on its side at the entrance of the closet. The other shoe lay deep inside; red spots stained the front. On the closet floor, officers found an opened white security box with an envelope stuffed with $600 in cash. They sent evidence to the FBI forensics lab.

At the FBI laboratory, analysts examined the bloodstains on the jacket. Now they could compare it with JJ's. The jacket had blood on the collar, the cuffs, and the lining of the hood. The analysts found DNA on the collar, but it was from at least three different individuals. Crime lab technicians had gathered Ben's DNA at the initial crime scene investigation. They now looked closer at Ben's and JJ's DNA. It appeared that both Ben's and JJ's DNA were present on the jacket.

Technicians tested a small paring knife for the presence of blood using chemicals. They conducted a two-step process after looking for discoloration. The first step was a screening test. The second was to determine if blood was present. Unfortunately, the test result was inconclusive. There was not enough material on the knife to conduct the second test.

Next, Anthony Onorato, the FBI forensic analyst, tested the stains on the Nike Sever Max shoes from JJ's closet.

"On the right sneaker, there were multiple stains. There was a stain on the heel and a stain on the toe and the sides of the toe. The stain on the top of the toe was, in fact, blood. The DNA profile that I obtained from that bloodstain matched the DNA type from Benjamin Varner," said Anthony Onorato.

The team of FBI analysts and police detectives were connecting the dots about who likely killed Ben. The time for an arrest was drawing close, but most of the campus community was unaware of this. Yet something was amiss for a small group of friends.

Manda recalled that day, February 12, when she knew something was very wrong. "JJ came to my room in Peet Hall. He looked very worried and kept asking why the police were talking with Melani. He paced back and forth in my room, sat down, then stood up and paced more. When someone flashed my doorbell light, JJ jumped up to get the door but accidentally tripped over the bed and hit me. He said he was sorry, but he looked very nervous.

"When he left, my roommate, Michelle, told me that she thought JJ was the one who did it. I told her, 'No. I don't think he was in that room. No, he didn't do it.' I really didn't give it any thought."

After leaving Manda and Michelle's room, JJ went to Anna and Cappy's room next door. Anna and Cappy immediately knew that something was wrong.

"Cappy and I had had a silly fight about the temperature

in our room. Then JJ showed up," explained Anna. "I asked him, 'Are you okay?' He said that he and Melani had gotten into a fight. Cappy and I felt so uncomfortable. JJ had never before come to our room like this. He said he wanted to page Melani.

"JJ asked if we minded that he had come into our room to wait for Melani. I knew something was strange. Our friends just usually walk inside; they don't ask if it's okay to stay. JJ sat on the floor and asked us if he could sleep there. We gave him a pillow and a blanket, but we knew something was really wrong."

Anna and Cappy started to use their computers, but Cappy said she felt very strange. She left JJ and Anna in the room. With Cappy gone, Anna felt uncomfortable. She sent Cappy an Instant Message (IM):

Anna: "Where are you?"

Cappy: "Manda's room."

Anna: "Why? What's wrong?"

Cappy: "I'll tell you later."

Anna did not understand what was happening, but a feeling of foreboding overcame her. JJ was acting strange. Cappy's response on the IM was weird. She instant-messaged Cappy again.

Anna: "So you think it's a good idea to leave me alone

in a room with JJ like that? I don't think it's a good idea to be alone with him."

Anna then turned to JJ and told him she was going next door to talk with Manda and Cappy, that she'd be back in a few minutes.

"I grabbed my keys, my valuables, and my purse. I was so nervous, but I tried not to show it," said Anna. "JJ asked, 'What are you doing? Why are you bringing your purse?' I just walked out and went to Manda's room to ask what was happening."

Anna had known that JJ had stolen Chad's credit card, but she did not think he would do anything worse. Worried, she did not want to raise JJ's suspicions. She suspected his temper might erupt. So, instead of leaving the room, she texted Manda and Cappy to come back to her room.

Once they returned to Anna's room, JJ said he had to find Melani. A few minutes later, JJ flashed the door light again. Cappy answered the door.

JJ asked Cappy, "Hey, can I borrow your room key?"

"No," Cappy answered.

He persisted. "Come on, let me borrow your key."

"No. You can always flash the lights when you want to come in." Then she closed the door in his face. They sensed that something terrible was about to happen.

Chapter 18
The Confession

The night of Ben's murder, I was at a Bible study group. I remember the moment. We were talking about salvation. JJ had come into the room and abruptly turned around and left. After the group, I went back to my room, and suddenly, JJ showed up. I remember he was sweaty, and one of his hands was bleeding.

—*Melani*

On Tuesday, February 13, 2001, Provost Fernandes

received a call from a worried mother calling from Florida early in the day. The parent had tried unsuccessfully to reach her son, Joseph. Joseph's mother was frantic. She begged Dr. Fernandes to locate Joseph to make sure he was alright. Dr. Fernandes contacted DOSS and asked if they would find Joseph and bring him to her office to call his mother. A short while later, a DOSS security officer called the office to tell Dr. Fernandes that Joseph had been located and was now on his way to her office.

A few minutes later, Dr. Fernandes's secretary told her that Joseph was in her sitting area. JJ and Melani sat shoulder to shoulder on the couch. Immediately recognizing JJ, Dr. Fernandes realized there had been a misunderstanding. It had not been JJ's mother on the phone. The parent was calling for another student named Joseph. Unaware of what would soon transpire, Dr. Fernandes apologized for the mistake and offered JJ and Melani some Valentine's Day cookies. After they left, Dr. Fernandes contacted the director of DOSS and explained the mix-up; they had sent Joseph Mesa, not the Joseph she needed.

The director finally located the other student and brought him to the provost's office. The student's mother, as well as the DOSS officer and provost, were relieved that the student was located and indeed alive. One problem with frantic parents, missing students, and chaos and frenzy on campus was that one could never tell who would be next. As the investigation continued and no arrests were made, there surely seemed to be another murder on the horizon. For this mother at this moment, her son was safe.

At 4:50 p.m., across campus and a few hours later, JJ and Melani went to the DOSS office and, through an interpreter, asked to see Detective Darryl Richmond. JJ asked the detective when he could go inside his room. He said he saw a police officer guarding his room.

"I'm not sure if we're going to finish with your room today," Detective Richmond said. "You might be able to return on Wednesday, but I'm not exactly sure what time you can get back in. Could we talk in a more private area?"

Detective Richmond and Lieutenant Pavlik, accompanied by two interpreters, went into a private DOSS office with JJ. "Is there anything else you'd like to talk to us about?" asked Detective Richmond.

"No," replied JJ.

"Is there anything else you can tell us that could assist in the investigation?"

"No, I already told you everything I know."

Detective Richmond persisted. "I don't believe what

you're saying. I didn't believe you yesterday either."

"I know you didn't believe me," said JJ. "I was being honest. I told you all of the information I know."

"I think your parents would be upset with you if they knew you had something to do with the murder and were being questioned but not cooperating with the police. There are tests that are being done in Mr. Varner's room that will tell us more information," Detective Richmond continued. "We will have the results back in just a matter of time. They'll tell us if you did, in fact, commit that murder or not."

JJ stonewalled. "I didn't have anything to do with that."

JJ and Melani left the DOSS office but returned within an hour to talk with the detectives.

Detective Reed said, "I saw Mr. Mesa coming towards DOSS with his girlfriend. She had clearly been crying. As he entered through the doors at DOSS, I followed behind him and grabbed Detective Richmond and two interpreters. We went up to the interview rooms."

The detective escorted JJ into an interview room. They sat at a table set up in the room. JJ appeared calm and collected. The detectives did not know what JJ had planned to tell them, but they were sure he knew they were getting close to solving Ben's murder case. Detective Reed grabbed a pen and paper, poised to take notes. JJ began the conversation.

JJ said, "To be honest with you, I did it. It was Thursday, two weeks ago," JJ signed. "I went to Ben's room. That's my jacket. I got the check, forged it, signed it myself, and used a knife and killed him. I went to the bank on Friday morning. The reason I killed him was because of the check. I just explained all this to Melani. She's shocked too. I had to stop it. I had to keep it quiet. I wanted the campus to be safer. I am willing to accept what I did."

JJ's words flowed from his hands in a flurry. Detective Reed scribbled notes, trying to keep up with the interpreters.

"I know I am going to jail. I don't know for how long. I don't want the Gallaudet community to be so worried and afraid. I threw out the jacket and the knife. I borrowed a dolly on Thursday night and went back to Cogswell Hall. Then I went back to Krug Hall. Then again, I went back to the fourth floor of Cogswell and rang Ben's light. When he answered the door, I asked Ben if he had his checkbook. It was tempting. I saw the knife under the microwave. Ben was sitting and looking at his computer. I picked up the knife and stabbed him." JJ gestured how he had stabbed him, pointing to his neck.

Detective Reed struggled to keep up with notetaking. The signing and interpretation were too fast to be written. She asked JJ if he would go down to police headquarters so they could videotape his statement. JJ agreed. The detectives ushered JJ and Melani out of the building through the basement doors; they wanted to avoid the news media camped out in front of the DOSS office. The detectives drove JJ in Detective Richmond's pickup truck. The other officers drove Detective Reed's police cruiser with Melani and two interpreters.

By 7:00 p.m., Detectives Darryl Richmond and Pamela Reed sat with JJ in the Cold Case Squad Interview room at 300 Indiana Avenue. Detective Reed handed JJ a Miranda card and read it to him through the interpreters.

"You are under arrest. Before we ask you any questions, you must understand your rights. You have a right to remain silent. You are not required to say anything to us at any time or to answer any questions. Anything you say could be used against you in court. You have the right to talk to a lawyer for advice before we question you and to have him with you during the questioning. If you cannot afford a lawyer and want one, a lawyer will be provided for you. If you want to answer questions right now, without a lawyer present, you still have the right to stop responding at any time. You also have the right to stop answering at any time until you talk to a lawyer. Have you read or had read to you the warning as to your rights?"

Detective Reed gave a paper to JJ and asked him to write his answers.

JJ wrote yes.

"Do you understand these rights?"

JJ wrote yes.

"Do you wish to answer any questions?"

JJ wrote yes.

"Are you willing to answer questions without having an attorney present?"

JJ wrote yes and signed the card.

Chapter 19

The Interrogation

    Mr. Mesa picked Mr. Varner because he knew that Mr. Varner had money, and he knew that Mr. Varner lived alone. And one of the awful ironies, in this case, is that one of the ways Mr. Mesa knew that Mr. Varner had money is because Mr. Varner had been kind enough to lend him money around Christmas time. Around Christmas time, Mr. Mesa asked Mr. Varner if he could borrow forty dollars, and Mr. Varner was nice enough to give him sixty dollars. Mr. Mesa picked Mr. Varner as his victim in advance; he thought very carefully about how he was going to carry it out. He pictured the whole thing in his mind before he did it, and when the time was right, on the night of February 1, he went over to Mr. Varner's dorm room.

—Jennifer Collins, Prosecuting Attorney

The detectives asked JJ if he knew where the video cameras were in the interrogation room. JJ pointed to them. The detectives asked him if he was ready to begin. JJ nodded yes.

JJ explained that when he saw police had taped off his room, he knew he would need to talk to Melani. She had known there was some bad news; he couldn't wait any longer. The detectives asked him to go through that Thursday night again. JJ began a long monologue.

"I went to the fourth floor and rang the bell light between 9:00 and 10:00 p.m. Ben opened the door and asked me, 'What's up?' I asked if I could talk to him for a short minute. He invited me in.

"I went in and closed the door. I sat down and asked if he had a checkbook; Ben said he did. He asked me why, but I just told him I was curious. That was all. And then he looked at the computer. He put all of his attention on the computer. I walked over and grabbed the knife sitting under the microwave. I put it in my jacket, the one that's been posted everywhere. It's my jacket. Then I took it off. I had the knife. I got myself ready and stabbed him and stabbed him and stabbed him until he died.

"Then I looked for his checkbook and found it in the first drawer. I forged his signature. I filled the amount out for $650, and in the memo, I wrote that it was for a laptop. I took his wallet, credit card, ID, and Gallaudet ID. I took all of his checkbooks.

"I was bleeding several places. Ben tried to defend himself. I pushed him, and he fell down. I continued to stab him until he died. I saw that I was bleeding on my eyebrow, eye, and finger. I used my shirt to wipe it off.

"Then I went to the bathroom on the fourth floor to wash my hand and eye. There had been blood spattered on my arms. I washed that off. I used Ben's towel to wipe myself off; then, I threw it in the trash. I left to go back to my dorm. My finger was still bleeding. So, I taped it up.

"My girlfriend asked me what happened, you know, to my finger and eyebrow. I told her I had been wrestling with one of my friends. My girlfriend told me to be careful.

"Inside, I was feeling very guilty, just thinking

about things. Later around 11:00 or 12:00, I went back to Cogswell to check and see if he was still alive or not. I used his key to get into his room. I checked and then moved the mattress to try and cover him so he wouldn't smell. I always locked his door when I left.

"Inside, I started to feel worse and worse. I started feeling scared and paranoid. I knew I had made a big mistake. I just decided to accept what I had done and not say anything to my girlfriend.

"On Friday morning, I had the check and went to Riggs Bank on Eighth Street. I got the cash for it, then went back to Krug Hall over at Gallaudet. I put the money in my lockbox case and put it away. I used my own money to buy things. I kept the other money in the box.

"I threw away my jacket in the trash behind Cogswell Hall. It had blood spattered on it. I went back to his room again to check on him again and again, about three or four times. I used the side stairwell to walk directly to his room.

"Then I went to Union Station on the following Tuesday or Wednesday and finally threw away Ben's room key, other checks in the checkbook, wallet, and ID cards at Union Station."

Detective Richmond interrupted JJ's lengthy

soliloquy to clarify. "How did you get into his room?"

"I had his key. I had taken it. I went back to the room to check and check again. Then I went to Union Station. I had the key in my jacket. I took it out and threw it in the trash at Union Station."

"When was that? What day and time?" asked the detective.

"That was Tuesday... Thursday, maybe... I'm not sure exactly. I'm thinking maybe Tuesday or Wednesday."

Detective Richmond interrupted. "What about the rest of Ben's checks? What happened to those?"

"I threw them out along with the checkbook," answered JJ.

Detective Reed asked, "You started to explain earlier to us that once this first incident occurred, you left Ben's room. You went directly to the bathroom to wash, and then you left Cogswell. What entrance did you use, and how did you get out?"

"The front door. I saw a lot of people near the back door. So, I decided to use the front door."

The detectives asked JJ to slow down; they wanted to understand the details of the crime. JJ had locked Ben's door when he left each time. Detective Richmond wanted to document JJ's actions precisely after he brutally stabbed

Ben.

"So, when you went to the bathroom, did you go back into the room again before you left the building?" Detective Richmond asked.

"Yes, I went in again."

"I mean, that was the second time you went in after you stabbed Ben?"

"Yes. I went back in to check."

"Okay. Then you came back out again," said Detective Richmond. "How many more times did you come back and check on Ben after that?"

"See, after that, I think I checked on him three times, maybe three or four times. The last one is when I saw my jacket lying there. I had forgotten about it. It had blood on it because blood had spattered on it. So, I threw it out behind Cogswell in the trash."

The detectives asked JJ to describe his actions over and over again. From the gruesome crime scene, the detectives knew that the blood would have saturated more than just his jacket.

"The t-shirt that you were wearing, what happened to it?" asked Detective Richmond.

"I threw it out. I put it in with the towels together. I stabbed him; I stabbed him," JJ signed. "He got up, walked over, and then fell. I stabbed him in the cheek. He started bleeding, and he tried to defend himself. He tried to get away, and he came towards me, and then he got blood all over me. Then I tried to choke him. I tried to choke him. I had his neck in my arm, trying to choke him that way. He started bleeding more," JJ continued. "Then I saw that there was blood over me, and my arm was sticky. I saw that he was still alive. Then I stabbed him right in the head, on one of the sides. I can't remember where but on the side of the head. He fell forward. So, I had my jacket, and he had a t-shirt. I wore his long-sleeve jacket to cover myself so you couldn't see the blood on my arms. I had seen it hanging, the jacket. I picked it up because it was a long-sleeve jacket. I walked to the bathroom to wash my arms. I used the jacket; I used everything to wash my arms off. I went back to his room and took another t-shirt of his that was clean. It was Mossimo. It had this emblem right here in the center."

    The detectives asked JJ if he had kept Ben's shirt. JJ said that he had. In fact, Ben's t-shirt was still in JJ's dorm room. JJ described it carefully. It was red and black striped with a blue collar. JJ then described the shoes he was wearing when he checked on Ben. He had worn his black and gray Nike shoes.

As if suddenly remembering something, JJ interrupted the detectives. "Oh, I forgot to add, when I was killing him, I kicked him in his head two times. His blood got on my shoes. I went to the bathroom and tried to wash off the shoes. Then I went to Krug, but I could still see that there was still blood on them. So, I kept trying to wash them off to make sure that you couldn't see any blood on my shoes. You could still see a little bit on the edge. There's a little bit of, like, red stain."

The detectives asked JJ where they could find the shoes. JJ said they were still in this closet in the dorm. They continued to ask him to be specific about what he was wearing, where the blood was on them.

JJ explained, "I was wearing black pants. They had a lot of blood on them. There was blood on it because I actually sat on the bed, and there was blood on it. Also, on the floor when he fell, I sat down, and I sat in his blood. When I was trying to hold him with my arm, I could feel that blood was there. So, I tried to wash that off. I knew that by wearing black pants, you couldn't see the red blood. I knew that."

Again, JJ told them where to find his Old Navy pants in his dorm closet. They asked him for details about the jacket he wore, but they also wanted to know how he positioned Ben's body when he finished killing him.

JJ explained that after the final visit to Ben's room, he had covered Ben with his own bed mattress and canvased the room to ensure there was no evidence left. He described how he escaped down the side stairs and into the parking lot. He detailed how he returned the dolly and went back to his dorm room in Krug Hall.

"I saw my girlfriend and some Christian students sitting in my room. I was holding this bag with everything in it. I left her alone, closed the door, and went into the basement of Krug. There was a fraternity party going on there, so I left and went back upstairs. I decided to throw things away in separate places," JJ explained.

Detectives Reed and Richmond continued to ask for more details again and again. Curious whether there was some sort of relationship between JJ and Ben, Detective Reed asked JJ if he and Ben were friends.

"He was, I would say, a little bit of a friend of mine, I guess. I had a lot of patience with him. The way I signed, he didn't really understand. The way he signed, I didn't really understand. So, it was a little difficult talking to each other."

JJ had wanted to befriend Ben and gain his trust. JJ would ask to borrow things from Ben.

"I had gone to his room before and borrowed a folding chair. I'd borrow the chair for a week, and then I would give it back. Then I'd borrow it and return it again. He bothered me because he kept asking me if I had a boyfriend. I was disgusted. You know, I asked him if he was gay. He said, 'Yes, but please keep it quiet.' So, I said okay."

JJ explained he had confessed to the murder because he had hoped it would help him in court. If he was going to be caught, he wanted to have a lesser charge and thought a confession would help. Though JJ said he felt guilty, the admission only came as detectives closed in on him as the prime suspect. JJ's spiel about feeling guilty and concerned about the anxiety of the campus community fell hollow. The campus community had felt anxious, worried, and in turmoil since the murder of Eric Plunkett a mere five months earlier.

Detective Reed must have sensed this because she said, "Since you have decided to clear your conscience about what happened to Ben, it would be a good idea if you have anything else on your conscience that you tell us about it now so that it can all be over at once."

JJ looked at the two detectives. "Okay. Also, Eric Plunkett, I did that one too."

Chapter 20

A Surprise That Was Not A Surprise

Around ten years old, I started having bad behavior. I started stealing from teachers, interpreters, and my parents. I knew I had behavior problems, but I couldn't stop. Then it got worse. I stole from students at MSSD and ELI. Then I wanted new experiences, so I killed.

—JJ

At 9:00 p.m., Detective Reed asked, "Do you want to tell

us about Eric's death?"

"Yeah, I want to explain everything clearly," responded JJ.

Detective Richmond excused himself from the interrogation room to get the lead detective on Eric's case. Detective LaFranchise joined Detectives Reed and Richmond in the room. Detective Richmond asked JJ to continue with what he said before the break.

"It was a long time ago," started JJ. "I'm trying to remember exactly what I did. The reason he was killed is almost the same as Ben, to get his credit card.

"My girlfriend and I were in my room. My room was right across the hall from Eric's room on the first floor of Cogswell Hall. That night my girlfriend was studying. I didn't know what to do, but I needed to get some money. Eric wasn't home. I knew he was kind of weak. I also knew he was gay. I knew that he kind of limped a little. I thought I was pretty strong. I didn't think he could really be that strong.

"I was trying to figure out how to do it. I decided to tell my girlfriend that I was going to go to the bathroom and talk with the R.A. as a cover. I rang Eric's door light. He opened the door and said, 'What's up?' I felt a little guilty, and I thought, should I do it? Should I go ahead and do it or not? I had this guilt, you know. It really hurt my feelings. So, I said, 'Oh, you know, I'll talk to you later.' He closed the door.

"My girlfriend's room was in Krug; I lived in Cogswell. So, I walked over there to get books for school or whatever and brought them back. I saw that Eric's door was open. So, I went back into my room and closed the door. Then I said to my girlfriend, 'Oh, I've got to go. Let me go to the bathroom, and then I'm going to talk with the R.A.' She said, 'Again?' She wanted to continue to study. I didn't want to bother her because I had already finished my homework.

"So, I walked out and saw that Eric was sitting at the computer. There was no one else in the hall. So, I closed the door slowly because the door was right beside him. I wanted to make sure that Eric couldn't see me behind him. Then I went behind him and put my arm around his neck. I kept holding it there. Then he breathed slower and slower. Then he laid down. Then I kicked him and kicked him, and I used the chair and hit him in the face.

"I looked for his credit card. I looked in his drawers. I found his wallet and put it in my pocket, and left him lying there dead. I closed the door. I had his key. I didn't think that his other IDs or anything else was important. So,

I threw them out. I put his credit card in my wallet.

"So, then I went and talked to my girlfriend. He had fallen asleep. I went back [to Eric's room] and checked again over there. I saw blood all over the wall, blood all over, coming from his mouth. I was trying to think why because when I killed him, it wasn't splattered all over the wall.

"So, I went back in and checked on him the second time; I saw blood all over. I tried to figure out what had happened. I was shocked. I thought, okay, he's not alive; he's dead. I closed the door and went outside because his room was right by the exit. I threw out the key, that's all."

The detectives asked JJ to confirm that he threw out Eric's key in the same dumpster where he had thrown out his jacket, towels, and shirt. JJ confirmed that it was the same dumpster. Detective LaFranchise asked JJ what he was wearing the night he killed Eric. JJ could only remember wearing black boots that came to his ankles. Detective Reed asked if his boots were back in his dorm room, but JJ said that no, he had thrown them away and bought new ones.

Detective LaFranchise asked JJ to sketch where he had left Eric after killing him. JJ drew a picture, but the detective knew Eric's body had been moved.

He asked, "Did you move him at all after he laid on the ground?"

JJ said that he had. "I pulled him back farther away from the door. So, he was closer to the middle of the room."

Detective LaFranchise wanted to know the details of the injuries JJ had inflicted on Eric.

JJ responded, "I kicked him a few times. I used this part of the chair, the ends, and the knobs. I hit him with the chair up and down, up and down, maybe about ten times."

The detective asked JJ how many times he had kicked Eric.

"Same thing, maybe about ten times."

The detective asked JJ if he had left anything in the room.

JJ explained that the day before the murder, he had intentionally left his Quick Silver jacket in Eric's room, hanging over his light so it could dry. It could provide the perfect excuse for JJ to return the next day for the murder.

JJ had taken Eric's credit card and gone to the Safeway grocery store and bought some food. He told the detectives that afterward he had cut up the credit card and threw it in the trash, but Detective LaFranchise knew Eric's credit card was used for other purchases. JJ said he could not remember details because the incident occurred so long ago.

Detective LaFranchise reminded JJ, "Did you try to use the credit card on the internet at all?"

"Oh yes, that's right," recalled JJ. "Yes, to order a bike on the Web. That's right."

"Was there anything else you used the credit card for on the internet that you remember?" asked the detective.

JJ said he couldn't remember anything more but then recalled the website from which he had ordered the bike.

"How much was the bike?" asked the detective.

"About $4,000. I just, like, randomly picked some stuff, then put the credit card number in there and gave the name and expiration date."

JJ remembered that the bike company had rejected the purchase. Gradually, the detectives coaxed JJ to recall the details of the crime. It was as if Eric's murder and the details afterward were a foregone conclusion, something to forget and move on.

Detective Richmond asked, "How long had you thought about approaching Eric, about getting money from him and killing him?"

"August or September," recalled JJ. "Maybe the

first week of September. My girlfriend and I bought a new bike, and it was almost $800. Then that left me with not much money left. So, then when I saw Eric alone, him sitting there looking at his money. I knew he had a credit card. So, then I thought about it and then started planning it. The more I thought about it, the more I started to plan exactly how or what. It increased from there. So, when it was time, then I killed him."

Detective Richmond, seeking whether premeditation occurred, asked, "How many days had you thought about it before you did it? What was your plan?"

"About three or four days. The plan was to make sure that his door was open; he would often leave the door open. He'd sit there watching TV with his back to the door. So, I was thinking, okay. I'd go in and kind of see if he could see me. I'd wave my hand around to see if he could see me. He couldn't. So, then I knew and planned that. Then I looked over and started to wave my hand around. He couldn't see me when I walked in. That made me feel like... okay, that's one thing. Then I developed the plan more. Then I thought, okay, I can close the door, and then I'll put him in my arm, around him. So, that basically matched right along with what I had pictured."

Detectives LaFranchise and Reed asked questions

about whether he had bought anything for his family. JJ said he made purchases only for him and Melani. They asked him if he had ever bought anything from Union Station for his family, like clothes. Then JJ added another surprise to his confession.

JJ admitted, "No. I stole my ex-roommate Chad's credit card, but he didn't realize it. He usually put his wallet right there in the desk drawer. So, I knew where he always put it. I took out his credit card. I went to Staples and bought a scanner, which was $200. Then I went to Union Station and bought some new toys for my nephew and goddaughter. I bought a silver watch. I think that's it, I guess."

Now that JJ had admitted to stealing Chad's credit card, they peppered him with questions about the details–where, how much, what. Detective Reed asked JJ if he had ever stolen money from anyone else.

"When I was a little kid, I did steal some money from my parents," said JJ. "They yelled at me, and I stopped. Then later, as a college student, I got those feelings again, that feeling where I needed to have money. So, I stole, stole, and stole."

Detective Reed wanted to know if there had been other murder victims. She asked JJ if he had ever been violent with anyone besides Eric and Ben. JJ said that the only other person was Chad, but he clarified that their interaction was not violent. In fact, according to JJ, he said that he easily told Chad about the purchases after Chad found out he had stolen his credit card.

Detective LaFranchise wanted to know more about why Chad was not a murder target. "Why didn't you do anything to Chad just out of curiosity?"

"He's my roommate," explained JJ. "It would be hard to do that. If it's someone who lives alone, it's a little bit easier."

Detective Richmond, picking up on JJ's comments about both Eric and Ben being gay, asked, "Did you have an intimate relationship with Ben or Eric?"

JJ said, "I had no relationship with them. I killed them because I was trying to steal money. I had no relationship, no argument with them. Ben was mad at me one time when I bothered him when I interrupted him with his homework, but that was last fall. That was all."

Detective Reed asked, "Was there anybody else that you thought about doing this to?"

"Chad. First, with Eric, I took the credit card and just used it for like two or three days, then cut it up. Then I moved to Krug from Cogswell. In November, when I was roommates with Chad, I saw what he had in his wallet. So, I decided to plan some things. I figured out what time he was leaving and exactly when he was coming back. It was, like, one morning when he left. I took the card out and closed the drawer. I knew that he wasn't going to check his wallet.

"Then, when I came back to Gallaudet after Christmas break, about a week later, I was like, oh, I still don't have enough money. So, one day I was thinking, oh, why don't I do this again, but with Ben? Because I knew he was alone now. So, I thought and planned. You know, so then the next night I was ready. I walked over and killed him, took his checkbook, and cashed his check."

Again, JJ said he started to feel guilty after the chaos ensued after Ben's murder. As the detectives made rounds again to ask for more specifics about the crimes, JJ admitted that he also used Eric's credit card to purchase internet porn. He said that Melani had been asleep in his room when he went into the websites. JJ remembered then that he had bought his nephew and goddaughter t-shirts. JJ revealed he had mailed the gifts to his parents' house in Guam.

The detectives asked JJ if he had known about Thomas Minch and Eric's relationship. Detective

Richmond asked, "When Detective LaFranchise talked to you earlier, did you have an idea that they were looking at Minch and that the students also were thinking it was Minch? Did you participate in making sure that he was the person that took the beef, took the role for this?"

"Yes," JJ answered.

Detective Richmond pressed for more details.

JJ said, "I said there was a relationship and that they argued. I didn't expect that he would be arrested. And actually, I felt somewhat relieved. I still felt guilty, but it lessened that.

"I talked about Thomas too. Then when I was interviewed by you and the other detective," JJ said to Reed, "you were asking me questions, I kind of changed my story. I had done it, but I still was changing the story and talking about Thomas and how he did all these other things. I don't understand why I did that."

JJ admitted he had indeed seen Thomas and Eric argue, but about a week before, JJ killed Eric. Detective Richmond told JJ that they had searched his dorm room and found photos of Thomas Minch standing at Eric's door. He asked him why he had taken and saved them.

"I don't understand why I took the picture," explained JJ, "but I think it was so that I'd have that as a memory. I was actually planning on sending my parents, you know, my package of pictures, but I didn't follow through. I kept it. My girlfriend was going through the pictures, and she said, 'What's this?' And then, after that, it reminded me that I hadn't sent that. I said, 'Oh, I was going to send that.' I put it aside and put it back into the package with the rest of the pictures."

JJ admitted to memorializing both Eric's and Ben's murders. For Eric's murder, JJ had the picture of Thomas Minch standing outside Eric's door. For Ben's murder, he took his t-shirt and planned to wear it. He felt a rush that the students would not recognize Ben's shirt on JJ. Detective Reed asked JJ if she could return to his dorm room to retrieve Ben's t-shirt and JJ's black pants.

JJ said, "Yeah. Here's my key."

The interrogation finished at 11:05 p.m. on February 13, 2001. JJ was arrested and sent to the Washington, D.C. jail.

Chapter 21

The Announcement

He made our whole group of friends look foolish. He also impacted the Asian deaf community. Our whole group couldn't believe that an Asian would dare kill someone. We had never heard of an Asian deaf murderer. He made us look stupid.

—Sara

On Valentine's Day, February 14, 2001, Dr. Fernandes received word of JJ's confession and arrest. She called an assembly of the campus community in the Kellogg auditorium for Chief Ramsey's announcement. Teachers, students, DOSS officers, police, and news reporters from numerous media outlets packed the hall. Anna, Chad, Manda, and Cappy sat together close to the stage in the third row. They scanned the crowd but did not see Melani and JJ. The restless crowd waited in the auditorium for an hour. While waiting, the group of friends worked on their homework. Shortly, the auditorium lights flashed, indicating that the assembly was about to begin. Two interpreters stood at the ready, one on the left side of the stage, the other on the right.

Chief Ramsey spoke first. "We found the person who committed the murders."

Everyone cheered, pleased to have the murderer in custody. Manda, Cappy, and Anna watched the interpreter on the right while Chad watched the interpreter on the left. The interpreters signed the name of the murderer at the same time. However, the interpreter on the left signed the letters "J-J." Manda, Cappy, and Anna looked at each other, confused about the name the interpreter signed. The interpreter on the left signed the full name "Joseph Mesa." Chad covered his mouth in surprise.

Manda, Cappy, and Anna turned to Chad and

signed, "What?! What?! Who?!"

The interpreter fingerspelled again, "J-o-e-s-p-h M-e-s-a."

Anna grabbed Manda and signed, "Pay attention! Joseph Mesa! Your roommate's boyfriend!" Anna screamed aloud, drawing attention from the hearing officials on stage and in the audience.

"Shut up!" someone nearby signed to her.

"Stop! Stop!" someone else admonished.

Anna signed back, "I can't. I can't."

Manda screamed and signed, "Why did JJ do that to us? Let's get OUT OF HERE! OUT!"

A growing number of people were staring at the group of friends. The group stood up and slid past the knees of those sitting around them. Manda and Anna were crying.

Distracted by the drama from the group of friends, other students in the auditorium waved their hands for them to move out of their sightlines. They wanted to know more about the investigation. With the student body being so small, surely other students who knew the group were concerned by the friends' outbursts. Knowing that most everyone would know JJ and his girlfriend, Dr. Fernandes made sure there were counselors available right there in the auditorium.

As the students explained to each other who JJ was and his connections to them, they realized that malevolence was close at hand. As is typical in the deaf world, each person connected themselves to JJ through his acquaintances, his friends, his girlfriend. Their interactions with JJ, Melani, and his friends sent roiling waves of newfound knowledge and distress through the crowd. The shock of a deaf killer among them revealed layers of dawning understanding and horror. Many had actually talked to, studied with, and ate meals with a killer.

The months of trepidation caused by the unsolved crimes now came to a dramatic end that sent undercurrents of relief, giddiness, and excitement. JJ could have targeted any one of them. Chad had lived with him. Manda had traveled with him. Cappy had hung out with him. Anyone at Gallaudet could have been the next victim. Maybe they came close without realizing it. The group of friends knew that JJ had called both Eric and Ben his friends. How close had they been to becoming his victims?

Dr. Fernandes tried to control the emotional chaos erupting in the assembly hall. The director of the Mental Health Center stood on stage and offered counseling services. Another counselor approached the distraught group of friends. She asked Anna, Manda, Cappy, and

Chad if they needed help. If they wanted to talk, a counselor would be available to them any time.

"All of us were reluctant," Anna explained. "I don't know why. Maybe the counselor would tell the police. None of us went to the counselor's office. None of us wanted to go. I couldn't go even though I could not sleep for two or three days afterward. It was good to know who the killer was so that all of the students could stop suffering, but I was very sad to know it was my friend. Why did he do that to us?"

Manda, Cappy, Anna, and Chad returned to Anna's dorm room. A friend found a picture of JJ on the internet from the Washington Post, which confirmed their worst fears.

"I wish JJ was never my friend. I wish I never met him," said Anna.

All that evening, no one had seen Melani. They wondered how much Melani knew about the murders. Surely, she must have known what was happening. The group speculated about how JJ had murdered Eric and Ben. Then the door light flashed. Anna looked out the door's peephole. Melani stood on the other side. Anna asked the group whether they should let Melani come inside. After a minute of deliberations, Anna opened the door.

"Melani looked like she was crying. She was holding onto a doll," said Anna. "She looked sad and grief-stricken. We huddled around to comfort her."

One friend asked, "If JJ needed money, why didn't he just ask us?"

"I don't know. I don't know," said Melani.

The group tried to help Melani calm down. They asked where she was sleeping. Gallaudet's administrators arranged for her to stay at the Kellogg hotel on campus. They felt it would be safer for Melani to be at the hotel when they announced JJ's arrest. Her clothes were still in her dorm room at Krug Hall. The group of friends called for the delivery of Chinese food. They wanted to know more details, but Melani seemed fragile, tears slipping down her face. They had lost one of their friends and didn't want to lose another. Melani needed to be with her friends. She received permission to stay in Anna and Cappy's room temporarily.

The professors were lenient with homework assignments and deadlines for the friends. However, some students were not as friendly or understanding.

"After JJ's arrest, my friends and I went to lunch together in the cafeteria," said Anna. Many of the students gossiped about us, often right in front of our faces. We tried to ignore them. A few people would tell them to stop, but they didn't. I couldn't look at anyone. I just stared at my food and ate. All of us, with heads down, just stared down and tried to ignore everyone. The students would talk about us. We were grieving, but at the same time, I wanted to tell the others to shut up and leave us alone."

"There was already a lot of tension on campus, but when the students found out that JJ's parents couldn't sign and that he was Asian and that his friends were Asian, it made it a lot worse for them," explained Dr. Fernandes. "The Asian deaf community at Gallaudet was very accusatory and blamed them after the arrest. The group of friends was stigmatized because of their connection to Mesa."

Manda said, "The Gallaudet community didn't say much until Melani came out after the arrest and started hanging out with us again. The other students said, 'Look! That's the killer's girlfriend!' and everyone would stare at her. I told them to stop because Melani didn't know anything about it. I almost got into a fight with one girl who was gossiping about Melani, but the girl left. I just wanted people to respect us and leave us alone."

The news of JJ's confession traumatized the group of friends. Their close friend had killed Eric and Ben. Their other close friend, Melani, struggled to cope with everything happening. The campus community was furious that the murderer was another deaf student. How could a deaf person kill another deaf person? Students were angry and discontent. Upset and anxious students and their parents flooded the University with calls and questions. Were their children safe at Gallaudet? How could an insider be responsible for these atrocious crimes? Should parents bring their children home and enroll them in universities closer to home?

    Though the shock of JJ's confession was still raw, Manda and Melani worried about JJ. Police had incarcerated JJ at the Washington, D.C. jail. The friends had many questions as well. How was JJ coping with being locked up? Why had he done this? As a deaf man, how was JJ dealing with being in jail with hearing offenders? Did JJ know what he was doing? Was he insane?

Part Two: 2002

Chapter 22

Letters To Melani

You and your family were never in any danger when I was at your house at Thanksgiving.

—*JJ told Manda*

On February 14, 2001, JJ was arrested, booked, and incarcerated at the Washington, D.C. jail on South 1 unit. The South 1 unit was a high-security area where high-profile cases are houses individually. There was no congregation outdoors with other inmates. One inmate to a cell, JJ was alone. Inmates on South 1 were under close surveillance. South 2 and 3 units were mental health units, but all three units had the consistent presence of psychiatrists and psychologists.

Here JJ was, a twenty-year-old college student from an affluent family, accustomed to having his needs met, and now he was sitting in a jail cell, alone, along with other criminals, all hearing. He had never been to jail before. Now he was facing murder charges. JJ likely did not know the District of Columbia did not have a death penalty option for murder. However, he knew that his punishment might last him a lifetime behind bars. He needed to sort things out, unravel the mess of his life.

Potential answers to his problems came from other inmates, those who were more experienced in deception, misdirection, and calculation. JJ networked inside the jail, looking for help from those who knew the legal system better. One inmate counseled JJ in the different approaches to an insanity defense. He could claim that he had taken the hallucinogenic drug Ecstasy, which erased all memory of his actions. How could he be criminally responsible for a murder of which he had no memory?

JJ could accuse both Eric and Ben of making homosexual advances toward him. These advances could have caused JJ to fly into a rage, to lash out violently when they pressured him for sex. Surely, a jury could understand how these advances would offend the sensibilities of an upstanding, conservative, young college student.

JJ could feign mental illness, one inmate suggested. A mental illness could make him do things he would not ordinarily do. A mental disease could explain why JJ murdered his two friends. He was not a horrific, premeditating murderer, no. He was a sick man who needed medication and therapy, not jail time. This explanation, JJ contrived, was something that he thought he could pull off.

JJ had nothing but time sitting in the D.C. jail. The more he learned from other inmates, the more reflective and calculating he became. He had to find a way out of his predicament. So, In March 2001, he started writing letters to Melani.

March 20, 2001

I understand you are confused with me about Eric's situation. Me too; I am confused with this. I did it [killed] Eric at about nine or ten p.m. You were sad that I was then with you at nine and ten p.m. Don't worry about it. Let me work on it and beat my charge. Smile.

—From JJ, D.C. Jail, 1901 D. Street, SE, Washington, D.C.

March 25, 2001

...I asked the officer to give me permission to use the phone. He let me call my family. I was so excited to call my parents, but I really wanted to call you. I really didn't know how we could contact each other. Anyway, I talked to Patrick first and already told him to hide the watches and baby's toys. He will take care of it. Thank God he will help me.

Then I talked to Dad. [It was hard] for Dad and I because we really love each other. He gave me my name after him. We are the same skin and blood. Well, I talked to him about my situation, and he really wants to help me.

Let you know that the police stopped by the Mesa house and searched for the children's clothes. They found it. That's all. But I already told him to put the toys and Patrick's watch away, and the police can't find it. He will do it for me. He knows what to do for me. I feel better.

You better keep talking to my mom and ask if she already put away the toys. I will explain more about it to you this Tuesday. Anyway, I want you to throw out all the letters I wrote about the case. I know that the detectives will go into your room with their warrant. Throw away all the letters I have written about the case, please, right now. It will not make more charges or more evidence or more guilty.

—From JJ, D.C. Jail, 1901 D. Street, SE, Washington, D.C.

March 26, 2001

Dearest sweetheart Melani. To my best wife. How are you, my baby? I hope you are okay and attending the class in a day. Go for me. I am okay but sometimes worried. One thing I really worry about is the police might stop by the Mesa family house and search for the things that I bought for the kids and Patrick's watch. I really need to talk to them to throw all the things away so the police will probably not find them. If the police don't find the things, the judge will probably dismiss Chad's case. I have three cases: Eric, Chad, and Ben. If the judge dismisses Chad's case because the police can't find some things, then they can drop it. Then focus on Eric's and Ben's cases.

Don't worry about it. I know what to do. But what I really want you to do is to refuse to answer the questions. That's okay. The detectives will search the things in your room. Make sure you [put] the things in Manda's room. You know what? The detective has a warrant. Okay to search for the things, that's all. You still can refuse to answer the questions.

Please be strong, wife, and help me out of this jail.
—From JJ, D.C. Jail, 1901 D. Street, SE, Washington, D.C.

April 7, 2001

(The word "IMPORTANT" is written along the side margin of the letter.)

This is the worst, blown-up, so bear with me, please. I think you are confused when I asked you for your help. So please help me [with a] defense for me. Let me know. If we make up stories, it will make the detectives confused; that's good.

If the detectives ask you, did Joseph move your bed drawer, do something in your room with a big dolly while you were in Joseph's room, the answer is yes. If the detectives ask you why didn't you help Joseph in your room, the answer is because I had a lot of homework and went to his room to use his computer.

If the detectives ask you what time you slept with Joseph on February 1, your answer is, I remember I slept with him at almost 12:00 a.m. I saw the clock next to my bed. If the detectives ask you are you sure one hundred percent that the clock says almost 12:00 a.m., your answer is yes.

If the detectives ask you if you slept with Joseph on September 27, your answer is yes. If the detectives ask you what time, you say about 12:00 a.m. If the detectives ask you if Joseph left the room while you slept, you say no, I could feel him hold me all night. And every time you saw the clock was 1:00 a.m., 2:30 a.m., and about 3:00 a.m. Joseph's roommate came in the room after that.

[Tell them] Joseph was there with me all night. If the detectives ask you, do you know how much money he had left on September 27, you answer, must amount to $1000, I believe.

Please remember all of these questions and answers. Please don't be confused and make [me] guilty, okay. Please be strong and confident. I need your help. The detectives will mess up. Remember that.

—From JJ, D.C. Jail, 1901 D. Street, SE, Washington, D.C.

April 23, 2001

[Another inmate] gave me a big book of law that he told me to read. The title is 'The Insanity Defense.' You can go to yahoo.com and look for the book if you want to learn. Smile. We are still learning more about the law.

—From JJ, D.C. Jail, 1901 D. Street, SE, Washington, D.C.

April 25, 2001

I can always plead temporary insanity. That is a very good defense theory for a case like this. I can say I took a drug called Ecstasy. That drug can blank out some of my memories, making me not responsible for my criminal actions I did while on the drug. Might work.
—From JJ, D.C. Jail, 1901 D. Street, SE, Washington, D.C.

August 6, 2001

Anyway, I would like to ask you something related to my case. I've been trying to raise an insanity defense. I found a good [theory] about insanity, but it isn't true, but again, I hope it will work anyway.

I can tell the jury that Eric Plunkett touched my butt and penis. I told him to stop and leave me alone, but he's stubborn. I was going too crazy and beat him up. I know that is not good, but I think it might work. Is that okay with you? If you're not sure about it, I will explain it clearer, and you will understand. Maybe someday the people will think that I am gay, but in your mind, I don't care what they think. I can get out of jail. Smile.
—From JJ, D.C. Jail, 1901 D. Street, SE, Washington, D.C.

September 9, 2001

Last night Kofi [another inmate] and I talked about my case and tried, hoping [to help] with my defense. As a matter of fact, it doesn't sound hard. However, I always worry about Plunkett's death because I don't think the police kept the evidence or interview files of him. Well, I don't give up anyway. I wrote about ten pages of the story. I am always careful with the alleged story so the government will not be able to catch my lie.

—From JJ, D.C. Jail, 1901 D. Street, SE, Washington, D.C.

JJ trusted Melani and needed her to corroborate the information he wanted to use to get his case dismissed. He planned to get off the hook for the murders, despite his confession. He sought counsel from other, more seasoned inmates, many of whom had inside knowledge about the criminal justice system, and meticulously planned for his defense. JJ had always thought of himself as Melani's protector and mentor, but in this new situation, he needed her help. He would outline his defense and expected Melani to back him up. He would coach Melani about what to say and not say to investigators. An insanity defense and blaming Eric for sexually approaching him would be his best bet in JJ's mind. However, he needed Melani's help.

Chapter 23

A Shadow Life

I wish I was sentenced to a mental hospital. I'd have more freedom and could have more visitors.

—JJ

On January 3, 2002, JJ was sent to St. Elizabeth's Hospital, a psychiatric facility in the southeast quadrant of Washington, D.C., for a psychiatric evaluation to determine his competency for trial. The historic hospital was founded in 1852 for psychiatric treatment of military personnel and residents of the District. St. Elizabeth's Hospital operates a forensic psychiatry unit designed to evaluate and treat criminal offenders in prisons.

On January 29, 2002, JJ's attorney, Ferris Bond, sent a letter with a request that Dr. Robert Madsen, a forensic psychologist with a private practice in Washington, D.C., go to St. Elizabeth's hospital to evaluate JJ's competency and criminal responsibility for his offenses. His role was to use three critical pieces of information to make a determination.

Direct interviews with JJ would give Dr. Madsen information about his perceptions, thoughts, feelings, and actions concerning his offenses. The second piece of information was to read and analyze corroborative information obtained from secondary interviews from family members, documents, reports, transcripts, history and background, videotapes, and reports from the D.C. jail and St. Elizabeth's hospital. Results from extensive psychological testing would yield the third piece of information. In total, Dr. Madsen would spend fifteen hours throughout seven sessions with JJ beginning January 31 through April 24, 2002.

Dr. Madsen reviewed an extensive collection of corroborative data about JJ. He read through JJ's childhood medical reports from the Guam military base about JJ's birth through the time he left for MSSD in 1995. He reviewed numerous student conduct complaints, including six reports from MSSD in October 1998, three reports in November 1998, two reports from February 1999, and finally, two more reports from April 1999. There were reports from the judicial affairs council at Gallaudet University when JJ had been expelled from MSSD in May 1999. He reviewed another document from Mr. Alexander Quaynor, the coordinator at the English Language Institute, that outlined expectations for restitution from JJ to the people from whom he burglarized and stole. He read a psychological evaluation by Dr. Linda Lytle when JJ was preparing to graduate from high school at the Model Secondary School for the Deaf.

  Dr. Madsen sifted through the police reports from JJ's arrest to incarceration at the D.C. jail to the transfer to St. Elizabeth's hospital. He watched the videotaped confession from February 13, 2001, as well as Melani's videotaped statement from February 14, 2001. He read the arresting reports filed by Detectives Richmond and Reed. The doctor read the transcript of the grand jury indictment from May 7, 2001. He read many of the letters JJ had sent to Melani while incarcerated at the D.C. jail. He read JJ's letters to his parents and his brother.

Dr. Madsen's evaluations were laborious, mostly because facets of the case did not make sense to him. His initial impression was that JJ was cold and calculating, lacking remorse and empathy. With more frequent meetings, JJ described his life experiences.

"After I saw him a second time, he talked about the despair that he had as a youth growing up in Guam, not being able to communicate with people, not even with his own family, other than somewhat with his brother," said Dr. Madsen. "When he talked about his sense of frustration and, what seemed to me, a tinge of some real bitterness and anger, then I started to reassess.

"Mr. Mesa seemed to lack the ability to communicate and that he felt very isolated. Mr. Mesa would typically withdraw when he was feeling frustrated, upset, depressed, distressed, and that he usually would come back and do something positive for the person that had made him angry or upset in the first place."

JJ explained that, for example, when he became angry at his father, he would go back to him later after he had calmed down to do something nice for him, like helping with chores or building something in his home workshop. JJ told the doctor that he often had difficulty discussing his feelings, especially about an unpleasant event. Still, he could show the person he cared about by doing something special instead.

"It became clear to me that he had something I called a 'shadow life' that he carried in Guam," explained Dr. Madsen. "That shadow life involved not only his subjective sense of being oppressed and being mistreated, being rejected, being treated as if he were a child without the dignity of communication coming his way from other people and going out and doing very mean things, even vicious things."

JJ described to the doctor various incidents on the school bus when he was a child in Guam. He had taunted another student who used a wheelchair. JJ explained he would tap the boy's shoulder and pull his hair to agitate the classmate. JJ engaged in physical fights with classmates. His anger extended into injuries and killings of animals, including his sister's cats. Dr. Madsen asked him to give more detail.

"I asked him how many cats he had killed. He said, 'maybe ten.' I asked him if there were other animals that were the brunt of whatever was going on inside. He told me he had whipped a dog once with a stick after his father had whipped [Joseph]. He said he had once punched a dog in the face with his fist. I asked him about other things that happened over time. That's when the floodgates opened even further.

"He talked about punching walls and trees and tiles, essentially lashing out. With most of these things, he said he wasn't even angry and didn't have relief after he did them. He would avow never to do these things again. He knew they were wrong and that, on some level, he said they scared him. He even used the term that he was disgusted.

"He said, 'I can't do this again. I can't do it. This is bad,' but he would never seemingly link up the why or any kind of situational things that might have led up to what he did. For example, he couldn't say that he had killed his sister's cats because his sister was the least likely in all the family to have communicated with him. He said he had always had a great deal of upset with those two sisters, in particular, the one who had the cats.

"He didn't make the link in his head that maybe he killed her cats because he had a great sense of resentment toward his sisters for talking at the dinner table, carrying on conversations, being convivial, laughing, and enjoying life while he was left in solitary silence to wonder about what was going on. They wouldn't even respond to him many times when he wanted them to."

Dr. Madsen speculated that JJ was primarily influenced by his father's disapproval or approval. JJ thrived on positive feedback from his father. When his father praised him, JJ would feel immensely happy and proud. Yet, according to Dr. Madsen, positive praise did not often occur, leaving JJ feeling depressed, disconnected, rejected, and unappreciated.

These experiences led Dr. Madsen to shift away from his initial impressions. "There were some things that didn't seem to fit the psychopath that I thought he was. I saw that he had sudden and genuine feelings that are unlike most psychopaths that I had ever seen. He had genuine behaviors that would indicate a loving, caring relationship with someone that I didn't anticipate to see."

Dr. Madsen started formulating a different hypothesis about why JJ would commit these murders. Yet, a contradiction remained. The murder victims were not hearing people who mocked or excluded him from social activities. Eric Plunkett and Ben Varner were like him: deaf, young, aspirational, and shared some of the same stresses and strains in the hearing world that he had. JJ came to MSSD, then Gallaudet, a world in which communication was fluid and accessible, where inclusion was the norm, and integration with peers was a matter of natural discourse. There was no strain about being understood and being left out.

According to early childhood school records from Guam and his parents' reports, JJ did well in the mainstream educational program before going to MSSD. School personnel told his parents that JJ was doing well in school and that his peers looked up to him. JJ never spoke rudely to others, even when he would become angry and walk away.

JJ was living with inner turmoil. "One time, Mr. Mesa (JJ's father) had asked JJ to make a rooster coop," explained Dr. Madsen. "Mr. Mesa, Jr. (JJ) had used the best wood to make the rooster nest, not the scrap wood that his father anticipated that he would use. When his father chastened him for having used the best wood that could have been used for another purpose, Mr. Mesa, Jr. Was said to get very red in the face and very upset, rushed out and tore down that which he had just made. He just ripped it apart. Ripped it asunder and then threw the good wood back to where it could be used for some other purpose."

Dr. Madsen had thought that JJ would blossom in a deaf environment. JJ did fairly well at MSSD academically, with a GPA of 2.5. Yet, JJ told the doctor that he never felt like he fit in with his peers at MSSD. Indeed, there were several disciplinary actions. One time he was disciplined for punching and damaging a wall. Another time, he had a fight with a student. There was another disciplinary action for provoking a student to get angry. Another altercation occurred when he was wrestling with another student.

To complicate matters, JJ's IQ scores, administered by Dr. Lytle, a deaf psychologist who worked at MSSD, were at a 2.7-grade level. He had difficulty with language mechanics and expression, low study skills, low science scores, and low overall problem-solving scores. JJ's aspirations to go to college and become a teacher for the deaf would remain virtually unattainable. He would need a lot of tutoring and remedial effort to get up to a level that would allow him to perform at a college level.

So, as JJ entered MSSD with aspirations of a promising future and helping future generations of deaf children, dreams that he had held for many years of his life, his hopes for grabbing hold of those dreams came to a halt. In fact, after graduating and when he came to Gallaudet for his first year, he did not enter as a college freshman. Instead, he was enrolled for a year as a remedial student.

"It's not where he wanted to be," explained Dr. Madsen. "He didn't particularly like to be at MSSD in the first place. He wanted to be at home. He wanted to be with his family, with his Chamorro people. He didn't like the food. He had trouble fitting in, but he came back because at least it had some kind of hope. So, he said to me of that first year that there was a rash of criminal activity, 'Far more than they knew,' he told me."

Dr. Madsen's assessment of JJ's behavior indicated it was all brought about from feelings of frustration, anger, and rejection. He characterized JJ as developmentally and socially backward, dramatically so. Surmising that JJ's deafness caused him to feel uncertain about himself, he pointed to a disconnect between JJ's thoughts and actions with behaviors. Dr. Madsen talked with JJ's parents, who said that he had never really expressed sadness as a child; he never cried.

Dr. Madsen said, "In his medical record was an incident that he had chopped his leg with a machete. In another record, he dislocated his elbow. I asked his parents, and they said, 'He didn't cry.'"

Dr. Madsen believed JJ suffered from alexithymia, characterized by an inability to understand his emotions and how they affected his behavior. He thought JJ's motivations were linked to deep-rooted anger and frustration, resulting in intermittent explosive outbursts. He felt JJ suffered from a chronic, low-grade depression, called dysthymia, because of his life experiences of being deaf and isolated.

Given his assessment, Dr. Madsen said, "Mr. Plunkett was somebody that he was friends with, somebody that he helped, somebody that he tutored, somebody that he had gone places with and shared things with. It makes no sense to me that he is just a psychopath going off; he's always known what's right and wrong. He just goes berserk. And it's not just kill; it is overkill. It's not just simply doing away with him; it is just brutal. That is common with someone who is in a rage.

"Now, is the rage because he is just a mean, nasty SOB? Or is he in a rage as the end product of all these years of build-up of anger and resentment? It makes no sense to me in any other way than to assert that his behavior was a product of mental illness, a product of that conglomerate of dyscontrol, that affective turmoil going on inside, and that cognitive obsessiveness. I have to support the not guilty by reason of insanity."

Dr. Madsen determined JJ could not be guilty of his crimes because he suffered from a mental illness. JJ's underlying mental disease undermined his ability to understand what he was doing. He could not exercise his free will or control his behaviors.

Chapter 24

A Serial Killer

The standard posits that an individual is to be declared insane and not responsible for their actions at the time of the crime if the individual is either unable to understand what they were doing or unable to control their behavior. The fancy legal language is "unable to conform your conduct to the requirements of the law or understand the wrongfulness of your actions." But in plain English, did you know what you were doing when you were doing the crime, and could you control yourself?

—Dr. Mitch Hugonnet, Psychologist, St. Elizabeth's Hospital

In early March 2002, Dr. Mitch Hugonnet, a forensic psychologist at St. Elizabeth's Hospital, also evaluated JJ to determine whether he was criminally responsible for his crimes. Dr. Hugonnet, like the other evaluators in this case, reviewed the documentation the prosecution and defense had about the case. Dr. Hugonnet interviewed JJ specifically about the murders for five hours. He did not do formal psychological testing with JJ because the standardized tests he typically used were not normed for deaf populations.

"First of all, we have a unique advantage in that we have the patients on the ward twenty-four-seven," explained Dr. Hugonnet. "We have trained staff, many of whom have been working there at least as long as me, if not longer. They have been trained in being able to observe and evaluate symptoms. We have a continuous flow of information from the staff, at least two reports a day, one in the morning and one in the afternoon. We observe everyone on the ward twenty-four-seven.

"We do a series of interviews, both typical psychiatric and psychological interviews, mental status exams, the kinds of things where you just want to know what the patient understands he's there for. You're evaluating things like awareness, attention, perceptual disturbances, also called hallucinations.

"You're evaluating whether there is a thought disorder. In other words, is the thought disjointed? Or is it straight, goal-directed, linear, and rational?

"My office is on the ward," continued Dr. Hugonnet. "Somedays, I wish it wasn't, but indeed, it is on the ward. As a result, I'm in the nursing station all of the time. I'm walking the halls, bumping into patients, talking to the patients. If they need to find me for something, they know where to find me. We talk about matters both mundane and important."

JJ had been in St. Elizabeth's Hospital on ward nine for about two months, since January 3. In addition to the five hours spent talking with Dr. Hugonnet about the murders, he also spent about twelve hours, thirty minutes once or twice a week during the first six weeks JJ was at the hospital.

"We wanted to get a sense of the kind of person he was," explained the doctor.

None of the clinical staff on the unit had observed JJ exhibiting psychotic symptoms. He did not seem to respond to hallucinations; he was not talking to himself or acting bizarre; he did not seem to interact with or respond to an unseen entity or person. Dr. Hugonnet had learned of JJ's letters to Melani about his plan to appear mentally ill. The doctor then asked the hospital physician, Dr. Richie, to take JJ off the antipsychotic medication, Seroquel, to see if symptoms would appear.

"Dr. Richie was relatively new at the forensic psych game, despite the board certification in forensic psychiatry," said Dr. Hugonnet. "[Dr. Richie] put [Mr. Mesa] on it presumptively because he read some reports that, according to Dr. Richie, there may have been hallucinations. In the era of defensive medicine, it doesn't hurt anybody to put someone on an antipsychotic; it can't hurt them, but not wanting to be caught not treating, he treats. When in doubt, Dr. Richie treats.

"I approach it from another perspective. Since we didn't see any evidence for psychotic symptoms of any kind, both on the ward or in the records we were reviewing. In fact, some of the records correspondence to Ms. Melani DeGuzman said that he was going to feign symptoms and so forth, I requested that Dr. Richie take him off the medication, and he did."

Psychotic symptoms did not appear. Dr. Hugonnet considered JJ's young age when he started stealing, injuring, and killing animals. JJ's consistent rule-breaking, emotional volatility, disregard for other people, and of course, killing Eric and Ben for self-gratification fit not only the conduct disorder diagnosis, but was also a natural step toward an antisocial personality.

"The DSM-IV allows you to diagnose conduct disorder in adults if they meet enough of the criteria. There is a threshold where they give you a list of behaviors or attitudes that you have to meet. And if in the case of conduct disorder, you have to meet at least three of them; [Mr. Mesa] met twelve of them. Twelve is considerably more than three, or you could be rated severe conduct disorder if your conduct has severely damaged or hurt others. Again, certainly, these two crimes are quite severe.

"Early-onset, because he was stealing before he was ten, hurting dogs and killing cats around the age of ten or eleven. Conduct disorder is meant to describe an individual that could consistently break the rules, violate social norms, hurt other people in a consistent and volitional way," explained Dr. Hugonnet.

The fourteen-year history of JJ's behaviors fit the

developmental path of a serial killer. He started stealing from his parents and teachers around eight years old. He progressed to hurting then killing animals. In adolescence, he continued to rob people. From there, he graduated to killing his first victim, then his second before police arrested him. JJ had tried to cover his crimes by removing evidence, pointing his finger at other people, and keeping mementos of his kills. He redirected police to focus on the sexual orientation of his victims. Each action, even at an early age, was calculated and measured. As JJ got older and had more practice perfecting his antisocial behaviors, he escalated the risks he took. He needed increasingly more stimulation to pursue his fantasies. His ultimate fantasy, murder, was further intensified when he chose someone from the deaf community.

    JJ's behavior was goal-directed, rational, and planned. He kept returning to the crime scenes, opening windows so there would not be a noticeable odor. He covered Ben in a blanket to keep the blood from seeping under the door, and moved both Eric and Ben away from the door entranceway. JJ noticed the blood on his arms and clothes, went to the bathroom, and washed up to remove the apparent stains. He took Ben's shirt to wear, both as a trophy and as an accessory, to leave his room without being obvious. JJ returned to both Eric's and Ben's rooms after the murders and did so with stealth and planning so he would not be caught.

Whenever he went into and left the rooms, he unlocked and then locked the doors again. He never went into their rooms and left the doors open so others may see. He hid his presence in their rooms. When JJ stole Chad's credit card, he had thought about killing him, but it would be too obvious. JJ chose his victims, in part because they lived alone in their dorm rooms. JJ knew that what he was doing was wrong. His actions pointed to planning, execution, and cover-up. There was no mental illness, according to Dr. Hugonnet, that would account for his behaviors.

The repetitive and detailed accounts of the murders in the confession videotape showed Dr. Hugonnet that JJ had strong, emotional feelings connected to the killings. The doctor observed the same intensity when JJ reviewed the murders with him. The act of killing itself brought temporary gratification. Murder became a source of excitement and stimulation: excitement in the planning, committing, and anonymity of the murders.

JJ told Dr. Hugonnet that while he was killing Eric and Ben, he wondered about what each was thinking at the time. *Why is he doing this to me? I have got to get out of here.* The doctor termed this as imputing the victims' thoughts, imaging what his victims were thinking while they were being killed. According to Dr. Hugonnet, this, too, fit the profile of serial killers.

Dr. Hugonnet knew of the early profiling studies of Robert Ressler in the FBI during the 1980s and 1990s. Criminal profiling creates an idea of what kind of person the perpetrator is based on a set of behaviors and personality characteristics. Serial killings usually involve three or more separate murders with an emotional cooling-off period in between. A serial killer usually premeditates the killing and fantasizes and plans the details of the crime. After the first killing, there will be a cool-down, which can be days, weeks, or months.

In contrast to a spree killer who is not concerned with the choice of victims, the serial killer chooses his victims with care. He selects the type of person he wants. In JJ's case, they both were deaf, had regular social interactions with him, and lived alone in their own dormitory rooms. The serial killer does not expect to be caught. He controls the events when he plans, chooses, and kills. The primary intents of serial killers can be different. Some may kill as part of a larger criminal enterprise, such as mob-related activities. Others may kill in emotional outbursts, such as in family disputes. They can also be killers because of sexual motives. Sexual motives may only be known to the killer himself.

While JJ himself denied sexual motivations, there were sexual-related aspects to his murders. For one, JJ perceived both Eric and Ben as gay and informed police of his observations. He chose to distract detectives toward Thomas Minch, who had reportedly had not only a sexual relationship with Eric but an argument about their intimacy. JJ told officers that Ben was gay, seemingly to make a point about a connection between the two homicides.

Serial killers often demonstrate an escalation in behaviors. As Dr. Hugonnet observed, JJ's behaviors started at a young age and escalated in severity and frequency as he became older. Though JJ only killed two people, his development was interrupted by being caught by the police. Another characteristic that JJ exhibited was the collection of trophies from his victims. JJ had collected a picture of Thomas Minch outside of Eric's door and kept it hidden in a lockbox in his closet. Manipulation of the body after death is also part of the profile. JJ had moved both bodies of Eric and Ben after he murdered them.

Dr. Hugonnet was experienced enough in forensic

psychology to see JJ's behavior patterns from a broad perspective. He was knowledgeable about the characteristics and manipulation strategies of criminal offenders, and knew of the research into serial killing profiles. He also understood how mental illness could manifest and cause people to commit crimes. According to Dr. Hugonnet, JJ was not mentally ill.

"He could conform his conduct to the requirement of the law. He knew what he was doing was wrong; otherwise, there wouldn't have been the elaborate planning and the behaviors after the murders designed to cover up what he had done. There were many behaviors involving covering up what he had done or directing attention elsewhere to someone else. That indicated quite clearly that A, he knew it was wrong, and B, he was capable of controlling himself, and in fact, orchestrating and planning these events days to weeks in advance."

Chapter 25

Funny Feelings

The issue of mind/body relatedness is, I think, more of a medical matter. There are people that have medical problems that can present as looking like they have a mental illness. One of the most interesting phenomena that I have seen are people who have medical illnesses and look like they're "crazy." But I have also learned over the years that you get the amount of information that's necessary for you to answer the questions before the court. And in this instance, the questions were whether or not Mr. Mesa was competent for trial, whether he was competent to waive the insanity defense, if he understood what the insanity defense is, did he know he could use it or not use it, and whether or not he was criminally responsible for his behaviors in the alleged crimes.

—*Dr. Raymond Patterson, psychiatrist, St. Elizabeth's Hospital*

Three months after his arrival at the forensic unit in ward nine at St. Elizabeth's Hospital, on April 8, 2002, Dr. Raymond Patterson was to evaluate Joseph Mesa for the court. He planned three hours for the evaluation, 8:00 a.m. to 11:00 a.m. Dr. Patterson had known JJ since his arrival on the ward. He intentionally waited to conduct the evaluation after he had a sense of how JJ behaved on the unit.

"He had been at St. E's since January," said Dr. Patterson. "So, he had an opportunity to talk with other people who were mentally ill. I asked him whether or not he thought he had any kinds of symptoms like they had. His answers to those questions were, 'no,' but that he had tried to kill himself in jail.

"His explanation for the murders was that he had a 'funny feeling' come over him as he was walking to Eric Plunkett's room to rob him, and as he was walking to Ben Varner's room to rob him.

"I asked him whether or not he had ever had that kind of 'funny feeling' before and to tell me more about it. He told me that the funny feeling had happened when he killed cats when he was nine or ten or eleven or fourteen; he couldn't tell me the specific age, which I found to be very curious.

"He also told me the funny feeling came over him at the D.C. jail when he tried to kill himself three times. He said that he took his sheet, put it around his neck, tied it off, passed out three times, and then woke up. That's a very interesting presentation for someone to give to a psychiatrist."

Dr. Patterson did not believe JJ's story of attempted suicide. As a regular reviewer of every completed suicide in California, New Jersey, and in the city of Philadelphia, he had never read a report of anyone tying a sheet around their neck, passing out, and then waking up.

"When you pass out, you cut off the air supply, you

tend to die," explained Dr. Patterson. "The only time it could happen is if the sheet broke. If it came loose from wherever they tied it off, and they fell because it became loosened, yeah, people have awakened from that. But if the pressure is there, you cut off the air supply. There is no reason for you to wake up."

When the doctor asked JJ if he had reported these incidents to the personnel at the jail, he said no. The doctor asked what JJ told the psychiatrists and psychologists when they made their regular rounds to South 1, 2, and 3 at the jail. JJ said he told the mental health team that he was all right.

"Why did you do that?" asked Dr. Patterson. "If you were thinking about killing yourself and you actually tried, why would you tell the mental health staff that you were all right?"

JJ responded, "Because I didn't want to lose my pencil and paper and have them take things away from me. I wanted to keep writing to my family and to my girlfriend."

Dr. Patterson founds this interesting. He suspected JJ had never truly meant to kill himself. Initially, JJ told the doctor that the incident in the jail was his first suicide attempt, but later in the interview, he said there had been previous attempts as well.

"To me, that was a curious statement," said Dr. Patterson. "People who are legitimately suicidal, who really want to die, either are successful because they don't tell anybody, or when they recover enough to realize they 'came close,' they tell someone.

"And I know from my own experience that the psychologist and mental health staff ask those questions, 'How are you feeling?' 'Have you thought about hurting yourself?' or 'Are you feeling suicidal?' They don't just say, 'Hey, how are you?' and keep walking by. So, for [Joseph Mesa] not to tell them that, which I thought was at least curious and possibly a reflection that he was not genuinely trying to kill himself."

JJ told Dr. Patterson that he had trouble controlling his temper when he was younger.

"He told me that when he was younger and got into arguments with his girlfriend, he threatened to hurt himself. He snatched a mirror off a car; he punched a steering wheel; he threatened to jump off a building at Gallaudet; he threatened to go off Gallaudet into the community, so somebody could shoot him."

Rather than serious suicide attempts, Dr. Patterson characterized these incidents as reactions to relationship issues.

"This is very characteristic of conflict in a couple's relationship, or sometimes between parent and child. A young girl or young man may say, 'I'm going to kill myself if I don't get to drive the car' or 'I'm going to do this,' or 'I am going to take some pills.' With relationships, 'If you don't come back to me,' 'If you don't spend all your time with me, I'm going to go jump off a building.' These kinds of things get said fairly frequently. Those tend to be relationship issues, and with Mr. Mesa, he reported to me that it all occurred in his relationship with his girlfriend."

Rather than delve deeper into JJ's interpersonal relationships, Dr. Patterson redirected the conversation back to the murders and the "funny feelings."

"I had a funny feeling when I was in the room with Eric Plunkett and Ben Varner. When I was walking to the room with the intent of stealing from them, this funny feeling came over me. When I got there, the funny feeling was on me. I found myself killing Eric with a chair and then stabbing Ben with a knife," JJ told Dr. Patterson.

However, Dr. Patterson had seen the videotaped confession. JJ's story with the doctor did not match the confession. JJ told the doctor that the detectives had misunderstood him. At this point now with Dr. Patterson, he had decided to share the real story, the one about the funny feelings. The doctor questioned deeper.

"Had you had the funny feeling any other times?" asked Dr. Patterson.

"I had it with the cats, the three times in jail, and the two times I killed Ben and Eric. I didn't have it any other time," JJ responded.

"I saw the notes about two fights you've had with other patients here, one in January and one in February. Did you have the funny feeling when you had these fights with the other two patients?"

"No, I didn't have the funny feeling then."

"How did you feel after you had killed Eric and Ben?"

"I had the funny feeling, then I was scared," JJ responded.

"What about the black hands and seeing ghosts and monsters?" asked Dr. Patterson.

"I saw the black hands when I was around nine, ten, eleven, or twelve or fourteen; I'm not quite sure."

Dr. Patterson asked JJ to tell him more about seeing black hands.

"I had seen them around seven or eight o'clock at night when I was walking to my grandmother's house. I would talk to them. I would tell them, 'I love you' so they wouldn't hurt me. And then they would go away."

"Did you ever tell your grandmother about it?"

"No, I never told her."

"Did you tell anybody in your family?"

"No, I never told anybody."

"Have you had anything like that happen since?"

"No, not for a long time, not for several years."

The black hands that JJ referenced were related to a professional wrestler called The Undertaker. The wrestler wore long black gloves in his matches.

Dr. Patterson wanted to know more about how JJ felt when he killed Eric and Ben.

"I had that funny feeling. I was scared," JJ said.

"What were you afraid of?"

"I was scared that I would get caught."

"And what do you feel about these deaths now?" asked Dr. Patterson.

"I am scared," JJ answered.

"Scared of what?"

"Scared of what is going to happen to me."

"Do you have any feelings about the deaths of these two men and their families?"

"No."

"Do you think that's unusual or that is strange in any way?"

"No."

It was clear to Dr. Patterson that JJ had no remorse for the murders of Eric and Ben, the anguish caused to their families, or the havoc wreaked in the deaf community at Gallaudet. JJ had only been worried about himself and how to get himself out of jail.

"Why did you confess to the murders?" asked Dr. Patterson.

"Because they were going to catch me anyway. They had found the jacket; they found the knife. They were going to catch me anyway. So, I decided to go turn myself in before they actually caught me."

Dr. Patterson diagnosed JJ with malingering, when a person makes up symptoms to avoid an adverse event, like getting caught or getting out of some type of problem. It can also be when a person wants something, like making up symptoms to sue someone and get a monetary reward.

"In criminal cases, it is usually to avoid being locked up or found guilty of a crime," Dr. Patterson explained. "Mr. Mesa gave me this description of these 'funny feelings' that he says happened with he killed cats and didn't happen again until he killed people. It didn't happen again until he tried to kill himself.

"My experiences with people who have legitimate psychotic disorders, particularly those who have hallucinations, they don't necessarily have them every day. They don't go away for years and then pop up conveniently when you get caught for killing somebody. They don't do that. They don't just hit you when you kill cats, then disappear, then come back when you kill somebody in September, then come back in February when you kill somebody again, then disappear, then come back when you're locked up."

Though Dr. Patterson's primary diagnosis was malingering, he found evidence of an underlying, foundational disorder. Similar to Dr. Hugonnet's assessment, Dr. Patterson also diagnosed JJ with antisocial personality disorder.

"Here is a man who has a chronic history of taking from other people, of breaking the law, whether he gets caught or not, of not having remorse for what he does to people, of being deceitful. There is an externalization of responsibility. Antisocial personality disorders don't take responsibility for what they have done until they get caught. Once they get caught, then oh yeah, 'I did that,' but there was something wrong, 'you should have pity on me;

I'm a victim.' But until they get caught, they don't take responsibility.

"The hallmarks of antisocial personality disorder, first, is a chronic, repeated effort at getting what you want and violating the law. It's not considered a serious kind of psychosis because it's a choice; people choose to do it.

"I asked Mr. Mesa why he killed Mr. Plunkett and Mr. Varner. He told me that he knew they were alone; they were weak. So, the hallmarks of antisocial personality disorder are continued, chronic abuse of the law to get what you want to get; it's a choice, not a compulsion, not something that you can't stop. It's a choice. The other factors are deceitfulness, a lack of remorse, and externalizing behavior.

"In my opinion, to a reasonable degree of medical certainty, Mr. Mesa is not suffering from and has not suffered from any kind of hallucinations. He understood the wrongfulness of what he was doing. He could conform his conduct to the rule of law; he chose not to. And that, in my opinion, is a choice; it is not a compulsion. It is not psychosis or some mental illness. It is a choice; that's what he did."

Chapter 26

A Continuum Of Behavior

I have several disagreements with Dr. Madsen's methods. First, based on his report where he described how he went about the work, he had a number of interviews with Mr. Mesa that were not facilitated with the services of a certified sign language interpreter. As I heard in his testimony and is in the report, he describes typing back and forth in English on a TTY machine that would, through either the lights display, the liquid crystal display, or printed display would allow each person to read in English. It was inappropriate to conduct an interview with a deaf patient with a TTY because, by and large, in the deaf population, English fluency is often quite limited in the deaf population. So, conducting an interview in English is a method where misunderstandings could readily occur.

—Dr. Robert Pollard, Deaf Wellness Center, Rochester, NY.

On April 14, 2002, Dr. Robert Pollard, a clinical psychologist and expert in mental health and deafness, met with JJ at St. Elizabeth's Hospital for an evaluation. He disagreed with Dr. Madsen's assessment right from the beginning. Dr. Pollard's assessments differed from other professionals' because he used sign language to converse with JJ directly. He did not use a sign language interpreter like Dr. Patterson and Dr. Hugonnet. He also did not type on the keyboard of a teletype communication device (TTY) like Dr. Madsen. Dr. Pollard and JJ conversed using American Sign Language. Dr. Robert Pollard spent seventeen hours interviewing JJ.

Dr. Pollard had an extensive background in using psychological tests with deaf people. For example, he knew that using tests designed for hearing people whose native language is English would lead to inaccurate, biased conclusions with deaf people. The doctor knew that Dr. Madsen's test results would be incorrect and biased. Dr. Madsen's use of psychological tests with JJ was inappropriate. Even worse, according to Dr. Pollard, Dr. Madsen's conclusions were based on what he thought it must be like to be deaf.

"If anybody did their homework in this field, they would know," chastised Dr. Pollard, "even just reading a couple of articles, that particularly using objective personality tests with deaf individuals is wildly inappropriate, and a mistake that has brought shame and very negative things on deaf people for a long time.

"The tests he gave are based on the English language and include reading levels that are far beyond Mr. Mesa, and usually the average deaf individual. Even if the overall reading level is within an individual's capabilities, these types of personality tests can include phrases or cultural references or pieces of information which are not known to the average deaf respondent."

Dr. Pollard explained that a person who lives

without hearing or speaking might not be comfortable in social situations with hearing people who cannot sign. Giving a psychological test to a person for whom the test was not designed can lead to substantial biases and conclusions that are inaccurate and erroneous.

"For example," Dr. Pollard said, "Dr. Madsen's report had a number of comments about his personal feelings being involved in the conclusions. He describes, 'This has been one of the most difficult endeavors I've undertaken in twenty-plus years in clinical and forensic practice. The more I tried to steep myself in the subjective experience of those who are deaf, the more I found the defendant to be suffering from a number of disorders most of which have been outside his awareness.'"

Dr. Madsen imagined what it must be like to be deaf and allowed his imaginings to become part of a psychological report about JJ's mental health status. Although Dr. Madsen differed from JJ in culture, language, and lived experiences, he inserted his own beliefs into his assessment.

"By and large a hearing person who grows up all their life with a sense of hearing, with ease of communication with those around you, with the enjoyment of music or birds singing, can't imagine life with hearing loss as anything except horrific, full of mental-illness-producing experiences, pitiful, and awful. It's the kind of thing you see on television with movies about pitiful deaf people or in early literature about pitiful deaf people," said Dr. Pollard.

"If there's one thing that's well known is the horrible history of the 'psychology of the deaf field,' which is a misnomer in and of itself. It's the misuse of two things, both of which Dr. Madsen did; it was A, the misuse of psychological tests, and B, psychologists or other mental health professionals who based their conclusions on imagining what it must be like to be deaf."

Dr. Madsen had diagnosed JJ with an intermittent explosive disorder and conduct disorder. Dr. Pollard disagreed; he concluded JJ did not meet the criteria for the condition. He did not believe there was enough evidence to support Dr. Hugonnet's and Dr. Patterson's diagnoses for an antisocial personality disorder. Dr. Pollard saw JJ's behaviors on a continuum: they got worse as he got older.

"Isn't it strange for someone who has committed property crimes to all of the sudden commit murders?" asked Dr. Pollard. "Dr. Madsen says that those murders must be the result of some mental illness. It would not be strange at all to look back at a group of people who have committed murders, to look back over their histories, and say, well, things started out with petty thefts, then things progressed to crimes or behavior problems where there was a victim around, and then there was property destruction, and then eventually the first murder occurred. That process of more serious behaviors is not at all unusual in a population of persons who eventually commit murders."

JJ told Dr. Pollard that he felt urges and temptations to commit his crimes. He said that he had imagined the killings, not a hallucination type of psychosis, but more like fantasies. JJ had fantasized about killing his sister's cats, imagined their bloodied heads before he killed them. While at the D.C. jail, JJ noticed a nearby graveyard, which "gave him bad pictures in his mind." Movies, in particular, caused JJ to have evil imaginings. These images, JJ said, exerted control over his behavior.

Like the other professionals who evaluated JJ's mental health, Dr. Pollard reviewed an extensive list of documents and videotapes. He interviewed JJ directly and administered psychological tests specifically normed with deaf individuals. During the testing, JJ had some difficulty concentrating, but he was, after all, facing serious punishment for his crimes. JJ's IQ testing revealed him in the average range, like ninety-five percent of the United

States adults. Like the other assessments, Dr. Pollard also assessed JJ as being depressed. JJ seemed to have been depressed since first leaving his home country, Guam, to attend MSSD when he was a teenager. Leaving home to attend to the demands of a college student was difficult for JJ; he missed his family and culture. Like the other assessments, Dr. Pollard agreed JJ did not appear to have psychotic symptoms, such as hallucinations and delusions.

Because JJ's behaviors started at an early age, Dr. Pollard diagnosed JJ as suffering from conduct disorder, sometimes a precursor for later antisocial personality disorder. His history of rule-breaking, aggression, and destructive behaviors began around eight years old and continued to escalate age he grew older. Like the others, Dr. Pollard agreed that JJ's depressive symptoms worsened by leaving home to attend high school in Washington, D.C.

Dr. Pollard used a scale from one, meaning the behavior was good and right, to five, meaning that behavior is medium, neither right nor wrong, to ten, meaning that behavior is bad, wrong, and illegal. Using this scale, JJ indicated he knew that the murders of Eric and Ben were wrong, both before the killings and afterward. He knew his intentions with them were lethal. He expected the two young men would die as a result of his intentional actions.

His plans to murder Eric and Ben became a reality when he entered their rooms and closed their doors.

Given all the information gathered from JJ, Dr. Pollard determined that JJ had indeed understood the wrongfulness of his actions, he did not have an underlying mental illness that caused him to commit the murders or thefts, and he could control his behaviors to conform to the law, though he chose not to.

Chapter 27

Motion To Suppress Evidence

I don't know why I chose Ben and Eric. I had an angel on one shoulder that was helpful, friendly, and nice. But there was a devil on the other shoulder. A thought would pop into my mind. I'd try to control it, but I couldn't. The only way that I could get rid of those thoughts was to do what the thoughts were telling me to do. Only then would they go away.

—JJ

On Thursday, April 25, 2002, a little over fourteen months after his arrest and eleven days after meeting with Dr. Pollard, on Thursday, JJ's court case began. Ferris Bond, JJ's defense attorney, enlisted the help of another attorney, Jill Sege, because of her knowledge of the deaf community and her ASL skills. They would begin their case by first trying to discount any testimony from Melani against JJ. Mr. Bond and Ms. Sege would be up against formidable opponents, Jennifer Collins and Jeb Boasberg, the prosecuting attorneys.

Melani was to take the stand first, assisted by her attorney, Mr. Kahn. Mr. Bond began by asserting privileged communication because of a common-law marriage between JJ and Melani. Mr. Bond definitely did not want the letters to Melani to be entered as evidence against JJ. He could only do that if he could prove that as a lawfully married couple, Melani could not be compelled to testify against her husband. He called for Mrs. Melani Mesa to take the stand.

Melani approached the witness stand. She wore a ring on the ring finger of her left hand, which, she explained to the judge, symbolized her marriage to her husband. She said she did not want to testify against her husband. She stated that in consultation with Mr. Kahn, she intended to invoke the marital privilege in this trial.

Mr. Boasberg stood to cross-examine Melani. He said, "Good morning, Ms. DeGuzman," to which Melani interrupted with, "Excuse me, but my name is Mesa, not DeGuzman." Mr. Boasberg continued unfazed.

"On what date did you consider yourself to be married?" Mr. Boasberg asked.

"May 17, 2000," Melani answered.

Undaunted, he continued his questioning, pinning down Melani's answers, imploring her to be specific in the details. Did she use her name on official documents? Was she registered as Melani Mesa at Gallaudet? Did she have a wedding ceremony? Did she use the last name Mesa on her driver's license? Melani answered his questions with one answer: no. Mr. Boasberg reminded Melani of her testimony with the Grand Jury when she told them Joseph Mesa was her boyfriend, not her husband.

JJ's attorney, Ferris Bond, approached this from a different angle. He said that Melani's signature on a statement indicating that she understood the interpreters, with both the detectives during the investigation and to the Grand Jury, was misleading. He said Melani had, in fact, not understood what she was signing; therefore, the statements to the police and her testimony to the Grand

Jury should be eliminated as evidence at JJ's trial. Finally, Mr. Bond suggested not only did Melani misunderstand the statement to the police and Grand Jury, but so did JJ. Because JJ had not understood the interpreters in the first place, the entire confession should not be admissible in court.

The judge disagreed with Mr. Bond's interpretation. He ruled against his arguments in all three circumstances: that Melani and JJ were lawfully married; that Melani's testimony should be eliminated because she did not understand the interpreters; and that JJ's confession be stricken because he, too, did not understand the interpreters. The judge determined the detectives and the court had consistently and legally procured the sign language interpreters. The police and court officials had legally obtained written waivers for understanding, also consistent with the law. Police had twice explained to JJ about the interpreter waiver form, and twice, JJ agreed he could understand the interpreters during his confession. Legal marriage between JJ and Melani had not been established because Melani and JJ had lived in separate dorms. In their statements to the police, they had referred to each other as "boyfriend" and "girlfriend," respectively. Melani had admitted she created a "wedding book" and "marriage certificate" on her computer after JJ was arrested. Though they intended to be married at a future date, that date had not arrived.

The judge's final decision was that Melani's statements and testimony could be used against JJ in the court proceedings. Melani's and JJ's statements to the police could also be used. Their relationship was not considered a common-law marriage under the law. Therefore, the prosecutors could use all the letters written to Melani by JJ could be used against him. The prosecution would present the United States' case against Joseph Mesa, Jr. to jurors the following week.

Chapter 28

Trial Day One

Attorney: Had Eric done anything to you that would make you want to hurt him?

JJ: Never. He was a very good friend.

On Thursday, May 2, at 2:10 p.m., the jury trial for JJ began. Prosecutors Jennifer Collins and Jeb Boasberg had planned extensive testimony by numerous witnesses. Ms. Collins presented a summary of the facts in her opening statement.

She addressed the jurors. "In August 2000, three

young men came here to Washington, D.C., to Gallaudet University to start their freshman year; three young men who came to Washington, D.C. from all over the country; three young men who came here, no doubt hoping, as most college freshmen do, to start new lives and have new adventures in a new city away from home; three young men who perhaps obviously were deaf, because as many of you know, Gallaudet University is the premier university in the world for students who are deaf and hard of hearing; three young men who actually all moved into the same floor, the same wing of the same dorm, a dorm called Cogswell Hall; three young men who came here to start their new lives. But before their freshman year was even half over, two of those young men would be dead; two of those young men would be brutally, brutally murdered in their own dorm rooms.

"And the reason that those young men died is because that third freshman turned out to be greedy; that third freshman decided that he wanted money; that third freshman decided that he didn't have enough money to buy the things that he wanted to buy, like presents for his girlfriend, and things for his dorm room. And that third freshman decided that the way he was going to get money to buy these things that he wanted to buy for himself and for his girlfriend was to rob his fellow classmates, to rob fellow classmates that he thought would be easy victims. And that third freshman decided that he was going to murder those classmates so he wouldn't get caught stealing from them. And that third freshman, ladies and gentlemen, turned out to be a cold and calculating and deliberate premeditated murderer. And that third freshman is sitting right here, and his name is Joseph Mesa."

Ms. Collins outlined the parade of witnesses that were expected to testify. Eric's mother, Kathleen Cornils, would tell the jury about her son. She would explain that he had cerebral palsy and struggled with walking. Ms. Collins told jurors JJ had discussed Eric's infirmity with his girlfriend, saying "He was never going to be able to ride a bicycle, for example, because of the problems with his legs." Ms. Collins described how JJ was cold-hearted and calculatingly sought after a friendship with Eric to lure him into trusting JJ. Jurors would learn the graphic details and see photos of the murder to help them understand the brutal nature of the violence. The medical examiner would present the factual information of the murder, the wounds inflicted, and the causes of death.

Ms. Collins would call in as witnesses JJ's group of friends, Chad, Anna, Manda, and his girlfriend, Melani.

Diane Varner, Ben's mother, would be called to take the stand. She would tell the jury how her son loved apples and was fascinated by world cultures, geography, and history. She would say to them how excited Ben was to come to Gallaudet, which was considered home to deaf and hard-of-hearing students around the globe. Ben's friends, Sui and Mohamed, would testify to Ben's thoughtfulness and gentleness as a friend. As with Eric's murder, Ms. Collins would detail the brutal violence that Ben suffered at the hands of JJ. She would describe how he fought JJ with the remaining moments of his life. The medical examiner would describe Ben's wounds and the fatal ones that caused his death.

Ms. Collins would present the testimonies of the numerous detectives and investigators involved in the cases to shed light on their analyses of shoe prints, fingerprints, and DNA. The last part of the prosecution's case would be from the testimony of Melani herself, including the letters she had received from JJ and the confession with Detective Pamela Reed. The case appeared airtight, especially given JJ's confession.

The defense team's lead attorney, Mr. Bond, painted a different picture for the jury. He said he did not question the evidence the prosecution would present.

However, the jurors would learn that JJ was not the cold-hearted killer that the prosecution wanted them to believe.

Mr. Bond started, "You will hear during the course of the trial about a number of horrible, horrible things, murders of people on the same wing of the dormitory that he lived in, stealing from people that lived in the same wing of the dormitory where he lived. The evidence is going to show you that in at least one of these cases, a security guard, or police officer, was right down the hall.

"The evidence is going to show you all kinds of conduct, stealing from people that are close to you, bringing the things that you buy with the proceeds of that theft right back into the dormitory where everyone can see. Bringing to the attention of authorities that something smells funny so that a body is discovered.

"The reason I'm bringing these out to you, and this is going to be difficult for you, during the course of this trial, I ask you to pay attention to this. As you do, I want you to have one question in mind as you listen to this: Why? Why? Why like this? And when we have our turn, and we will, we will show you why."

Mr. Bond would point out that JJ was born a profoundly deaf child on the remote island of Guam. He would highlight his poor-quality schooling in a small, underdeveloped educational system. He would describe JJ as a deaf person frustrated by the limited communication in his social world, though he was raised in a loving military family. JJ would have trouble expressing his feelings, Mr. Bond explained. The pressure of his pent-up anger and frustration would one day erupt.

"His parents decided to what they call mainstream, and they put him in school with hearing people," explained Mr. Bond. "He had a lot of trouble fitting in. But he did everything he could to be a model citizen. He played football. He was a legend around the island. He was a caring kid who engaged in numerous acts of kindness, including helping people carry groceries. He was constantly trying to get approval by engaging in acts of kindness. And you will hear from people that they just can't believe what Ms. Collins described to you, is this young man right here. And again, the question that you are going to have to answer during the course of the trial is why, or how.

"And I'll tell you what our evidence is going to show you. Mr. Mesa had mental illnesses, not one, but you're going to hear that there are a number of things that are wrong with him." Mr. Bond's defense was going to be based on the fact that JJ was not guilty by reason of insanity.

Prosecutor Jeb Boasberg called Eric's mother, Kathleen Cornils, as the first witness. Ms. Cornils was a finance manager at a bank in Minneapolis, Minnesota. She explained she had three children, Eric being the middle child.

Ms. Cornils told jurors, "When I was twelve weeks pregnant, I had German measles or rubella. The impact of that illness on Eric was that he was born profoundly deaf and with cerebral palsy. The cerebral palsy was primarily in his legs. It affected the muscles in his hamstrings and his heel cords. And so, it prevented him from being able to stand up straight or walk with his legs straight. He walked with a limp or kind of shuffle, where his knees were bent, kind of a crouching position. He had difficulty picking his whole foot up off the ground when he took steps. It affected his balance in that it was easy for him to fall. He needed to pull himself up on something, some kind of leverage to pull himself up."

At five feet, nine inches and about 135 pounds, Eric's physical frailty was the primary reason JJ had chosen Eric as his first victim. He knew Eric lived alone and, combined with trouble walking much less running, Eric made easy prey. The prosecution's plan for Eric's mother as the witness for the first day was perfect. She conjured

Eric's spirit to life for a group of jurors who had never known her son. She wanted them to understand the innate goodness of Eric, how much pleasure he brought to his family and friends. She helped the jurors realize what had been stolen from her, how the murder of her son had cut her so deeply that she would never truly recover, how his murder would forever scar Eric's family.

The physical presence of Eric's mother put a face, albeit one of devastation, on the murder. Her words from the witness served as testimony to the dark corners of humanity where Eric's life, her own son's life, was considered not only as disposable but as a means of gratification for a sadistic killer. Her young, vibrant, deaf son was taken by someone he thought to be a friend. After overcoming all of the challenges he faced, Eric Plunkett had finally achieved a significant milestone, only to be robbed of it by a friend. The prosecutors' choice to present Eric's mother first created the context for tragedy, unfairness, and loss.

Officer Grant Greenwalt stepped to the witness stand next. In contrast to the raw pain from Eric's mother, Officer Greenwalt would present the crime from an investigator's eye. He described what this murder crime scene looked like when he arrived. This professional, objective, and concrete perspective would jolt the jurors into the harsh reality of what had occurred in Eric's room that night. As an experienced mobile crime lab processor, Officer Grant's job was to process violent crime scenes, such as murders, rapes, arsons, and suspicious deaths. In the trial, he presented the physical evidence of that very first encounter with Eric.

He explained his job. "We're really there for documentation purposes, and we do it in several forms so I can preserve the evidence, document it through photography or sketch diagrams. Then I eventually disseminate it out to the different laboratories. I get it back here so I can bring it to a courtroom and present it to a jury.

"For indoor crime scenes, there are more considerations. There is a lot of evidence that is left behind, trace evidence, hairs, and fibers, different bodily fluids that may not be present on an outdoor crime scene. Indoor scenes are usually confined into a really small area. It's a lot more tedious for us."

Officer Greenwalt presented jurors with crime scene photographs and sketches to show the layout of the room, the position of Eric's body, and evidence collected and documented during the six-hour scene processing. The gruesome, extreme violence of Eric's murder set against the deep, heart-breaking wounds of a mother's dead son allowed the jurors the opportunity to empathize with Eric's family and simultaneously harden against the man who had caused so much destruction.

The last witness of the day was the resident advisor of Cogswell Hall, Lauren Buchko, who found Eric's body. Her testimony allowed jurors to understand the context in which this crime occurred. This murder was not a random act of violence seen with disturbing regularity within the District of Columbia. It was not a drug deal gone bad. Nor was it an act of violence in the context of domestic violence. There was no million-dollar bounty the killer could claim from Eric's death. The murder would not serve as a weapon for revenge or retaliation.

Lauren Buchko described the close, connected, tight-knit deaf community on campus at Gallaudet University. Deaf herself, Lauren told the circumstances from a typical resident advisor's perspective, her job duties, the context in which she knew both Eric and JJ. She normalized the environment in a way that outlined the deep betrayal of one deaf person's trust against someone else in the same deaf community, the same deaf family. Lauren showed the jurors what a typical deaf student looked like, for she was one herself. She could try to describe the indescribable connection between deaf people to jurors who most likely were not college students themselves nor deaf.

Lauren told the jurors how Joseph Mesa led her and her co-worker, Thomas Koch, to Eric's door. "Joseph Mesa was the one who reported to me when I was on duty in the R.A.'s office," she said. "He said something smelled funny in Eric's room. I asked, 'Was it something related to drugs or alcohol? What do you mean?' He said, 'No, something else, something smells funny.' So, I said, 'Okay.'"

Lauren's testimony revealed the sinister, mocking underbelly of JJ's game plan. She and her co-worker were guided to Eric, to the gruesome, blood-spattered, horrific scene, by the person who had caused it all. JJ had manipulated the discovery of his conquest. As if in a horror movie scene, he directed how each actor would behave, all the while with him watching from the sidelines.

Chapter 29

Trial Day Two, Morning

Detective: Did you ever take any photos of Minch at Eric's door after the police had come?

JJ: Yes. I don't know why I took a picture of Thomas standing outside Eric's door, but I think it was so that I'd have that as a memory.

On May 3, 2002, the prosecution attorneys, Jennifer Collins and Jeb Boasberg, were prepared for another day with the jurors. The next witness would be graphic and likely impress upon the jurors the true nature of what had occurred to Eric Plunkett in his dormitory room on the evening of September 28.

The Washington, D.C. medical examiner, Dr. Gertrude Juste-Hjardemaal, took that stand and explained her job to the jurors.

"We investigate the deaths that fall under the jurisdiction of the medical examiner's office, such as violent deaths, deaths that occur as a result of blunt impact trauma, gunshot wounds, deaths that result from accidental or intentional ingestion of substances, deaths that occur in the hospital sometimes, deaths that occur while in police custody," she explained.

She described the autopsy process of examining Eric's body. "We perform an autopsy by examining the body, documenting evidence, injuries or lesions as we see them externally, photographing the body, x-raying the body when necessary, and then opening the body to look at the injuries or disease process in the organs that are affected by these injuries and determine how and why this person came to us." She then showed the jurors a copy of Eric's autopsy report.

The autopsy report for Eric Franklin Plunkett was written on a standard form from the Office of the Chief

Medical Examiner. It noted that Eric's age was nineteen, that he was white and a male. It listed his address from Burnsville, Minnesota.

Date and Time of Death: September 28, 2000, 2300 hours

Date and Time of Autopsy: September 29, 0950 hours

Cause of Death: Blunt impact trauma to head and neck with subdural, subarachnoid hemorrhages, and laryngeal fractures

The M.E. sketched Eric's wounds on a pre-printed diagram of a male's head. One page of the report presented five different perspectives of the head: a frontal view, a back view, a left side view, a ride side view, and from the chin up. Handwritten descriptions of the type and size of the wounds accompanied outlines of the wound darkened by a black pen on specific areas of Eric's head. One read "2 1/2" x 3/4" laceration" with a line drawn to a small tick on the left side of the diagram's head. Another indicated "3 1/4" x 3/4" abrasion" with a line drawn to an area just below the bottom lip.

The prosecutors had enlarged each of the five

perspectives so the jurors could carefully see just how many injuries were inflicted on Eric's head. The projections highlighted the numerous and violent injuries. The final two sketches detailed Eric's frontal and rear views of his entire body. Though there were scrapes and scratches along Eric's body, the injuries to his face, neck, and head seemed to be the target of the violence. From the autopsy report, it was clear JJ had been very close to Eric when he put him in that first chokehold. His face was likely right alongside Eric's, his breath brushing against Eric's ear as he compressed and fractured his neck.

At some point, rage took over. Eric's wounds were inflicted by a savage, someone out of control and agitated. Dr. Hjardemaal explained the brutality of the murder in medical terms that jurors could understand. She presented the diagrams, measurements, and sketches of the wounds, which brought Eric's struggle for his life to the forefront.

Next, the prosecutors personalized the murders, guiding jurors back to the fact that this event wreaked havoc on many levels. They called three of JJ's friends, Manda, Anna, and Chad, consecutively to the witness stand.

"Every day since Eric Plunkett was murdered, JJ had started sleeping in my dorm room with Melani and me," Manda said.

She described how after the murder, Melani and Manda had hung pictures of him in their room. JJ told Manda to take them down; they made him feel uncomfortable.

She recounted the day JJ had told her about how he had smelled something strange and led the resident advisor to Eric's room.

"He said that he saw him lying on the floor with his shirt off and holding his shirt and blood all around."

She described the altercation between Chad and JJ for the jurors when Chad realized JJ had stolen his credit card. Manda explained it was then that she decided that she did not want to live with Melani the following semester. The intensity of JJ's rage toward Chad had scared her. She told jurors that he had become a different person from the one she met at the start of the school year.

Anna's testimony came next. She took her place at the witness stand and pointed her finger to identify her friend Joseph Mesa. Jennifer Collins asked Anna to recall a conversation with JJ about finding Eric's body.

"I was in Mr. Mesa's dorm room in Cogswell Hall. I asked him if he was okay because he said he was the one who reported the smell to the R.A. He described the entryway to his door, that he had seen something black in the doorway, plus the smell. That's what made him go to the R.A."

Anna explained she had moved into the dorm room with Melani after Melani and Manda stopped living together. Anna said after JJ's arrest, she noticed Melani and JJ were writing letters to each other. This piece of information was necessary for the prosecutors to show the jurors. JJ's defense relied on an insanity plea that he could not control his behavior and did not know right from wrong. The letters sent to Melani were proof that his entire defense was a pretense.

"I saw them corresponding through the mail and on the phone too," Anna said. "I've seen her writing letters. I'd see the letters she received from him too. I would just see the address from Melani to JJ; I'd see the letters pretty often. When she would get a letter, she'd read it and leave it on the table. When the letters piled up, she put them in a metal cabinet. There were many, many letters coming almost daily."

Finally, Chad stepped into the witness box. The prosecutor asked him if JJ had seemed strange or abnormal after Eric's death.

"He mainly talked positively about Eric. He said he

helped tutor him in math."

Jeb Boasberg homed in on the incidents when JJ had stolen Chad's credit card and when JJ denied taking the card.

"I didn't believe him. He could not produce any proof that he had purchased those items. I told him, 'I don't believe a word; I'm sorry.' Then he got mad. He threw a bracelet that he had on into the air.

"Another time was around Manda's birthday. I was sitting in my room using my laptop. JJ and Melani had left. They went to buy a gift for Manda. When they came back, they brought some things from the Gallaudet University bookstore; he told me he had bought the gifts for Manda from some vocational rehabilitation money. I told another friend about the purchases made with the V.R. money. The friend didn't appreciate that and told me I should tell him to buy stuff with his own money, not V.R. money. V.R. money is supposed to be for educational purchases only."

Under cross-examination, Ferris Bond wanted to establish that JJ's behavior had become increasingly volatile.

"The first argument occurred when you and Joseph Mesa were roommates, correct?" Mr. Bond asked.

"Yes, the first one."

"The second one occurred when you were not roommates, correct? Did he ever kick you, grab you, hit or choke you during one of those arguments?"

"No, he did not do those things."

"And one of the reasons Mr. Mesa didn't do those things is because you turned around and walked out of the room, correct?"

"Right. And another reason is that people stopped him."

Jeb Boasberg wanted to make one thing clear to jurors.

"When his personality seemed to change, did he attack you?"

Chad responded, "No."

"Did he kill you?"

"No."

"Thank you, Chad."

The three friends closest to JJ had finished their testimonies. The prosecution used their testimonies to not only establish facts of the case, but also to demonstrate that JJ was indeed in control of his behavior even when he was angry. JJ's behavior also validated an ongoing pattern of antisocial behavior. He continued to steal from others and brazenly exhibited his purchased items with others' money.

Now the prosecution team needed to present evidence of Eric's stolen credit card, which police had not discovered until after JJ's arrest. Jeb Boasberg called Detective James LaFrancise to testify about Chad's stolen credit card investigation.

"We learned that [Eric's] credit card had been used on the 28, specifically, of September. It had also been used at least five or six other times throughout October and November. We thought that the person who may have committed the murder had actually used the bank card.

"It was later learned that the bank card was missing along with his identification and wallet. We went to the bank itself and obtained records from them to show us where the actual credit card or bank card had been used, what stores, or what places it had been used at.

"We found out the names of the stores. I went to the stores and recovered the receipts from both of those. I also contacted a porn website that an account that had been started using the bank card. I called the company and got as much information from them as I could. Unfortunately, all the information we had was in Mr. Plunkett's name."

JJ had shopped at Union Station with Eric's bank card on September 28, the day after he murdered Eric. JJ had purchased items from the Made In America store and

Bon Voyage. He sent the children's clothing he purchased to JJ's father.

"The return address for the property to be sent to was Mr. Eric Plunkett, at 800 Florida Avenue, Northeast, Washington, D.C., but it had Mr. Mesa's mailbox number, which was 810," said Detective LaFranchise.

"So, he was giving you a trail leading right back to him?" asked Mr. Bond.

"After we found out about it, after he told us about it, yes, sir."

Had the police discovered these purchases soon after he made them, JJ may have been arrested earlier. Instead, JJ left the same trail of breadcrumbs for the police to follow after the next murder.

Chapter 30

Trial Day Two, Afternoon

After the announcement that the killer had been caught, I withdrew from Gallaudet. I was having problems and struggling with being there. It took me a long time to heal, but I tried to think positive.

—Manda

Back from lunch, prosecutors would present evidence of Ben's murder. Like the first day, they would allow the grieving mother to humanize her son for jurors. Diane

Varner took the stand.

"Ben was deaf from birth; it was genetic. He was the tenth in line on my husband's side of the family. He was profoundly deaf, having less than ten or fifteen percent hearing in one ear and no hearing at all in the other.

"He graduated from high school in May of 2000 and spent the summer with us. In August 2000, I brought him up to Gallaudet, and he entered as a freshman and lived on the first floor of Cogswell Hall.

"Shortly after the murder of Eric Plunkett, they moved him to the fourth floor in Cogswell Hall. He had lived with a roommate on the first floor; they both decided they would both move up to the same room and share that room. When he came back from Christmas break to start the second semester of his freshman year, Ben emailed me on the second day and said, 'I don't have a roommate. I'm surprised.' He continued to live alone."

Mrs. Varner described the shopping trip she and Ben took to buy items for his dorm.

"I bought a knife, but I didn't want one too long. I didn't want a six-inch knife or a six-inch blade or anything like that because I thought it looked like a weapon. I chose one that was sturdy, so it wouldn't flip around, so it wouldn't be wobbly when he was peeling apples, and he wouldn't accidentally cut himself."

The prosecutor showed Mrs. Varner a photograph of Ben's shirt; she identified it was her son's. The defense attorney decided not to cross-examine Mrs. Varner.

The prosecution consecutively called to the stand two of Ben's closest friends, Sui and Mohamed. Sui was twenty-six years old and had been at Gallaudet University for five years. She had first met Ben in November 2000.

"We were classmates. We had math class together. We were close friends, best friends. He was very reliable with his job and with his classes. He loved to go to class. He helped me with my homework."

Sui described the Thursday evening when she and Ben had dinner, which she had cooked for him. She had sent him home around seven o'clock that evening with boxed leftovers and plans to meet the following day. Sui would never see Ben again.

Mohamed was thirty-eight years old and had been at Gallaudet for six years. He met Ben through a mutual friend, a Muslim student. Mohamed and Ben spent a lot of time together.

"He was very interested in Islam. We very often spent time together. We were first introduced in December. Then in January, we saw each other more often. He wanted me to be roommates with him and asked for that frequently."

Mohamed described the Thursday evening, the last time he had seen Ben.

"He came to my room around seven o'clock to visit. He brought with him rice from Sui. I could tell it was from Sui. Later Ben left and said he would be coming back that same night.

"We had agreed to see each other on Friday at ten o'clock. I had class at that time, so he would come to get me at eight o'clock, and then I would wake up. He would come and get me by flashing the light. Then I would drop him off, and then I would go to class. That was the agreement that Ben and I had made. But Friday morning, he didn't show up at all."

The prosecution then called Scott Pfaff, a twenty-three year old senior student who was a resident adviser in Cogswell Hall and lived on the third floor. The R.A. said a fire alarm had gone off in the early hours of the morning. Mr. Boasberg asked Scott how the fire alarm system worked at a university for deaf people.

"Most of the time, [the fire alarms] are malfunctioning. Sometimes someone actually sets it off, but this time, it was a malfunction. In each room, there is a light that flashes, a strobe light that flashes just like a fire alarm elsewhere.

"After the fire alarm goes off, all of the R.A.s are required to go down to the office, to our main office on the first floor to retrieve the master keys. Then we all agree on which floors we are going to check and which wing. The R.A. who arrives first at the office gets the first choice of which floor and which wing. Everyone doesn't want to go to the fourth floor because it's far, and you can't use the elevator because of the fact it's a fire alarm."

"So, who got there last?" Mr. Boasberg facetiously asked.

"I did."

Several people laughed in the courtroom.

"I went to the women's wing first. I unlocked each door and open it up and made sure the resident is out of their room. They need to go outside since it's a fire alarm. If the person is still asleep, I have to wake them up and get them to show me their ID, just to make sure that everyone is out of the room.

"I checked all the rooms. It took longer because many were still asleep. I had to get them up until maybe five or ten minutes later; the fire alarm then stopped. Lauren Buchko came up to me because she told me to stop looking because the fire alarm had stopped.

"We both went down to the first floor. Our boss, Carl Ewan, is the head of the dorm. He wanted to know if all the wings had been checked. We said no; we only completed the women's wings. So, he told me to go back upstairs and finish the job. So, I went back up to the fourth floor. I checked the first door on the left, then on the right, then on the left, and that was where I found the body of Ben Varner.

"I ran. I ran out of the room. I went to the middle of the two wings and waved to my boss, Carl, to get his attention. He looked up and asked, 'What's wrong?' I said, 'Come up here right now. This is serious.' He asked, 'What is it?' I said, 'Get up here now.' He knew something was really serious, and he ran upstairs to check."

Prosecutors next brought in evidence from police. Detective James Trainum took the stand. He described how he had searched for evidence in a dumpster outside of Cogswell Hall on February 4, 2001, after discovering Ben Varner's body.

"I had gone into the back parking driveway area behind Cogswell Hall. There was a dumpster back there. I went into the dumpster and began removing items to make sure that there was a thorough search done of the entire dumpster. It was at that time that I located a paring knife that was under some of the trash that was inside the dumpster.

"There had been a jacket found earlier that was suspected of being involved with this investigation. We decided that it would be best to make sure that every item was taken out of the dumpster so that it would have been searched thoroughly.

"We pulled up this pickup truck that belonged to Detective Darryl Richmond up to the dumpster. We didn't want to have everything all over the street. I got into the dumpster itself and began to hand items out of the dumpster, placing them in the pickup truck from the top, working towards the bottom."

The knife was hidden under some of the bags of trash. Detective Trainum confirmed that the knife in the evidence bag was the knife he had found in the dumpster.

Prosecutors wanted jurors to see how JJ revealed details of his murders to his friends, a little more with each retelling. Jeb Boasberg called Christopher Beyer, JJ's most recent roommate, to the stand. Chris had come to Gallaudet as a sophomore, transferring from another university. He had known both Eric and Ben as well as JJ. Chris said that JJ had told him about Eric's murder a few days after the discovery of his body.

"He talked about how he left his room on that night when the police were there investigating. He described the scene, how there was blood on the wall and on the floor. He said he saw it when he went into the room the night they came to investigate."

After Eric's murder, when students were relocated, Chris moved to Krug Hall with his roommate, Daniel. In early December, Chris began sharing a dorm room with JJ.

"Daniel wanted to be a roommate with a different person. So, the dorm director said that I couldn't live alone. I had to pick a new roommate; so I moved in with Joseph Mesa. I was roommates with him until his arrest."

Mr. Boasberg asked Chris about JJ's personal habits.

Chris responded, "He would tend to lock his closet door. I didn't. That's the only thing that seemed strange.

"The Saturday morning that Ben's body was found, around 8:30, I was still sleeping. JJ woke me up and told me to look out the window. There were police everywhere on campus. That's when I realized that something was wrong. JJ and I were watching the news, and we found out that Ben had been killed.

"JJ was very concerned about what was going on on

campus because most of the students didn't know what was going on that day. JJ kept asking me questions to see if I knew anything from the media, but I didn't know more than what the media was reporting.

"Later in the day, the late afternoon, JJ and I were in our room. JJ was sitting at the desk. I was sitting at my desk. He asked me how to spell the word 'fifty.' He was writing on what looked like a piece of paper.

"That same Saturday, I noticed that he had bought for his girlfriend a new RCA thirteen-inch TV. I was already in the room when he came in with the television for his girlfriend."

One other friend was to testify. The prosecution called Cappy to the stand. Cappy described how she became a friend to JJ and Melani.

"After NSO week ended, I was waiting for the Gallaudet bus at the Kellogg stop. I noticed this man on my left. He seemed to be a person who was friendly. He introduced himself and his girlfriend to me."

The prosecutor asked her if JJ had discussed Eric's murder with her.

"Yes. He said that Eric had been killed, but he didn't know who did it. He explained about his death from the chair and the blood in the room and everything. He said that Eric was hit with a chair and there was a lot of blood, that Eric had fallen on the floor."

Mr. Boasberg asked, "What did he say happened with the chair?"

"He described grabbing the chair and hitting him again and again."

"Did he ever tell you how he knew all of these details?"

"He didn't exactly tell me that, about how he knew it, but he really wasn't emotional about it. His face had no emotion when he was explaining."

Again, JJ had revealed more and more of the details of his murders. Had the group of friends talked to put together the puzzle, they may have detected something amiss with JJ. It appeared JJ needed to retell the story of what he saw in Eric's room to keep the momentum of excitement rolling. Each retelling bolstered JJ's pride about his strength, cunningness, and sophistication at not being caught. Ultimately, his adventures would come to an end.

Shortly after JJ was arrested for Ben's murder, Cappy and Melani had visited him in the Washington, D.C. jail. A few weeks later, Melani showed Cappy a note from JJ.

Cappy explained, "The note was from JJ. He had

written it to his parents. The note said, 'Dear mother and father, I would like to tell you that I'm sorry that I have confessed that I did kill two people. Please forgive me.'"

Cappy continued to describe the night before JJ's arrest when he went to her dorm room asking for Melani. She told jurors that JJ's behavior started to change after Eric's murder. Like his other friends, she noticed he became more withdrawn from everyone except Melani.

The mothers' and friends' testimonies conveyed to jurors the essence of two aspiring young men who had come to the university to fulfill their lifelong dreams. JJ's friends highlighted JJ's calculating and scheming nature. The patterns of behavior seen in childhood, including theft, taunting, anger, and violence, had continued into his freshman year. JJ had not changed for the better; he had developed more sophistication in his methods. He operated with relative anonymity after killing Eric. Bolstered by what he had seemingly achieved, he continued into the spring semester. For the next day of trial, Jennifer Collins and Jeb Boasberg planned to call the police investigators to the stand the following day to present a full line-up of evidence.

Chapter 31

Trial Day Three

Ferris Bond: Before you had him captured on videotape cashing Mr. Varner's check, was Mr. Mesa assisting you in closing the investigation?

Detective Reed: No. In fact, he threw a wrench into it by approaching Detective Leadmon and coming up with this gay theory.

Ferris Bond: Did that cause MPD to spend some time looking into whether Mr. Varner's murder was a gay hate crime?

Detective Reed: Yes.

The prosecutors had planned May 6, 2002, to be a day for the detectives' investigative findings. Their tone was formal, professional, and exacting. Detective David Murray from the Mobile Crime Unit detailed the crime scene on the morning he found Ben's body. He described how Ben's room was in disarray that morning, drawers open and clothing strewn. The bed mattress had been pulled off the bed; Ben was lying on the floor entangled in his bedsheets. The prosecutors showed him the computer-generated diagram of the crime scene that morning. Detective Murray confirmed that this was correct.

Jennifer Collins asked the detective to highlight the critical features of the crime scene.

Detective Murray said, "The location of the decedent was in the middle of the floor with the fitted sheet and the other sheet on top of him. He had a clothes rack on top of him as well."

He pointed to Ben's left leg on the diagram. "The comforter was near the front entrance to the door. There was a portion of a trunk covered with blood and a pool of blood on the floor. The southeast closet door was open with the light on. There was a workstation with the front portion of the door open, a dresser open."

The detective pointed to the diagram to indicate locations of the microwave and Ben's broken eyeglasses on the radiator. He showed jurors where the eyeglasses lens lay, having shot out of its frame. He pointed to where the bloody hearing aid lay.

Ms. Collins showed the detective photographs taken of Ben's room on February 1, 2001. One picture showed Ben's ransacked room and a bloody chest of drawers. Ben lay at the center of the room. She showed photographs of the extent of the blood splatter covering all four walls of the room.

Detective Murray described, "Government Exhibit 31 depicts the decedent lying on the floor; also, some blood spatter that was on different items, different furniture there, such as the chest, the scale, the bed, the radiator, and the blinds."

Jennifer Collins presented photographs and diagrams and asked the crime scene processor to describe each. One by one, Detective Murray described each piece of furniture, each part of the room, and each piece of evidence connected to the violent crime, all covered in blood.

By the end of Detective Murray's testimony, jurors understood the extent of the violence inflicted upon Ben during his final moments of life. JJ had inflicted a great deal of viciousness upon Ben, and Ben had fought hard for his life.

Jennifer Collins called Detective Lorren Leadmon from the Violent Crimes Unit to testify. The detective pointed to JJ and identified him as the man who had approached him in the cafeteria on the day Ben's body was discovered.

"The students were allowed back and forth, they put the people from Cogswell on the second floor and were trying to interview them individually.

"It was about seven o'clock that evening. Chief Ramsey came to me, and he wanted to address the student body. So, first, Chief Ramsey and I addressed the second-floor level from the people that were up there from the dormitory. Then we went downstairs, and we addressed the rest of the general students. That was when [Mr. Mesa] and his girlfriend came up to me in the cafeteria."

JJ would tell the detective that Ben was gay. He tried to distract the police as before when he hinted that Thomas Minch had killed Eric. Apparently, his tactic worked once; perhaps it would again.

Ferris Bond asked the detective, "Did you ask Mr. Mesa what led him to believe that Mr. Varner was gay?"

"He said that Mr. Varner had told him he was gay," responded Detective Leadmon.

"And that didn't affect your investigation, did it?"

"Absolutely not."

The detective was permitted to leave the witness stand. Jennifer Collins next called Detective Pamela Reed. Ms. Collins asked Detective Reed to identify the dormitories where the murders occurred and their relation to where JJ had lived.

"And, so we're clear," said Ms. Collins, "Cogswell Hall was where both Mr. Varner and Mr. Plunkett were murdered?"

"Yes."

"And what relation does Krug Hall have to this case?"

"It's adjacent. Mr. Mesa lived in Krug Hall in February 2001." Detective Reed pointed to two locations on a campus map.

"This is where Cogswell was located, which is now named Ballard North. This is where Krug was located, which is now Ballard West."

She pointed to an area between Cogswell Hall and the Central Utilities building to indicate where the dumpster containing evidence was located.

The prosecutor asked the detective for her conclusions about when Ben had been murdered.

"February was a Saturday," said Detective Reed. "But we had concluded that it would have been between Thursday evening, approximately 9:00 p.m. on February 1, to the morning prior to 9:00 a.m. on February 2. Mr. Varner was fully clothed. He had shoes, socks, no PJs, or that sort of thing. So, we assumed it would have been the night that he went in, that Thursday night, or in the morning since he was fully dressed. He was fully dressed as if he were going out or had just come in."

The prosecutor showed the detective a picture showing purple and smudged images and asked the detective to describe what it showed.

"It's the processing by the Secret Service. They processed this for fingerprints, as well as conducted a handwriting analysis before it was smudged."

Jennifer Collins showed the detective Government Exhibit 37A.

"This is a copy of the front and back of the check prior to its processing," explained the detective.

The prosecutor asked the detective to read from the check.

"The date was February 1, 2001, paid to the order of, written in was Joseph Mesa, Jr. The amount $650 was written in both numbers and spelled out, and it is signed Ben Varner, and the memo says 'used laptop.'"

Jurors now knew that the "fifty" JJ had been practicing in his room with Chris Beyer was actually a forged check taken from Ben's room the night JJ had murdered him. Detective Reed reviewed her visit to Riggs Bank and how she obtained the video and still photographs of JJ cashing the check. She described finding the truck with the check en route to its destination at the depository. She said that after she acquired the forged check and saw the photo of Joseph Mesa in Riggs Bank, she and her partner, Detective Richmond, decided to interview JJ.

Meanwhile, detectives had continued to run JJ's key card to trace his whereabouts during the time of Ben's murder. The detective detailed the process of obtaining the sign language waivers and questionnaires they used with all interviewed witnesses. She described the initial interview and then the one after Melani and JJ had approached another detective, saying that he now remembered a check from Ben. She recounted how Melani and JJ came to her and her partner for the last interview on campus and how they moved to the station when JJ confessed.

The courtroom took a lunch break. The prosecutors planned an afternoon with Detectives Michael Murphy and Darryl Richmond, along with the interpreters who were at the station during JJ's confession. Jennifer Collins would help the jurors understand the qualifications and roles of the interpreters. Then they would show the lengthy videotaped confession in its entirety. The afternoon session concluded at 4:48 p.m.

Chapter 32

Trial Day Four

I know that keeping it inside built it up more. I really wanted to get that out so that it wouldn't continue. Now for my relationship with [Melani], I didn't want to keep things inside and build things up that way. I really wanted to be able to talk to her; that helped. I promised her that I would not do that again. She said, you know, if you need any money, come to me; that's what she told me. She made me promise that I would do that. So, for all of you here and for everyone else, I also promise the same thing.

—JJ during the videotaped confession.

On the morning of Tuesday, May 7, the prosecution planned to show jurors the remainder of JJ's videotaped confession. The courtroom watched the videotape until lunch break around 1:00 p.m. They returned an hour later to resume testimonies.

Jeb Boasberg called Dr. Jacqueline Lee, the medical examiner. Like Dr. Hjardemaal, Dr. Lee detailed her experience as a medical examiner. She explained how she systematically examines bodies to look for the causes of death.

"The office of the Chief Medical Examiner is responsible for determining the cause and manner of death for those people who die suddenly and unexpectedly. That can be a result of natural disease or can be a result of trauma or injury that is inflicted on a person as a result of an accident."

Mr. Boasberg handed Dr. Lee a copy of Government Exhibit 58 and asked her to identify it.

"This is a copy of the autopsy report for Benjamin Scott Varner, which has medical case number 01-0497, which I produced."

The prosecutor asked her to describe her impressions of Ben's body when she first saw him.

"The clothing was pretty much soaked with blood, particularly his shirt. There were defects of the clothing which were consistent with stab wounds on the body."

She reviewed what she had written in the autopsy report about Ben's various injuries and traumas. Like Eric's autopsy report, Dr. Lee presented diagrams and sketches of Ben's injuries. She noted Ben had defensive wounds on his hands, evidence of an actual fight for his life. She methodically explained each bruise, laceration, abrasion, and puncture found on Ben's body. In total, she recorded sixteen or seventeen stab wounds to Ben's eye, face, neck, chest, and abdomen. She described Ben's bruised and scraped skin.

Mr. Boasberg showed Dr. Lee the original knife and a duplicate knife and asked her to state whether she thought they were consistent. Dr. Lee stepped down from the witness box to demonstrate.

"This is the same as the original knife, the knife that I examined before. The wounds that were inflicted were caused by a single-edged instrument, meaning that there's one side of the blade that is a cutting edge, then there's the other side of the blade that is a dull edge. The characteristics of most of the wounds have that distinctive characteristic. The other thing for this knife, even though it's a small knife, you will notice that the blade actually passes through the entire handle; it's bolted in place by three bolts. So, this is a professional knife. The blade is secured into the handle. What's significant is that this anchors the blade, makes it secure so that this blade can actually pass through bone and not be broken off into the bone. And particularly for wound A, which passes into the skull and comes out of the skull without being broken off; this knife can do that in spite of the fact that it's small. Because of its construction, it can inflict that type of wound."

Dr. Lee concluded her testimony with an analysis of the contents in Ben's stomach, which was the dinner Sui had prepared. Mr. Bond asked only one question for cross-examination about which of the wounds would have been fatal.

She responded, "The single stab wound to the head could have resulted in his death, the stab wounds to his neck and chest. All of the ones could have killed him. They were all in and of themselves would have been fatal. It's just that together death would have come more quickly than just a single wound."

Jennifer Collins called Lamon Wright, a Riggs Bank teller, to the stand. He testified about the videotape that showed JJ cashing the check. He described the identification system that the bank uses for cashing and tracking checks.

Deborah Leben, a Secret Service agent, testified to the fingerprint analyses. She described her duties.

"Some of my duties are to examine items of evidence for the presence or development of latent prints and to compare those latent prints to any subjects in the case. I then report my findings to the respective field office and testify, if requested. I also aid in the training of Secret Service personnel. I have conducted lectures, had workshops and conferences, as well as other duties.

"A latent fingerprint is an outline or reproduction of the friction ridges of your skin transferred from an object once the object is touched. If you look at the underside of your palms and fingers, you will see raised portions of the skin. These are friction ridges. Along the center of those ridges are small openings called pores, which exude perspiration that eventually covers the ridge surface. When an object is touched, a transfer of that outline and any perspirations or contaminants that were on the finger may transfer to that surface. The word 'latent' is applied because many times, it's invisible and can be made visible by various chemicals and powders.

"I would examine the object for any visible prints initially. I would then subject that to a fluorescent examination using a laser and alternate light source to see if there were any fluorescent deposits on the item. Following that, I would follow up with some chemical processing on a porous item to determine or see if there is any chemical reaction with the chemicals we use and the residue that may be left on that item. In between each one of these processes, the latent prints that are developed would be photographed and used later for comparison."

Agent Leben used these procedures to process the check that JJ had cashed at Riggs Bank. She had chemically processed the check, so the original writing on it was not visible. Based on the results of the processing, she concluded that five of the seven latent prints matched copies of the fingerprint card that JJ had submitted when he was arrested.

Jeb Boasberg then called Officer Monica Coleman to the witness stand. He asked her to describe her job duties.

"I'm assigned to the K-9 patrol division. Patrol

consists of looking for suspects, looking for objects that were dropped by suspects, or objects that were dropped in the commission of a crime, looking for lost children or senile adults. The term K-9 refers to the police dog."

Officer Coleman testified about the procedures she used with her K-9 patrol dog in locating any evidence.

"I was advised that they had a crime scene; they wanted me to conduct a track, which is to actually pick up the scent of a suspect that had left the scene."

She described how her dog picked up a scent from blood droplets in the basement of Cogswell Hall and then to the dumpster outside. Mr. Boasberg presented her with photographs of JJ's jacket taken from the dumpster, which she identified as being collected as evidence. After her testimony, she was dismissed from the witness stand.

The final witness for the day was Anthony Onorato, an FBI DNA analyst. Mr. Boasberg asked him to describe his job duties.

"It's easiest to think of someone like myself as the lab's biologist. Really, it's our unit that's responsible for looking at items of evidence that we get into the laboratory for biological material. Typically, that's going to take the form of body fluid stains, such as blood or semen, which is male reproductive fluid. Sometimes we are working with things like cigarette butts or envelopes, those kinds of things where people come into contact with those objects. They might not leave behind body fluids necessarily with respect to blood or semen but what they will leave behind is something like saliva or skin cells on clothing, something like that. And really, it's our job in the lab to try and find those materials and, if we can, characterize them. Can we find a stain? Can we characterize that stain as being blood? Is it possible to isolate DNA from those stains, from those biological materials? If we can isolate DNA, we can type the DNA. If we can type the DNA, we can compare that type from that bloodstain, let's say, to the DNA type that we get from known blood samples or known saliva samples that we get from individuals who might be the source of that blood.

"DNA is deoxyribonucleic acid is the material that is present in virtually all the building blocks in your body, and it's this material that contains all the information for all the physical traits that make you who you are. So, if you think about it, what DNA really is, it's the chemical blueprint that makes you first a human being, and second, it's also the chemical blueprint for those physical traits that make you unique as a human being.

"When we type the evidence material and then type

the known blood sample or the known saliva sample from an individual, we are going to run thirteen tests on the evidence material and thirteen tests on these known samples. When you boil down what we do in the laboratory, it's isolating the DNA from the bloodstain, whatever the evidence is, and doing thirteen tests to get twenty-six answers, and we are comparing those twenty-six answers for the same tests that we are doing on the known blood sample that came from a specific individual. If those twenty-six answers match the sample, that particular person could have been the source of the blood."

Mr. Onorato explained to jurors how the lab examines DNA from dried body fluids as well as wet. Dried stains will retain the DNA longer than wet stains. The DNA analyst received DNA from two individuals in this case, Joseph Mesa and Ben Varner. He also analyzed biological material recovered from the jacket found in the dumpster.

"When evidence comes into the lab, like this jacket, the first thing that we do in the lab is really simply take the item and look for discolorations. Now, in lab lingo, that's called 'looking for stains,' and what we were able to determine is, in fact, that there were stains on this jacket. Once these discolorations or stains are identified, we do a series of tests in an effort to determine whether those stains are or are not blood. In this particular case, we did, in fact, identify bloodstains on the inside of the hood of the jacket, right here where the hood is actually attached to the top of the jacket. We identified bloodstains on the lining at the bottom of the jacket, down near the hem on the inside, and on what would be the right-hand side of the jacket about the level of the lower chest, near the zipper."

Mr. Onorato conducted thirteen tests on all the bloodstains and compared them with the DNA from Ben and JJ. He discovered that the DNA from the bloodstains in the jacket did not match the DNA from JJ's saliva sample. Rather, the DNA analyses revealed the DNA from the bloodstains matched Ben's DNA.

The prosecutor asked about the DNA recovered from the knife found in the dumpster.

"The knife was, for the laboratory's purposes, designed Q154. We attempted to do chemical testing for the presence of blood on the knife. The result we got suggested that blood may have been present. There was not enough material on this knife to do the second test. So, I can't tell you conclusively if blood was on this knife."

Mr. Boasberg asked about the DNA typing on the sneakers found in JJ's closet. Again, DNA results were inconclusive. Blood on the heel of the sneaker revealed a mixture of DNA from at least three individuals. One person's DNA, a "major donor," was identified. That donor was Ben Varner.

Chapter 33

Trial Day Five

Prosecutor: Now, you have been asked questions about whether or not you love Joseph. My question for you is, despite the fact that you love him, would you be willing to lie for him under oath?

Melani: No, I would not lie. I would only tell the truth. JJ would want me to tell the truth.

On the fifth day of the trial, the prosecution would present its last witnesses. They planned to call an FBI analyst,

Melani, and Detective Reed as their final testimonies. Mr. Boasberg first called FBI analyst Sandra Wiersema. She described her training after working for the San Diego police department.

"During my time in the [San Diego] police laboratories, I attended several FBI classes, two of them on shoe print and tire tread analysis. I have gone to factories that manufacture shoes to determine how the manufacturing methods might affect the shoe prints that we would see at a crime scene.

"I have also taught footwear evidence at the FBI training facility in Quantico, Virginia. I have trained internationally in Warsaw, Poland, in Budapest, Hungary, and in Estonia, teaching footwear and tire tread examination."

Ms. Wiersema was indeed an expert in shoe prints and tire treads. She told jurors about collecting evidence of a shoe print found outside of Ben's room. Mr. Boasberg asked her about February 4, 2001.

"I responded to Gallaudet University, and I noted that there were some bloody footwear impressions that were on a floor leading from a room down a hallway. And those impressions had already been previously marked by the Metro Police Department.

"I had those impressions photographed first to be sure that we would have a record of what they looked like at the time that I arrived at the crime scene. Then I decided to chemically enhance the bloody impressions, and I did that using ametoe black, which is a chemical that reacts with the protein in the blood. It turns the blood from the reddish-brown color that you normally see to a deep blue/black color.

"We enhance these footprints, for one thing, to increase the contrast. The impressions were on a tile floor that was reddish-brown, pretty similar in color to the color of the blood. And frequently, if you do chemical enhancement, you will enhance impressions that are very, very faint and difficult to see with the eye without enhancement.

"I had them rephotographed to record the appearances of them after chemical enhancement. We had the photographs printed at the laboratory. And I chose the photograph that I thought was best to have printed natural size so that at some point, I could make a comparison. I compared this footprint with a pair of shoes that were submitted to the laboratory [nine days later].

"The morning after I had enhanced these impressions at the scene, I went into the laboratory. We have a footwear database in the laboratory which has a number of shoes in it that are coded by design. By that, I mean if there is a circle on the bottom of the shoe, then it would be coded into the database by circles. I can actually then do a search of the shoes that are in the database to see if I find anything. Based on my memory of the impression that I had developed the day before, I searched the database, and I found a shoe that had the same design. It was a Nike Air Sever Max, the model name of the shoe. This was on February 5.

"Nine days later, on February 14, I was given a pair of Nike Air Sever Maxes. The first thing I did was I had the shoes photographed just to record the outside of the sole. After I had them photographed, I made test impressions from the bottom of the shoe to compare the impressions that we had developed at the crime scene."

Mr. Boasberg showed her photographs of the JJ's shoes. Agent Wiersema stepped from the witness box to point to the relevant areas on an enlarged photograph of the shoe impressions. She pointed to the enhanced areas where the ametoe black turned the blood into a blue-black color on the brick floor of the dorm. She said there were four different places on the dormitory floor with bloody shoe prints.

The prosecutor asked the agent to hold up the actual shoe recovered from JJ's closet to the photograph so the jurors could see how the markings were the same. Agent Wiersema explained how she made a test impression for comparison.

"I made that test impression by dusting black fingerprint powder on the bottom of the shoe. Then I put the shoe on my foot and stepped down on clear adhesive material. When I did that, the fingerprint powder that was on the bottom of the shoe would stick to the adhesive.

"I use that impression to lay over a natural size photograph. In other words, this is the size of that impression at the crime scene. Then I would take the test impressions and actually lay them over the impressions on the floor to see if everything aligns. Is the design in the same location? Is the design the same size? Are the design elements all the same size?"

She explained that when a size is larger or smaller, the design elements change in relation to the size.

"The designer wants all the shoes to look the same, whether you buy a size six or you buy a size fourteen. The elements have to change as the shoe gets bigger. So, we compare the size of the design with the size of the impression. I determined in this particular instance that the design and the size of the shoe corresponded."

Based upon the matching of the impression and the actual shoe print, the agent concluded that JJ's shoes were the ones that left the bloody imprint on the dormitory floor. One of the telling signs was a defect in the shoe, a slight dent along the edge, most likely caused by wear. The pattern in the impression and in JJ's shoes was identical in the enlarged photographs. There was no doubt that JJ's shoes had made the imprint.

After a morning recess at 10:20 a.m., the prosecutors, Mr. Bond, and the judge discussed their next witness, Melani. They wanted her attorney, Mr. Khan, to remain in the courtroom. The judge admonished the attorney for leaving the courtroom without being excused. Mr. Khan informed the judge that Melani would assert marital privilege to avoid testifying against JJ. The judge asked him on what basis. Mr. Kahn was concerned that she would be named a co-conspirator in the case.

"Are you alleging that she took any action in response to the letters [Mr. Mesa sent her]?" asked the judge.

"She did not give the letters; she did not come forward to the police or anybody."

The judge said, "She doesn't have an obligation to

do that. I'm going to order her to testify, Mr. Khan. I don't see any basis for a privilege here. If she still doesn't want to testify, if the Government wants her locked up, she will get locked up."

Mr. Boasberg assured Melani's attorney that they were not focusing on the letters. They did not plan to identify her as a co-conspirator nor accuse her of obstructing justice by withholding the letters. Again, the judge told the attorney that Melani was ordered to testify.

"Why don't you find out whether she wants jail or to testify?" asked the judge.

"I have talked to her," said Mr. Khan. "She is asserting a privilege, but if the Court orders her to testify, she has no choice."

"That's the case. So why don't you bring her in," the judge responded.

At 10:30 a.m., the judge called Melani to the witness stand.

Jennifer Collins went through the formalities, reviewing how Melani knew JJ from childhood and moving to Krug Hall at Gallaudet. She asked about how much time Melani spent in Cogswell Hall with JJ and how she knew Eric Plunkett.

Melani told jurors the last time she saw Eric

Plunkett was the day of the murder.

"Eric had a limp. He told [JJ] and me that he couldn't ride a bike."

When asked if JJ had mentioned that Eric lived alone, Melani said no. Ms. Collins asked for a copy of Melani's Grand Jury testimony from February 15, 2001. She asked Melani to look at page ten, lines eight through eleven. Melani said she did not remember making those statements to the Grand Jury.

Ms. Collins read, "Did Joseph ever talk about the fact that Eric didn't have a roommate and lived alone? Your answer was, 'Yeah. He said Eric's so lucky; he has this huge room and no roommate.' Do you remember being asked that question and giving the answer?"

Melani said, "No, I don't because it was a while ago. I don't remember what questions were asked."

Ms. Collins asked Melani about the night before Eric's body was found, the last time she saw him alive.

"I saw him the night before the murder. I saw Eric typing. His door was open. He was sitting in his room with his back to the door." She said later that evening, she saw that his door was closed.

Jennifer Collins asked Melani to tell the jurors more about what she and JJ were doing that day.

"We had gone to class that day, and then I think we went to the cafeteria. Then we came back to JJ's room. We decided to make pasta for dinner that night and cooked it in the microwave.

"I had gone to get water for the pasta and walked away. When I walked back toward his room, JJ was standing near Eric's door. I asked him what he was doing. JJ said he smelled something funny."

"Did he describe to you what he was smelling?" asked the prosecutor.

"No, because I told him that I didn't smell anything because the pasta smell was so strong."

Ms. Collins continued to push, "But did Joseph tell you what he thought he was smelling?"

"No, he just said it was a funny smell."

"Melani, I'm going to ask you to look at the transcript again. And this time, you can look at page twenty, lines nineteen through twenty-two. Do you remember being asked this question: 'What did Joseph tell you it was that he thought he was smelling?' You answered, 'He said something, he smelled something funny, maybe it was blood or something.'"

"I don't remember. I just remember that he said something smelled funny. It puzzled me. So, I told him,

'Why don't you go get an R.A. so they can go check on it.'"

JJ had left his dorm room to get the R.A. Ms. Collins asked what happened next.

"The R.A. opened the door. Then they turned around and told us to get into JJ's room and shut the door. I said, 'Something had to be fishy because I hadn't seen Eric all day.' So then JJ looked through his peephole. He said he could see a bunch of people hanging around Eric's door, like the police. And then he said he could see Eric lying in his room.

"Then I had to go to the restroom. I opened the door and told the officers that were there that I needed to go down the hall and go to the bathroom. And when I stepped out, I could see Eric's body on the floor."

"Did Joseph himself ever describe the appearance of Eric's body to you?" asked Ms. Collins.

"He did say after he had looked through the peephole in his door that he saw Eric's body and it looked like there was blood, that it was covered in blood, his face and so forth."

Melani said she and JJ had gone to visit Ben in his room on the fourth floor of Cogswell on other occasions.

Melani read again from her Grand Jury testimony.

"It was around Christmas time, the first time JJ borrowed money from Ben. I told JJ, 'You know, you really shouldn't do that. It's embarrassing.' And JJ said, 'Don't worry. I'll borrow forty dollars from him. I'll pay him back later.' When he asked Ben for the money, Ben gave him sixty dollars instead of forty that he asked for.

"But he didn't pay him back. He said, 'Oh, I'll pay him back later.' He knew that he was aware that he owed him. He figured that once he got his SSI check, he would pay him back. And I said, 'Look, you ought to pay him back now, rather than put it off. You owe him.' But JJ said, 'Look, I will, just hold on.' But, you know, he never did."

The prosecutor asked her about the night before Ben's body was found.

"Our Bible study group was talking about salvation. JJ had come into the room, then turned around and left. After the study group finished, I sat down and used the computer for a while. Then I went back to my room. When I got back to my room, all of a sudden, JJ showed up there. He was sweaty. I asked him about it. He said that he had just finished wrestling with some friends in Cogswell. I told him he shouldn't be involved in wrestling. One of his hands was bleeding. He was bleeding over one of his eyebrows too.

"I asked him what had happened. He said that he had been wrestling with some friends from MSSD, like former students of MSSD. I was angry with him. I told him, 'I'm mad because you shouldn't be wrestling. You'll hurt yourself.'"

The prosecutor read from Melani's Grand Jury testimony. "JJ was sweating and pacing. He didn't have the same outfit on that he had before. He had different clothes on. He was out of breath. You know, he had like a polo shirt on. It was short-sleeved, different. Originally, I saw he was wearing a running outfit, but he had changed his clothes.

"And then he left. I went in search of him. I said, 'Where did you get these clothes?' He said, 'Well, I borrowed them from a student, this MSSD student who planned to withdraw.' I said, 'Oh, well, these clothes are all dirty or something.' He said, 'Well, you know, I was out wrestling.' I didn't really think anything about it."

Melani told the jurors she remembered her testimony. Ms. Collins asked her how she found out about Ben's murder.

"JJ was staying over in my room. In the middle of the night, we saw a bunch of flashing lights and sirens. Then JJ's roommate, Chris, sent him a page saying that there had been another murder. JJ told me they found Ben's body. We started to talk back and forth about that. It puzzled me; I wasn't too sure about that."

She said later that day, after Ben's body had been discovered, she and JJ had gone shopping. They bought a television, a purple computer pad, and a purple mouse.

Next, the prosecutor wanted Melani to tell the jurors what happened on February 13th.

Melani said, "We had slept together and woke up that morning. When we got up, JJ was going to go to his room, but it was blocked because the police were still investigating the area. He wanted to get clothes, but we decided not to go. Then JJ said he wanted to go to the DOSS office. I went with him but waited outside. I don't know what they talked about. When he came back out, JJ told me that we were going to Union Station. JJ and I bought a mocha and some food. JJ handed me some money, but I told him I had money. He told me to hold onto his money. I remember JJ saying something about if he went to jail, but I wasn't exactly sure why he was saying that. I remember him handing me $54 and saying, 'Here, you hold on to this in case I go to jail.' I was taken aback, yes. It sort of made me suspicious, as if something were wrong.

"He looked unhappy," she said. "I remember the

two of us stepping outside for some fresh air. We went to the area near the fountain outside of Union Station. I was saying something about a good memory I remembered. As I was talking, I noticed that JJ started to cry. When he started to cry, I asked him what was wrong and hugged him. He just said that what I had been talking about was such a good memory that it really touched him and made him cry."

When the two went back to campus, they stopped at the post office. Then they went back to Melani's dorm room. JJ had wanted to talk in private. They went to the top floor of the dorm because no one was around. JJ then told her what had happened.

"He said that he killed Ben. We talked about our relationship. I was crying. I was mad at JJ. I was totally overwhelmed. We were both crying. It made JJ cry that I was crying. We hugged, and then JJ said that he needed to go to the police."

JJ had not revealed to Melani that he had also murdered Eric. Though JJ's father had sent spending money to him, he told Melani he stole the money so he could buy her presents.

"After his interview with the police, it was pretty late at night. He went to be videotaped to confess. Then after that, when it was all over, we were sitting together. The police were around. I asked him, 'Is it true that you killed Eric?' He said, 'Yes. I thought I already told you.' I said, 'No.' He couldn't remember if he had already told me or not. I was angry. And then that was it. I told the two police officers I needed to go home, back to Gallaudet."

When the judge excused Melani, Jennifer Collins called Detective Reed to the stand a second time.

She asked, "During the videotaped statement you took from Mr. Mesa, on one occasion, were you and Mr. Mesa referring to some drawings?"

She presented Government's Exhibit Numbers 76, 77, and 78 as evidence. Detective Reed recognized them as evidence confiscated from a search warrant on February 13, 2002, a year to the day of JJ's arrest. Detective Reed had presented a warrant for Melani and Anna's dorm room to a DOSS officer, who escorted them. Detective Reed wanted the letters that JJ had written to Melani.

"She had a lot of letters," said the detective. "One batch was in a plastic container, like twice the size of a shoebox. And we found a few stray letters amongst her other items. There was another stack of letters we also obtained. In the end, it filed up a shopping bag."

Many of the letters remained in their original

envelopes with the return address as the Washington, D.C. jail at 1901 D Street, SE. The prosecutor showed jurors an enlarged photograph of the letters the detective removed from the room. The letters showed JJ's calculated attempts to hide evidence and create alibis that would lessen or drop the charges. This was not the actions of someone with a mental illness.

Defense attorney Ferris Bond cross-examined Detective Reed. He handed her a copy of Melani's Grand Jury testimony. He asked the detective to confirm that police did not prompt Melani in her testimony, to which the detective confirmed.

Mr. Bond asked, "Has anyone ever asked Patrick Mesa if he had the watch, and if he did, would he be willing to turn it over to the authorities?"

"I'm not sure if anyone asked that specifically. There was a law enforcement agency sent out to the house, but I don't know if they asked that specifically."

"Has anyone talked to Mr. Mesa's father to ask him if he had what you were looking for and whether he would be willing to turn it over to you?"

"No. I can't say that one way or the other because I wasn't actually in Guam asking, but there were some police agents sent out there."

"Was there a search warrant?"

"No," answered the detective. "I believe it was a voluntarily asked."

"The fact of the matter is the police came, did they not, and the Mesas told them to come in and look around for whatever they wanted to look for, right? You have no information to the contrary. Is that correct?"

"I know what came back from the agency, but I don't exactly know what the exchange was."

Mr. Bond seemed to be redirecting the cross-examination to imply that JJ's family was cooperative with the police. With the prosecution's objection, the judge shut down the line of questioning.

Mr. Bond focused on the book about the insanity defense that JJ referenced in his letters. He asked if JJ had also had a book related to psychological testing. Mr. Bond's line of questioning did not serve to conjure reasonable doubt. Instead, he seemed to speak just to speak. The final testimony concluded the prosecution's case. The court would close for the next several days for annual training. When the trial resumed, the defense would present their case.

Chapter 34

Trial Day Six

Prosecution: Isn't it strange for someone who has committed these property crimes then all of a sudden commit murder? Didn't Dr. Madsen say that those murders must be the result of some mental illness?

Dr. Pollard: When the evidence of the conduct disorder is sufficient at an early enough age, you have a worse prediction about their future behavior. That's the framework in which I see the facts of this particular case.

As he's getting older, things are getting worse.

Mr. Ferris Bond and Ms. Jill Sege, the defense team, began its case on Tuesday, May 14, 2002. They planned to show the jurors that JJ was not a monster; rather, he was just an unhappy deaf kid with all sorts of problems. His first witness would be JJ's father, Mr. Joseph Mesa, Sr. However, Mr. Bond approached the judge's bench before the trial started.

"Since we last talked to you, apparently Mrs. Mesa's status had changed; she apparently has very, very high blood pressure right now. She's down with a nurse. They're having her sit down and trying to get her to calm down and relax. If the blood pressure goes down, she will come up here. If it goes up, she's going to need to go to the emergency room. My first witness I'd like to call would be Mr. Mesa. In the event it goes up, he's probably the one that would have to take her over there. I may, at some point, be asking the court to indulge us somehow, but I don't expect him to be a witness that's going to take hours and hours of testimony."

The judge agreed to be flexible if the situation required it. Clearly, the Mesa family felt a great deal of stress and sadness after learning of their son's actions from the prosecution's witnesses.

Ferris Bond called JJ's father, Joseph Mesa, Sr., to the stand. Mr. Mesa told jurors he was a chief warrant officer with the United States Army in Guam, specializing in logistics. He explained that when he and his wife, Grace, discovered that JJ was deaf around four months old, they immediately sought medical help. After multiple medical tests, JJ was diagnosed as profoundly deaf within the year. Both father and mother had rudimentary sign language skills. They used primarily fingerspelling, forming words and sentences by signing individual letters. As was the custom on the island, the parents sent JJ to school.

JJ's father was a strict disciplinarian. He used corporal punishment with all of his children, JJ included. The family members struggled with sign language communication. Mr. Mesa understood that his son might have felt excluded and frustrated. Though Mr. Mesa tried to instill hardworking and disciplined values, he conceded that JJ rarely understood why he was sometimes punished.

As JJ got older, his tolerance for being left out worsened. His frustration turned to punching objects, destroying property, and increasing aggression. JJ's internal conflict with wanting to be helpful and connected to his family was at odds with feeling left out, ignored, and often in trouble.

"When we'd have a gathering," explained his father, "I didn't even have to ask him help my in-laws set up the place for the gathering. He would go up there and help out without being told. When we asked him to pick up my mother from the hospital, he would do that. Whatever we asked him to do, he would do. He would never turn around and ask why he had to do it, like my other kids."

In Guam, JJ had worked a couple of jobs. One was with the government for the summer and another at the Army-Air Force exchange. Within a year at the exchange, JJ was named the month's employee. Mr. Mesa's pride for his son swelled as he watched his son receive congratulations from military personnel and even the territorial governor. Yet JJ still seemed troubled to his father.

"One time in frustration, he punched the plywood. We were playing; we were all laughing and joking; we're all patting each other, but for him, he doesn't see that. When he makes a mistake, like in volleyball or basketball, all of a sudden, he just punches the ball doesn't care where it went. It wasn't a game. When he gets frustrated, he also, you know, goes and looks for a quiet place. He moves away. Back home where I live, there's a lot of trees and air, that stuff. There are no houses in the back. So, I'd see him walking in the back. He just wanders the fields. Sometimes he will just sit right underneath the coconut tree, just watching the animals."

In Guam, JJ was very active in his community.

"The activities back home," said Mr. Mesa, "we had him participate in the youth football league. Basically, that's the community type activity where kids from certain villages come together as a group and play games; they play football. So, he participated in that for about two years. He played volleyball for the school. He also assisted the coaches in managing the basketball team. Apparently, he tried to get into basketball, but because of his disability, they felt that there wasn't anybody there to sign the moves or, you know, when to give signals to pass the ball. He tried to participate in track also."

To prepare to attend MSD, JJ's father opened an account for JJ at the Pentagon Federal Credit Union. He would replenish his account so that JJ could use a debit card when he needed money. His father provided him with a student credit card to help him establish his own credit. If JJ needed money over the weekend when the bank was closed, JJ's father would wire money through Western

Union. JJ's parents ensured that their son's financial needs were met.

Ferris Bond now planned to craft JJ into the image needed to fit the defense.

"Have you ever observed your son appear to blank out?" asked the defense attorney.

"Just one time. One time I saw him actually blank out and fall on the pavement. He was in a daze. It's like his eyes were fixed."

Mr. Bond asked him to clarify what he meant by "fixed."

"They were fixed, you know. He wasn't blinking. We were talking to him. His eyes were wide open, but he just seemed like he couldn't see us. That happened at one of the gatherings we have back home. There were some cases when we were together, normally when we were doing work. I had a lot of expectations for my kids. They needed to concentrate on what they were doing. Sometimes I caught JJ just kind of wandering, like he was just not engaged with what he was doing."

Mr. Bond asked Mr. Mesa to describe what JJ was like when he came home from Gallaudet for winter break after Eric was killed.

"During Christmas in 2000, there were a lot of

things that needed to be done to prepare. I came home and saw JJ in bed. I asked him, 'Why are you in bed? How come you're not out there helping, doing what I asked you to do?' He said, 'I got a terrible headache.' Then I said, 'Are you sick?' He was perspiring. He said that he just had a terrible headache and needed to rest. I asked, 'Are you sick? You look like you're hot. Do you want me to turn on the air-conditioning higher?' He said, 'No, no, no. I just need to take a rest. I got a terrible headache.'

"I was worried because my father, throughout the years, also complained of headaches. Not knowing that, one day, he got into an accident. They did an x-ray and found a tumor. So, when it comes to headaches, I try to pay particular attention."

Mr. Bond asked Mr. Mesa if he had ever seen his son get angry.

"Oh yeah, sir. A lot of times. Playing games. It's just the lack of communication; he gets angry. The last one I'll never forget was just before he came back to Gallaudet in January 2001. We were fixing the car in one of the hobby shops on base. I found myself doing all the work, and he was just standing there. I got upset. Then he looked at me and turned red and said, 'Why? Why? Why? Why are you so angry? What did I do?' Then he started crying."

"Have you taught your son to express his emotions or taught him not to express himself?" asked Mr. Bond.

"No, sir. We never taught our son how to express himself. It's more like if you want something, let us know. But, you know, I can't recall a time where he actually sat down and even talked about that topic of expressing himself."

Mr. Bond asked how JJ would react when whipped for a misdeed.

"He wasn't like my other kids. When I spanked them, they were running around and yelling. Joseph would just sit there or stand there, and he would just take it. I noticed that only tears would come out, only tears. Eyes red, tears came out. He was a lot different from my other kids. I spanked them, and my next-door neighbors could hear them, but with [JJ], he never ever yelled.

"How hard did you hit him?"

"Many times, it was hard enough that even my brother-in-law, my sister-in-law, would come over and tell me to stop it."

Mr. Bond then excused Mr. Mesa from the witness box. Mr. Boasberg stepped forward for cross-examination. He clarified for the jury that JJ had been doing fine academically when he was arrested for the murders.

Besides doing fine in school, Mr. Boasberg claimed JJ was also never treated for mental illness as a child in Guam. He clarified that no one in JJ's family had a mental illness or been treated for one. There were no suicide attempts or psychiatric interventions as a child. JJ had never used illegal drugs or alcohol. JJ had never witnessed trauma or violence as a child. He had never been sexually or physically abused. He had never spoken of the devil or Satan commanding him. Even when JJ complained of headaches, his family treated him with Tylenol or aspirin. Step by step, the prosecution chipped away at Mr. Bond's facsimile of JJ as a disturbed, mentally ill child and now an adult.

Mr. Bond had wanted to call Mr. Andy Noble, the defense's investigator, to the witness stand. Mr. Boasberg objected because anything Mr. Noble said would be hearsay. Mr. Bond explained that Mr. Noble was with Mr. Bond once when visiting JJ at the D.C. jail. He could attest to JJ's statement that black hands had forced him to commit the murders. Mr. Bond insisted that this testimony would show jurors that JJ was indeed mentally ill. The judge disagreed; he ruled the testimony as hearsay and that it had no independent relevance to the case. It would not be heard.

His point squashed, Mr. Bond called Patrick Mesa,

JJ's younger brother, to the stand. At one year old, Patrick moved from San Francisco to Guam. He worked as a sign language interpreter for Augeda Johnston middle school. His brother, JJ, was two years older than him. As children, he and JJ shared a bedroom. He felt they were close.

Mr. Bond asked Patrick to describe when he had seen JJ lose control.

"The first time was when we wrestled. We had an understanding where if he knows I can't get out of a hold, all I do is tap him on the leg, and he'd let go. That's it. There were times where it seems like he blanks out or zones out and applies pressure to the point where it really, really hurt me. I'd start to cry. The only way for me to get out of that is I'd have to hurt myself even more, trying to get out. I never understood why he did that. I'd look at his face. He'd be looking the other way in a zoned-out manner, paying no attention to me."

Patrick explained JJ would perspire heavily during these times, especially when he would zone out.

"After he hurt me and I got up, I would cry. It's like he'd still be out of it. He would retreat, you know, run out. He would go somewhere to be by himself.

"The second time I remember my brother losing control again was when we were wrestling, and he had me in a headlock. He just threw himself down with me in the headlock. That really brought a lot of pain in my neck, and this was during a typhoon. So, I got out, but I was in pain. It was like he zoned out, like he wasn't paying attention to me. He was looking the other way."

JJ and Patrick had an understanding that when one of them tapped the other's leg or arm, the restraining brother would release the wrestling hold. JJ often pinned Patrick but was reluctant to release him. Patrick described repeated tappings while he cried for JJ to release him. Patrick would struggle and slap him, panic rising. For Patrick to escape, he often needed to hurt himself more to get out. Mostly, it was JJ's sweat that allowed Patrick to slip from his grip.

"One night, we were wrestling, and he picked me up. I didn't want to wrestle anymore because I wanted to go outside into the kitchen and eat, but he picked me up. He had a blank stare, then picked me up. There is a nightstand in my parents' room. He picked me up and slammed me down. My head hit the corner of the nightstand; I was bleeding. I got on the bed, and I was holding my head. I picked up my head and looked at my hands; I saw blood all over them. I ran to the bathroom to check. I looked in the mirror. He was right behind me, staring. He wasn't staring at me. He was staring at himself. I ran out, but he stayed behind in the bedroom. I had about ten stitches. When I came back from the hospital, he was sleeping in the other bedroom by himself."

Mr. Bond emphasized JJ's blank stares and profuse sweating during these violent incidents for the jurors. Patrick said that sometimes JJ would hurt himself while in a rage. He would cut himself as he punched or head-butted walls and wall tiles.

"When you use the term 'zoned out,' can you describe how his face appeared?" asked Mr. Bond.

"He had this dead look on his face. He wasn't paying attention to his surroundings; he was paying attention to something else."

Mr. Bond asked Patrick to relay the details of several incidents where JJ's explosive anger resulted in injuries to himself or other people. Patrick described numerous occasions when that had occurred as a child.

"He punches the wall hard, like full force. Sometimes he would go up to the wall, either facing the wall or the side, and he goes like this." Patrick demonstrated how JJ banged his head. "You can hear it. You can hear the thudding. A lot of times when he does harm to himself, he's frustrated or mad at somebody, something, or himself."

Mr. Bond asked Patrick about the winter break in December 2000.

"While [JJ] was in Guam, he would isolate himself from everybody at that time. He never wanted to go out. He was always tired and emotional.

"At times when he was by himself inside the room, he would sign to himself. It's really fast fingerspelling. I caught him on a couple of occasions doing that. And like I said, this is also when he had a dead look. He's just signing. And if I ask him [what he's doing], sometimes he either gets mad or he just says, 'never mind.'"

Mr. Bond asked Patrick about household animals.

"We have cats. Sometimes we get stray cats, and we just take them in. There had been a couple of occasions where we would have a cat for a couple of months, and then all of a sudden, they were gone. We also had a family cat who gave birth at one time. Then they were just gone. We didn't know what had happened to them.

"We had one dog; we never knew what happened to it. But I was too young; I didn't really pay attention to that one."

Patrick said that JJ complained of headaches on multiple occasions during the Christmas break. He described JJ as looking flushed and without energy.

"It was like he was lazy. He didn't want to do anything. He just wanted to lay down."

Ferris Bond wanted the jurors to see JJ as clearly plagued with some sort of problem. He injured himself, his brother, and his household animals. So, when Mr. Bond called Melani to the stand, he would add information that would render JJ even more disturbed.

He first asked her to describe her childhood experiences in Guam with JJ. She said they started dating officially when she was about sixteen years old. By the time she had come to Gallaudet, they had been dating exclusively for three years.

"When we first met, he was a sweet boy. We used to teach each other. Then, at one point, we decided to date. He taught me about relationships, about love. He treated me the best. Everything he's done for good for me. He taught me everything, even about education and family values."

Melani witnessed many of JJ's explosive tantrums. She had seen him lose control numerous times, pounding his head and hurting himself. She described an incident that occurred shortly after Eric's death.

"[JJ] tried to jump out of the third-floor window of

Krug Hall. We were talking, having some kind of argument. He actually got up onto the windowsill. I told him he was being ridiculous. I grabbed him and pulled him back in. He wasn't looking at me when I told him that. He was looking everywhere, but then he calmed down. I calmed him down by making him look at me by forcing eye contact. That was usually the way I could make him calm down. That was the only way we could resolve things."

"Did he tell you why he wanted to commit suicide?" asked Mr. Bond.

"No. He didn't give a reason. It was just him being out of control. I would try to ask him what was wrong with him; he wouldn't respond. He wouldn't tell me why.

"[In December] during final exams in the Hall Memorial Building, JJ got angry. He punched a glass case that had a fire extinguisher inside; he grabbed it. As he was walking away with it, I tried to grab him, but he was so angry he wouldn't talk to me. He tried to get away. So, I basically left him alone. I didn't know what was going on with him. He came back and put the fire extinguisher back.

"Another time when we were in Krug Hall, he grabbed another fire extinguisher that was just around the corner from my room. It was right near the fire door exit. We were having some kind of fight with each other. He grabbed the extinguisher and was going to walk down the stairs with it. I tried to talk to him. I don't think he even knew what he was going to do with it. So, I just left him alone. It caused me a lot of frustration."

The defense attorney asked Melani to describe the situation with JJ's and Chad's altercation about the missing credit card.

"Chad, my roommate Manda, Elaine, and Sara were in the room when it happened. It was the first time they had seen any kind of incident happen. [JJ] almost punched Chad, but luckily, he was able to restrain himself because there were other people there. He took off."

After the court's break for lunch, Mr. Bond wanted the jurors to know that JJ had killed his friends, and he wanted Melani to explain this in more detail.

"We first met Eric at the Edward Miner Gallaudet building. Eric was there doing some stuff on the internet. JJ and I met him and talked with him. Then Eric's room was right across the hall in Cogswell. We were surprised to find that out that evening. JJ introduced himself to Eric. They talked about their families and where they were from. Eric seemed very interested in Guam. Eric said that he wanted to visit because he was curious. They were kind of teasing each other, having fun.

"JJ helped Eric with tutoring because he was kind of weak in math. JJ tutored him, and he was able to pass his test. Eric would sometimes borrow DVDs, or they would treat each other to food or share food sometimes. JJ showed Eric a bunch of pictures he had. Those pictures were of our friends and family back home in Guam. In return, Eric shared information about his parents and how much they looked like Eric. Eric talked about a young baby, maybe a sibling. But then Eric told me a little later that he was a little scared. He asked to talk to me privately. So, I sat down in Eric's room. He told me he was gay. I told him it was no big deal, that he didn't have to worry about it."

Melani explained JJ had also considered Ben Varner a friend.

"JJ asked Ben for help with computers because Ben was so knowledgeable about them. JJ would have a problem and ask Ben for help. I remember they were laughing and teasing each other. Ben then asked me about JJ, how I knew him, and all of that. I told Ben that we grew up together. Ben said to me, 'Well, JJ's such a cool guy. He's funny and nice.'"

Melani characterized JJ's relationship with Eric and Ben as close friends. Then, Mr. Bond reminded the jurors through Melani's testimony that JJ was often unable to control his anger, that something was wrong with JJ physically and mentally. Close to the end of the day at 2:50 p.m., the defense's next move was to call JJ himself to the stand.

JJ said he was twenty-two years old and from Guam. He said that he learned little while he attended school. Mr. Bond asked him about communication with his family.

"Growing up, I had lots and lots of problems with my family and relatives. My immediate family knew how to sign just a little, primarily fingerspelling, except for my brother. As far as the other relatives were concerned, they couldn't communicate with me."

JJ told jurors that the lack of communication made him feel upset, depressed, and sad.

Mr. Bond asked, "Mr. Mesa, do you have trouble controlling yourself?"

"Always."

"And do images come into your mind and tell you to do things?"

"Many times."

Mr. Bond asked JJ about his relationship with Eric Plunkett.

"I first met him at the EMG building, which is

where the computers are. I met him there pretty unexpectedly. I found out that he lived right across the hall from me in the dorm. My relationship with him was pretty good."

"Now, you told us just a little while ago that images come into your mind. Could you describe what those images look like for the ladies and gentlemen of the jury?"

"Black hands," JJ responded. "They are black hands up to the elbows. They are maybe seven by thirteen inches. They are covered in leather. The gloves go all the way down the arm, and they are sort of segmented going down the forearm."

"When you see these hands, what do they do?"

"The hands sign to me and tell me to commit crimes, and sometimes they are carrying weapons. Guns. A knife. A large knife."

JJ explained that he first met the black hands when he was young in Guam.

"They would have a weapon and show me what to do. There would be some awful pictures altogether. It wasn't signing, but kind of demonstrating what to do. It was a picture like of a cat and hands crushing the neck of the cat that led me to do something."

"What did you do? Tell the jury."

"I killed around ten cats. The first was in my living room at home. It was late at night; I was sitting down. I couldn't sleep. That was the first time I saw these black hands with the cat. I was puzzled by that. I felt like I was supposed to strangle the cats, that I was supposed to kill the baby cats. I tried to ignore it by keeping myself busy. I couldn't go to sleep. I went to get something to drink and watch television. I was restless. My mind was running full speed. I couldn't control myself. So, I got up and did exactly what the picture in my mind was telling me to do."

"And what did the picture in your mind tell you to do?" asked Mr. Bond.

"The picture was of taking hands around a cat's neck and putting the rope around [its] neck and hanging it from the ceiling or from something. Then I took a baseball bat; I went looking for it. I hit the cat several times with the bat. And as far as the kittens were concerned, I crushed their heads."

"When was the next time that you remember seeing the black hands, Mr. Mesa? Would you tell the jury about that?"

"I can't remember exactly when, but it was a while. I couldn't get Eric or Ben out of my mind."

Mr. Bond told JJ that they would talk about Eric

and Ben later. He wanted JJ to tell the jurors more about the black hands.

"Have there been other times, aside from when you killed the cats, that you had pictures in your mind?"

"Yeah. I really can't answer that question."

"Why can't you answer that question, Mr. Mesa?"

"Because I don't want to answer it incorrectly."

"Would you explain to us why you can't answer it?"

"I'm trying to tell you all that I remembered, but some of the things I don't want to say because I'm just trying to remember. I'm not sure I'll answer them right."

JJ said he had never told his family about killing the cats because he felt embarrassed. He did not want them to think that he had a mental health condition. Yet, the black hands would not leave him alone.

"They talked to me about Eric Plunkett, about taking things from Chad, about Ben, about my attorney, Mr. Bond, and the federal attorney, Mr. Boasberg.

"At first, I would be seated as usual at my computer. The black hands would start signing to me with pictures of Eric's face, beating him up, then strangling him. I tried to ignore the hands. I kept working at my computer. I talked with Melani, my girlfriend, but this kept running through my brain. Plus, I had some feelings going on inside about taking his credit card.

"I walked to Eric's door; he answered it. So, I tried to stop myself, asking myself If I should or shouldn't hurt my friend. I had to go back to my room. The only way I could prevent him was to go back to my room. I can't remember what I did when I was there, back in the room, but I had this strong feeling about beating him up and strangling him, these pictures of him. I tried to stop myself, but I couldn't. I closed the door, then grabbed him around the neck."

JJ explained to the jury that he saw Eric's body from the chest up in his mind.

"I saw him from the chest up; plus, I saw his face bloodied. I tried to prevent those pictures from staying there, but they kept bothering me and bothering me.

"It was like they were trying to force me to do something. I saw his face plus, really, his face bloodied. I started worrying. I was anxious and nervous. I tried to stop myself, but this kept running through my mind."

JJ told jurors he could not stop the parade of death images. The images, he told jurors, forced him to murder even though he and Eric were friends. The black hands had signed to him, commanded him to go into Eric's room. The hands showed him how to beat and strangle him. They demonstrated how to put him into a chokehold and squeeze the life from him.

"I saw the black hands beating him. That was something I didn't expect. Then kicking his head. And the black hands said to beat him up, but what I unexpectedly did was kick him, and then I was choking him. You know, I didn't expect that I would be kicking him. Then there was a chair there. I started hitting him with the chair up and down."

"Why?" Ferris Bond asked.

"I don't know why. Most of the time, I don't understand myself. For the same reason, I didn't understand why these thoughts were still in my mind. I always tried to fend them off, but I couldn't."

JJ's attorney asked him why he reported the smell coming from Eric's room. JJ told him he wanted to get caught. He was concerned, he said, that he would kill again.

"You did kill again, didn't you?" asked Mr. Bond.

"Yes."

"Why don't you tell the jury, if you would, what kind of relationship you had with Ben Varner."

JJ described how he and Ben were friends. Ben had helped him fix a computer and a fan in his dorm room. JJ had borrowed money on more than one occasion. He borrowed and returned a chair. He borrowed a scooter. Like Eric, JJ told the jurors, he had paid for and shared food for the two of them. The black hands paid another visit to JJ.

"The black hands had a large knife, with a black handle at the end, and a blade. The handle was a darker color than the blade. I forget how to spell the word, but it's something you use with coconuts and trees and leaves. To cut those kinds of things down."

"Tell the jury what you saw the black hands doing with that knife, that large knife that you used to cut coconuts down," said Mr. Bond.

"Sometimes, the knife would cut across the neck. Just like with Eric, I saw his body down to the middle of his abdomen with cuts on him and stab marks all over his body. First, I saw a wound on the right side of the neck. I saw a wound in the skull on the right side. I don't remember the rest."

JJ described how the thoughts kept coming to him, summoning him to kill again, and frightening him. The commands from the black hands were relentless. He told jurors he had tried to stop the hands from bothering him, but he couldn't.

"Tell the jury, if you would, why you were very

frightened, Mr. Mesa."

"Because of what had happened to Eric. I couldn't get it out of my mind. I just felt that I didn't want to kill again, and this I did; I would be even more scared and more worried. Inside, I really didn't want to kill him, but these thoughts kept on bothering me and bothering me; they were staying in my mind. I couldn't control myself. I had to do something to Ben, you know. The thing is, I was so scared about this and worried about what I had done to Eric and the very fact that I couldn't get that out of my mind."

"Did you get those thoughts out of your mind?" asked the attorney.

"No. No. They stayed a long time."

"Why did you kill Ben?"

"Because of the black hands. I tried to stop those black hands, but I couldn't. I felt that they were more powerful than I am, forcing me to do what I did."

"How long after you killed Ben did it take for those pictures, those images in your mind of the black hands, to go away?"

"That was longer, much longer than with Eric. Maybe three or four hours. I'm not just sure. Longer than with Eric.

"At first, I saw the black hands stab him in the neck

on the right side. I didn't expect that Ben would have a small knife. In my mind, there had been a larger knife, but this one was much smaller. I didn't want to take the knife, but something inside me forced me to grab it. I saw the black hands stab him in the back of the neck on the right side. It made me do the same thing; I stabbed him the same way. After that, I don't remember clearly. The last thing I remember was stabbing him in the head on the right side."

JJ told the court that though he did not need any money, he had forged and cashed Ben's check as a clue to the police. He said that he wanted to be caught and stopped. He described intense feelings of fear and hurt. In JJ's mind, he was a puppet of some sinister force. The black hands, telling him exactly how to commit the killings, had held JJ victim just as much as did Eric and Ben. JJ described a malevolent force entering his body.

"I've very, very frequently seen a professional wrestler by the name of the Undertaker. This person had those kind of gloves. Often I've felt that there has been this connection that I have with him."

"What kind of connection do you feel that you have with him?" asked Ferris Bond.

"I don't know what you call it, but these feelings that have come to me are really not mine. They are not my own feelings. I've tried to stop myself. I believe that these other feelings that have come into me, taking over, and I have often seen that person, you know, that professional wrestler. These feelings overtake me."

"I've often felt that there has been this connection I have with the Undertaker," JJ said. "I don't know what you would call it, but these feelings that come to me are not really mine. They are not my own feelings. These feelings come into me, taking over. I have often seen that professional wrestler when those feelings overtake me."

JJ had been an avid and skillful wrestler in his youth. He admired and emulated the WWE wrestlers. He wrestled with his brother, Patrick. He dominated over everyone with whom he wrestled. JJ knew a lot about wrestling and professional wrestlers. This knowledge and skill would fit well into his plan.

In the year that JJ murdered Eric, the WWE wrestler Mark William Calaway, aka the Undertaker, had a profound impact on JJ. The Undertaker stood at six feet, ten inches and weighed 300 pounds of chiseled, taut muscle. He was mean and lean, a tower of dominance and strength. The Undertaker wore his brown hair long. His tight, black, scalloped bodysuit and long pants he wore when wrestling helped craft a menacing presence. Tattoos lined the bulging skin of his arms and neck. He wore black leather gloves and a black hat. He was prone to sticking out his tongue as if possessed by the devil. With moves like the "suicide dive," the "big boot," and the "triangle chokehold," the Undertaker could toss competitor after competitor to the mat. JJ not only idolized the legendary Undertaker, but he realized the wrestler would be the perfect alibi for his murders.

To push the point even further, Mr. Bond asked, "Now you indicated that you had seen or had images in your mind relating to other people besides Ben and Eric. Is that true?"

"Yes. Yes."

"Name some of the other people that you had these images in your mind about."

"I don't know how to spell their names, but the government or the prosecutor. I don't know how to spell the men's names."

"What kind of images have you had in your mind?"

"Like just recently, today, the black hands were very angry. The black hands had a gun in them. I felt like the hands wanted me to strangle the prosecutor's neck and then use a gun. Sometimes the hands tell me to kill myself."

He described to the court multiple attempts at suicide using a nail across his wrist and hanging with a bedsheet. Mr. Bond allowed JJ to go on at length about how embarrassed he felt, how victimized he was by the black hands, and how mentally ill he indeed was.

Chapter 35

Trial Days Seven And Eight

I thought about Ben. I pictured him alone, studying, sitting at his chair. I was hoping he would have a knife. I thought about what I would do. Maybe I would be behind him and stab him in the neck or in the body, but it really didn't happen the way I had pictured it.

—JJ

On the seventh day of trial, May 15, 2002, Jeb Boasberg planned to cross-examine JJ's testimony. Before JJ was called to the stand, Mr. Bond needed to discuss a concern with the trial process. He addressed the judge.

"Judge, I know there are some real strong feelings in this trial. Believe me; I'm probably more aware of it than anybody in the courthouse because I deal with it every day when I walk into the court and every day when I walk out. And I know sometimes it's difficult when people are testifying, or things are coming out for people not to react and show a reaction. I think it's improper for that to occur in this or any other trial. I'd just ask you to caution the jury. We are doing our best, all of us here on this side of the counsel table, to give him a fair trial. I would request that people in the audience do the same thing by keeping their comments to themselves while they are in the courtroom. In one case yesterday, I saw a psychiatrist sitting in the back of the courtroom trying to get my attention and smirking. I think that's unprofessional. I think it's uncalled for."

The judge disagreed but still cautioned the courtroom audience. "All right. I mean, obviously, I'm facing the audience, Mr. Bond. I'm aware of what's going on. I think, as a general matter, the audience has been remarkably restrained throughout the trial. I certainly don't think anything has distracted the jury in any way. I think you are correct that certainly, nobody wants an unfair trial here. I would hope that people in the audience realize that their feelings and reactions to things are not appropriate to be expressed to the jury, who has to decide the case based on the evidence they see. If there has been or will be any responses to things, they need to be silent in the courtroom."

Jeb Boasberg continued with cross-examination and went directly for the black hands theory.

"Mr. Mesa, you testified yesterday that the black hands were telling you to harm or kill me. Do you remember that? But you didn't do it, did you?"

"No, not yet."

"Because this is a courtroom full of people, right?"

"No."

"And there are marshals here?"

"No."

"And you couldn't get away with it, could you?"

"No."

"And that's why you controlled your urge to kill me yesterday?"

"It was actually hard to control, yes."

"But you did control it, didn't you?"

"Sort of."

"Well, you made no effort to harm or kill me

yesterday, did you?"

"No, not yet."

JJ conceded it was hard to control his urges. He said that taking the oath before stepping into the witness box had helped him refrain from attacking the prosecutor. Mr. Boasberg's point was well-taken because it demonstrated that JJ could restrain his urges when he felt he would fail in his attack. He had calculated the risk, means, and opportunity and made the conscious decision not to attack the prosecutor.

Mr. Boasberg pointed out to the jurors that JJ had never even mentioned the black hands to any psychiatrists and psychologists who had evaluated him. JJ contradicted Mr. Boasberg's claims, but the prosecutor already had copies of the psychological and psychiatric reports. None who evaluated JJ reported that he discussed the black hands theory, not on any of the 120 pages of assessments. JJ had not discussed the Undertaker or command hallucinations telling him what to do. In fact, each mental health professional had written in the report an absence of psychotic symptoms.

JJ had confessed to the murders to Detectives Reed and Richmond but had never once mentioned black hands telling him what to do. He had provided exquisite detail of how he planned and executed his victims but never once claimed that black hands had compelled him. After fifteen months in jail, JJ had plenty of time and connections to create an explanation. There was an abundance of time to learn the strategies of other criminals seeking an insanity defense.

Mr. Boasberg referred JJ back to his original confession with the police. JJ claimed there was a misunderstanding.

"It depended on what the interpreter signed because what she signed influenced my answers. I used a lot of her words. Sometimes I wasn't paying attention to the question and just kept talking. I was telling the truth. When I was in jail, I didn't have the transcript of the confession. I told my attorney I needed one so I could look at it and read it again. It wasn't until a month or two later that I looked at it. Once I read it, I was very confused because it was impossible that I said these things. But I know I did say that, so I think there was a misunderstanding. A lot depended on what the interpreters were signing because what she signed influenced what I said. Like she mentioned something about planning to kill Eric two or three days ahead of the event. That wasn't true. So, that's why I think there was a big misunderstanding."

Mr. Boasberg knew JJ was trying to backtrack about what he had confessed when he was arrested. However, the prosecutor and the jurors had heard testimonies from the detectives. They had even watched JJ's confession directly.

Mr. Boasberg read from the confession transcript. "How long had you thought about approaching Eric and getting money from him and killing him? Answer: 'August. Maybe the first week of September. My girlfriend and I had bought a new bike, and it was almost $800. Then that left me with a little amount of money. So then when I saw Eric alone, and I saw him sitting there looking at his money, and I knew he had a credit card, I thought about it and then started planning it.'"

JJ tried to evade the prosecutor. "I think I remember saying that, but again, that comment was misunderstood," he said. "That comment about me actually planning it for two, three weeks, that was misunderstood, plus I don't remember actually saying that. What had happened was when I saw it on videotape that I had said it, it's the first time I realized it."

JJ insisted he had only half-understood what the interpreters signed during the confession. He said he was mistaken while he was talking to the police. He said he did not mean to tell the detectives that he had planned the murders. He should have told them about his mental illness. During the videotaped confession, he had given up control to the black hands.

Mr. Boasberg continued to apply pressure.

"You had never even told Dr. Madsen or Dr. Pollard that the black hands committed the crimes."

"Yes, I believe I did tell those two."

"But you told the jury yesterday that the black hands committed a bunch of the crimes you are charged with, didn't you?"

"Yes. They made me do them."

"But that's not what you told any of these doctors, did you? And you certainly never told the police in a three-hour confession anything about the black hands."

"Correct. I was focused on the situation at hand. I wasn't thinking about my own mental illness or mental capacity. I was focused on the actual crimes that they were asking me about. That's all, the robberies and the murders."

Mr. Boasberg continued to refer JJ back to the transcript of his confession. He read from the transcript for the jurors. Line after line, Mr. Boasberg tried to corner JJ with his own words. JJ continued to evade him. Then Mr. Bond interrupted the prosecutor and requested to approach the bench.

Jill Sege, an attorney for the defense, challenged the interpretation of the exchange.

"I had talked to Mr. Burton [the interpreter], indicating the tone of voice of Mr. Boasberg. Mr. Mesa doesn't understand that when he is asking some of the questions, there is a sarcastic tone of voice being used. He just thinks he is agreeing with him. I asked for the tone of voice to be indicated. Every time the tone of voice is there, it's not being indicated in the interpretation."

"I don't want the interpreter indicating the tone of voice," said the judge. "If you think that's a problem, I think the question itself is sarcastic; the tone of voice is not. But to the extent people are using voice tones, and no question, Mr. Bond was doing that very effectively in his questioning. Mr. Boasberg, a little less. Let's try not to use sarcastic tones if that's the feeling. I don't want the interpreters trying to interpret a tone of voice when it's not at all pertinent to the questions and answers. So, that is not the solution."

Ms. Sege continued to express concerns to the judge that JJ could not see Mr. Boasberg's expression; that JJ could not fully understand how a question was asked. The judges directed the prosecutor to redirect the questions for clarity.

Mr. Boasberg continued to cross-examine JJ's testimony. He repeatedly referred to his confession. He reminded him of how he distracted the police by blaming Thomas Minch. Yet, JJ reframed his actions as altruism.

"I [told them] about Thomas Minch. When I approached the police, I had planned to tell them I had done it. During the questioning at Gallaudet, I was very scared. At that time, I felt I wasn't ready to be honest about what I had done. That's why I tried to blame Thomas Minch. Until later, I didn't expect to kill a second person. At that point, I knew definitely that the bank had a security camera. So, I decided to go to the bank, cash a check, knowing that the camera would be on me because that's an easier way for the investigators to find me."

Mr. Boasberg challenged JJ that he had not gone to the police with Eric's wallet after killing Eric.

JJ responded, "I wasn't thinking about that then. The next day, I felt like I wanted to tell them. The reason I told them about smelling blood, the purpose of that, was to be caught. I was not thinking about the wallet or the keys."

JJ had evaded the police detectives until, at last, he knew he would be caught. He had simply gone to Detectives Reed and Richmond because there was nowhere else to go. The game was over; JJ's time was up. JJ's testimony concluded at 12:50 p.m.

After the lunch break, Jill Sege called Betty Colonomos, the interpreter for JJ's confession. They planned to weaken the impact of JJ's admission.

Ms. Colonomos was an interpreter and the director of the Bilingual Mediation Center. She had authored many published articles on interpreting, some of which involved the criminal justice system. She was certified, including a special certification called the Masters Comprehensive Skill Certificate, which, at the time, only a handful of people around the country held. She had worked for forty years as a paid interpreter. The police had obtained one of the best to interpret JJ's confession.

Yet the defense, Ferris Bond, and co-counsel, Jill Sege, tried to pinpoint areas of the confession where interpretation differed the police officers' speech. Ms. Sege, fluent in American Sign Language, focused her attention on those differences.

"Did the detective ask Joseph, 'How long had you been contemplating and thinking about getting money in that way?'"

"That's what I heard on the videotape," responded Ms. Colonomos.

"What did the interpreter convey to the defendant? Could you tell this jury in spoken English what the interpreter conveyed in sign language?"

"Okay. The question that was signed was: 'How long were you thinking about money and planning to do it? Was it one, two, or three weeks before? One, two, or three months before? How long was it that you thought about doing this?'"

The interpreter explained that, as part of the interpretation, she offered specific choices to JJ that were not part of the original question. She had wanted to help JJ understand the context of the police officers' questions.

Again, Ms. Sege challenged the interpretation. She went through the lengthy confession line by line, the details becoming laborious. Jennifer Collins cross-examined. Multiple sections of the confession were scrutinized. What did the word "memorialize" mean, and how was it signed? What about the word "planning?" The defense team referred the interpreter to multiple lines of the transcript. Then the testimony of Ms. Colonomos ended unceremoniously.

The prosecution asked for the parties to approach the bench. The defense's attempt to have the confession testimony thrown out because of interpreting issues was unsuccessful. JJ's interpretation had been adequate; the police had not violated his rights during the arrest and subsequent confession. His statements made to Detectives Reed and Richmond would stand.

The defense spent the rest of the afternoon and the subsequent trial day on May 20, 2002, reviewing testimonies from all the mental health professionals; Dr. Madsen, Dr. Pollard, Dr. Patterson, and Dr. Hugonnet. They would each take the stand and testify to their professional experience, the process of evaluation, and final diagnoses and determination of JJ's mental competency. Compared to the others, the beauty of Dr. Pollard's evaluation methods was rooted in his ability to communicate with JJ directly using ASL. JJ's tone, subtleties, and nuances of his interviews would be understood directly by the forensic psychologist. In contrast, an interpreter distills those nuances into a spoken version that resembles the original but is not quite at one hundred percent. Their rendering is not a pure form of direct conversation but a filtered version. Indeed, as Dr. Pollard warned in his testimony, using standardized evaluation procedures developed for English people can cause an erroneous evaluation. They can point to more pathology than is there. The closing arguments would proceed next after the defense's witnesses had been cross-examined.

Chapter 36

Closing Arguments

To be honest with you, I'm happy that I did tell you everything that happened. Now I'm not feeling that guilt. I feel much better inside because I got it out and told you. That really helped me a lot.

—JJ

The final day of the trial was on May 20, 2002. Jurors spent this last day listening to the closing arguments by both the prosecution and defense teams. Prosecutor, Jeb Boasberg, began first.

"If you believe that these calculated, deliberate, premeditated, and covered-up crimes were actually committed by some professional wrestler's black hands and not this man, then you go back to the jury room, you vote not guilty by reason of insanity," began Mr. Boasberg.

The prosecution team did not believe that JJ was mentally ill. They thought he was intentional about the murders and careful to cover up his crimes. They believed JJ had intentionally selected Eric and Ben to be victims beforehand and then set about to enact his plan. Mr. Boasberg reviewed the evidence presented by the prosecutors to the jurors. He read from the confession transcripts and statements made in the courtroom about how he had planned and executed both crimes. He explained the fifteen charges that JJ now faced, particularly the defense's claim that JJ was mentally ill.

"We've talked a lot about guilt; now I want to talk about sanity. The Government has the burden of proving that the defendant committed the crimes, but, and this is very important, the defense has the burden to show that he was insane. We don't have to prove anything. We do not have to prove that he was sane. They have to prove that he was insane.

"Only Dr. Madsen, the defense expert, believes that there was any mental disease or defect. You will remember that the other three doctors told you that the defendant had dysthymia, which just means mild depression, and that's not responsible for anything. He also has a conduct disorder or antisocial personality disorder, but, and this is another important point, that is not a mental disease or defect under the law."

Mr. Boasberg reiterated the testimony from the psychiatric experts. JJ did not discuss the black hands theory with any of them. He compared the ridiculousness of the black hands with JJ's testimony that he was trying to get caught by the police.

"He was trying to get caught by practicing Ben Varner's signature, by throwing away all this evidence in different trashcans, by going back and checking on the crime scenes to make sure everything incriminating was gone, by washing off the blood, by covering Ben Varner's body with the mattress... he was trying to get caught? How he was trying to get caught when he implicated another student in these murders, how he tried to get Thomas Minch, another student, arrested; that's how he was trying to get caught.

"All of the doctors he talked to, he told of instances

353

when he had urges that he controlled. When there were other people around, he controlled them. And how about me? He told you he had those uncontrollable urges to harm or kill me. Did he act on those? No, again, he controlled them. And why? Because all of you were here. All of you would have seen everything. It's a shame all of you weren't in Eric Plunkett's room on September 27. It's a shame all of you weren't in Ben Varner's room on February 1.

"Ladies and gentlemen," he concluded, "the defendant, Joseph Mesa, brutally murdered Eric Plunkett on September 27, 2000. He brutally murdered Benjamin Varner on February 1, 2001. Now he is coming here trying to get off by telling you all a whole bunch of tales. Why? Because it might work. Don't let it work, ladies and gentlemen. He killed those two young men, those two freshmen, during their first year of college. He did it, and he was sane. Convict him."

The court adjourned for a lunch recess until just after 2:00 p.m. When they returned, Ferris Bond stood to present his closing argument.

"At the beginning of the trial, I think I made it pretty clear to you that we weren't going to be contesting a lot of the evidence in this trial, as far as what happened, who was killed, how it happened, what happened afterward. The real issue that you had to decide during the course of this trial was not if, but why. As the defense sees it, it should be pretty clear to you why. He was insane. This whole incident is insane. It is a tragedy. It should have never happened, but it did. And the reason, the why, is that he is insane.

"You start with the fact that he is deaf. Since he was a little boy, he wanted to talk to his parents. You had to go to the bathroom, you point. You wanted to eat, you point. You get to the point where you can communicate a little bit with your hands. You're sitting around the dinner table and at school. You've got people talking like I am right now. All you can do is look around and not hear and not understand. I guess you can probably understand his frustration and how it might build up."

Then Ferris Bond misspoke. He told the jurors that the prosecution had the burden to prove that Joseph Mesa was sane. Judge Richter interrupted.

"Ladies and gentlemen, contrary to what Mr. Bond just said, the Government has no burden of proof to show that the defendant was sane. They have the burden of proving beyond a reasonable doubt the elements of the offense. As to the issue of criminal responsibility, the defense has the burden of proof," clarified the judge.

Mr. Bond continued. He listed JJ's actions that would make an ordinary person wonder about his sanity, slashing his wrist with a nail, driving at high speeds to hurt himself, and banging his head and body against things without provocation. JJ's behavior, according to Mr. Bond, was reckless and injurious. Indeed, JJ's periods of zoning out when he was wrestling his brother was indicative of some brain dysfunction. JJ complained of headaches and sometimes signed to himself.

"Let's talk about Joseph Mesa, Jr., or JJ, as Eric Plunkett called him. JJ didn't hate Eric. They were friends. He was talking about coming to Guam and visiting. They studied together. They ate together. JJ tutored him in math. He liked him. They were friends. They were doing things for each other. Why?

"The killings. For me to come up here and tell you somehow the Government missed something good about him, you're not going to get that from me. They are horrifying to me. They should be horrifying to you. They should horrify anybody about this case. One boy is choked and bludgeoned to death. Another boy is stabbed and mutilated. That's horrible, but it's sick.

Mr. Bond's next statement was unexpected and appeared to be an incomplete thought. "Son of Sam.

Doberman retriever next door supposedly was possessed, he admitted to this, by a demon that was 6,000 years old. His name, who was the son of Sam, he told him to do those things. There was another one that received impulses from a UFO. There was another one who was told to do things by voices out of a graveyard. Sick? Yes. Logical? Oh, no. Insane? Yep.

"You know, one of the things I submit to you that should really bother you about this case is, you know, we can all make fun of black hands. When he said he saw some hands, and when pushed on a little bit, he said, 'Well, they were inside my mind. I would see them doing things, and I would imitate or carry out what I saw them doing.' Everybody says, well, that's bunk. Yeah, if it's true, psychotic. There is no data to support that. How many times have you heard that? You know what really bothers me about this case? If this kid could hear, there would be all kinds of data one way or the other."

He concluded, "Folks, the evidence, in this case, is compelling. It is crying out for a verdict that is just, that is appropriate. Ladies and gentlemen, it's a verdict that each and every one of you is going to have to render courageously. Make him responsible for these killings. Make him responsible for his conduct but do it by finding him not guilty by reason of insanity because it's the right thing to do. That's what the evidence has been overwhelmingly telling you that you should do. It is the courageous thing to do."

Jennifer Collins presented the rebuttal for the prosecution. She emphasized that the evidence pointed out that Joseph Mesa committed these crimes beyond a reasonable doubt. There was no dispute of that between the prosecution and the defense. The sticking issue was whether JJ was sane.

"This case is about Mr. Mesa making choices, choices that perhaps no one else would make, choices that perhaps are difficult to understand, but his choices."

At 3:15 p.m., the jurors left the courtroom to deliberate the case. By 11:30 the following morning, the jury had reached its verdicts.

Charge 1: First-degree burglary of Eric Plunkett: Guilty

Charge 2: Armed robbery of Eric Plunkett: Guilty

Charge 3: First-degree felony murder while armed for first-degree burglary upon Eric Plunkett: Guilty

Charge 4: First-degree felony murder while armed, armed robbery of Eric Plunkett: Guilty

Charge 5: First-degree premeditated murder of Eric Plunkett: Guilty

Charge 6: Credit card fraud for the use of Eric Plunkett's credit card: Guilty

Charge 7: Credit card fraud for the use of Chad Shumaker's credit card: Guilty

Charge 8: First-degree burglary of Benjamin Varner: Guilty

Charge 9: Armed robbery of Benjamin Varner: Guilty

Charge 10: First-degree felony murder while armed for the burglary of Benjamin Varner: Guilty

Charge 11: First-degree felony murder while armed of Benjamin Varner attached to the armed robbery: Guilty

Charge 12: First-degree premeditated murder while armed of Benjamin Varner: Guilty

Charge 13: Carrying a dangerous weapon, a knife: Guilty

Charge 14: Forgery: Guilty

Charge 15: Uttering: Guilty

Question: Has the Government proven beyond a reasonable doubt that Eric Plunkett was an especially vulnerable victim due to the physical infirmity of cerebral palsy?

Answer: Yes.

Chapter 37

The Sentencing

For sentencing, Mr. Boasberg sent the Government's Memorandum in Aid of Sentencing, which outlined the factual background, the argument for sentencing, a request for a sentence of life imprisonment without release, and a rationale.

"The Court should impose a sentence of life without release [because] the murders were planned in great detail and were carried out in a particularly atrocious manner. In regard to the Eric Plunkett murder, the defendant contemplated this for several weeks. For example, he would go into Eric's room and wave his hands to make sure

Eric could not see him so he could approach him without being detected. On the night of the murder, he concocted a scheme to distract even his girlfriend, Melani De Guzman.

"As heinous as [Eric's] assault was, it paled in comparison to the violence of the killing of Benjamin Varner. In order to prepare for his planned violence, the defendant took off his jacket and, just like with Eric Plunkett, approached Ben from the rear. In all, Ben Varner suffered sixteen to seventeen different stab wounds.

"The psychological and emotional wounds suffered by the Plunkett and Varner families are immense. To see their beloved children finally garner acceptance into Gallaudet University and then see their lives extinguished in their freshman year has been an almost unsustainable trauma.

"The families have tried to describe the gaping hole in their lives the murders have left, but even these cannot convey the anguish and torment these families undergo on a daily basis.

"The defendant's psychological profile proves him an extreme danger to society. Even were these crimes of passion that we could with certitude predict could never be repeated, the defendant's sentence should be severe. In this case, however, where medical experts reach the contrary conclusion, it is all the more imperative that the defendant be segregated from society, whose members he could very easily attack again.

"The defendant himself attempted to make a mockery of the trial, with his letters planning out preposterous insanity defenses and then his staged performance discussing the black hands and his desire to kill one of the prosecutors.

"At bottom, therefore, the defendant is a rare type of person, like other serial murderers, who are killing for gratification and will continue doing so unless rendered unable to carry out their desires. The only way here to render him unable is to impose a sentence of life imprisonment without release. While few cases in this Court may merit the greatest sanction this Court can impose, this is certainly one of them.

"WHEREFORE, the Government respectfully requests that this Court impose a sentence of life imprisonment without release."

Judge Richter imposed six life sentences without the possibility of release.

Part Three: 2009

Chapter 38

Atwater Federal Penitentiary

When someone is bludgeoned that number of times or stabbed that number of times or the weapon is left sticking out of the head of the victim, there is a certain dominance that's being expressed there, a grotesque need for dominance.

—*Dr. Mitchell Hugonnet, forensic psychologist from St. Elizabeth's Hospital.*

Atwater Penitentiary was in the middle of a large, barren field next to a small airport in Atwater, California, 130 miles from San Francisco. Its location was on a former military base, Castle Air Force Base. A large sign, "United States Penitentiary," marked the entrance to the maximum-security institution. The long driveway curved toward the main building. A tall, expansive iron fence enclosed the compound. The rails were tall, with rounded loops of barbed wire at the top. Guard towers stood tall around the perimeter of the grounds.

Before arriving at the main building, smaller warehouse-type buildings lined the drive to the main building. Known as a minimum-security satellite camp, special prisoners called "camp inmates" lingered outside near the smaller buildings. A few camp inmates watered rows of potted trees. Others rode on small electric golf carts driving from one building to another. The camp inmates were preparing for their releases. Their infractions were minor, probably drug-related. They had more privileges than the other prisoners. They walked around freely, though their supervisors were in the vicinity.

This prison housed some of the most violent and dangerous criminals. Its history included the murder of a corrections officer, twenty-two year old Jose Rivera, on June 20, 2008. Mr. Rivera was a Navy veteran and had completed two tours of duty in Iraq only to be killed by two inmates after telling them to go back to their cell. Murders among prisoners were more frequent.

The main building was a nondescript concrete structure that looked the color of sand. Its front had a glassed entranceway but was otherwise devoid of windows. An inmate wearing a dark green uniform swept the front walkway to the main building. He said hello but always looked at the ground. A guard stood next to a long conveyor belt and door-sized metal detector near the front desk. Visitors signed in on the clipboard and waited for the guard to call one's name.

Visitors were prohibited from wearing gray or khaki clothing because of its similarity to the inmate uniforms. The guard asked visitors for driver's licenses then instructed them to remove shoes and place them on the conveyor. They asked that everything in the pockets be removed and turn the pockets inside out. In addition to keys and wallets, visitors brought bags of quarters for the vending machines. Visitors laid their belongings on the conveyor belt that pushed them through an x-ray machine. Once through the metal detector, visitors retrieved their shoes and other belongings. They sat on metal chairs to await the next guard's instructions. When most of the chairs were filled, the guard asked visitors to line up against the beige cinderblock wall to take their pictures.

Most of the guards looked formidable. They were fit, and heads shaved bald with flat, unimpressed facial expressions. They watched the visitors closely as they filed in a line behind them. The guards led them to a small alcove. Heavy metal doors slammed shut behind. The nook had a thick glass wall from which guards controlled the prison. Machines and levers surrounded the guards, the cameras watching over the prisoners. One by one, the escort guard called each visitor's name and pointed for them to step forward. Each person held up the driver's license so the guard behind the glass could make sure they matched. When all looked clear, he nodded to the guard standing in the alcove. Another heavy metal door then slid open.

The guards herded visitors on a fifty-foot sidewalk towards another set of heavy metal doors. As they left the alcove, the bars behind them slammed shut. Inside the next windowless waiting area, visitors could see a long hallway of cells. No prisoners walked the halls. At the end of the room, near where the group of visitors waited, another metal door with a small window opened. Inside the larger room were four guards, each as intimidating as the last. They sat behind a desk on an elevated platform. The walls were a faded yellow; the flooring was an institutional gray linoleum. There was a children's room with the Hulk, the Rock Man, and Dora the Explorer painted on the walls. A television played silently from its place on the wall.

As each visitor entered the room, a guard pointed to a numbered, plastic gray chair and instructed them to sit. Once the visitors all sat in their assigned places, the guards brought out the inmates, one by one. The first inmate who entered the room was African American, about six-foot five. He wore a small knitted green cap on the crown of his head. His gray beard hung down to his clavicle. As he lumbered forward, his dark, flat eyes scanned the room until they trained on a particular visitor. Immediately he smiled, transforming and softening his face. A plump woman with graying hair stood and opened her arms. The man embraced her as she stepped to him. She laid her head against his chest and closed her eyes. He snuggled his nose in her neck and wrapped his muscled, thick arms entirely around her. They stepped away, but he continued to hold her fingertips and allowed his eyes to linger on her face before they sat down in their chairs.

Another younger visitor with blond highlights sat in a nearby chair. Well put-together, her teased and sprayed hair stayed firmly in place. She wore a tight, short-sleeved, see-through white shirt with a skimpy fuchsia bra underneath. Her glittery earrings twinkled as she leaned forward to grab her plastic case that held the quarters. She wore heavy make-up in peach and mauve tones. She stood up to pull her shirt tight against her chest. Gold bangles slid down her forearm to her wrists. She walked comfortably in her three-inch heels to the soda vending machines at the far end of the room, a strong scent of cheap perfume wafting behind her. She slid in six quarters and pushed the button for Mountain Dew, then grabbed more quarters for a diet Pepsi and a pack of peanut butter crackers. She walked back to her seat and arranged the snacks as if for a picnic on the small plastic table.

  The guard's key clanged from behind against the metal door. A white man, a slender, tough-looking former meth-head, stepped into the room. His eyes fixated on the blond woman; a mischievous smile secured itself on his face. He waited for the guard to close the door behind him before he moved toward her. Dark blue tattoo ink covered his roped muscles on his arms and across his broad knuckles. Menacing tattoos arise from underneath his uniform to his neck and earlobes. Despite his ominous presence, he smiled and shuffled on his feet with excitement. He danced to her with outstretched arms and lifted her off her feet. His eyes shifted to the guards standing nearby. He put the woman down for fear that his quick movements would alarm the guards. The guards focused on the couple, watching for a contraband exchange. The man asked the woman how the hell she'd been. She whispered something to him, low and slow. A broad smile spread across his face. He leaned closer and whispered something back. She giggled.

The visitor door opened. A man and woman walked into the waiting area, each holding a brown leather briefcase. A guard escorted the couple to a glass room off to the side of the visitors' area. Dressed in business suits, the attorneys took a seat in the room. The inmate door opened. A lumberjack of a man stepped through, his wild salt and pepper mane framing his Pacific Islander features. The gargantuan man was covered with dark, inky tattoos from the ends of his fingers to the top of his head. His dark eyes were still and malevolent. He scanned the faces of each of the visitors. The other prisoners in the visiting area kept their eyes downcast. Clearly, this man held power in the prison. He walked into the glass room and sat across the attorneys at a table. They exchanged handshakes and pleasantries. The inmate's voice boomed with laughter; then, they sat to deliberate.

The door slid open for another inmate to enter. A

man, short, fit, and a Pacific Islander, stepped through the door. Like the others, his eyes were black and unmoving. Edges of a tattoo peeked from under the sleeve of his uniform. His face showed no emotion; then, his eyes registered my presence. I smiled. His lips fell short of a smile, but his face softened. In the etiquette of Deaf Culture, I stood and embraced him, even though we had never met before. Joseph Mafnas Mesa, Jr., JJ, sat across from me in a standard-issue, khaki uniform, cleaned and ironed, wearing heavy, black leather boots.

Chapter 39

My Life Is Good

I have everything I need in here. I can buy things at the prison store. I have a job and earn $175 a month. My parents send me about $100 a month. My expenses are about $200 a month. I don't have to pay for rent or electricity. I can go to classes for free. With my extra money, I mostly buy extra food and books. Last night on my unit, I made chili with onions and peppers and tomatoes that I bought from another inmate. I watch television with my friends, though we're not allowed to watch R-rated movies. I guess they think it will encourage us to be horny and rape someone. I write and use the TTY to call my family and friends. I have subscriptions to *Maxim* and *National Geographic*. It would be hard if I were released from prison. My conviction would follow me and make it hard to get a job. I've seen others get ready to be released only to then mess things up, like get into a fight, just to have their release delayed. Some of them don't want to go on the outside. Life is too hard there. I accept that I'll be here for life. I accept it.

—JJ

I signed first. "Hi. I'm happy that I could come to meet you. How are you doing?"

JJ paused a moment, his eyes intense and alert. He signed, "Wait. Slow down. It's been a long time since I've used ASL. You'll have to sign very slow for me."

I formed the signs slow and clear on my hands. I spelled my name, T-e-r-e-s-a, and showed him my name-sign with the letter "T" coming off just above my right ear and wiggling down to my chin. "This is my name-sign, but my students call me 'crow.'" I showed him the sign for "bird," a sign with a double meaning, a crow (bird) and my name. "How long has it been since you've signed?"

"About four years. That's the last time Melani came to visit me. I teach some of the other prisoners sign, but they don't sign ASL like you do."

JJ's khaki uniform shirt and pants looked freshly pressed, but a size larger than necessary. He told me he borrowed a "homeboy's" black books because his were too scuffed. He said he wanted to look nice for our first meeting.

"If you had seen me a week earlier, my head was shaved bald except for a long ponytail hanging from the crown of my head. I looked like a warrior. I thought that you might be afraid of the way I looked, so I shaved it last week. I haven't had visitors in a long time. So, it didn't matter before how I wore my hair."

He asked if I would get him some food from the vending machines. I picked up my plastic sandwich bag of $20-worth of quarters and walked to the far end of the room where two soda machines, two microwaves, and one food vending machine stood. I turned around and signed in large, exaggerated movements so he could see me from afar. When I fingerspelled, I paused between letters so he could follow what I was saying. I identified the kinds of food in the machines: cookies, crackers, pizza, burritos, and candy. He asked for a burrito and a Mountain Dew. There was no Mountain Dew left, so he settled for a Pepsi. I bought one for myself and put his burrito in the microwave. I walked back to my seat and set the food on the small plastic table between us. JJ unwrapped the burrito and took a small bite. He let the flavor linger in his mouth before swallowing. He told me he is always hungry in prison and had to buy extra food at the prison store to snack in the evenings.

"I hate being hungry. It's such a terrible feeling," he said.

JJ mentioned his uncle was in Atwater USP, where JJ was incarcerated now. I was shocked.

"You mean your uncle from Guam is here in the same prison? Here? At Atwater?" I asked.

"Yes, my uncle is here, too."

"What did he do to get here," I asked.

JJ broke eye contact. "I don't know. Prisoners don't ask each other why they're here. It's considered rude and nosey. I see him sometimes, but he doesn't ask me why I'm here. I don't ask him either. He lives in another unit. So, I don't see him often."

JJ explained that on the units, the inmates grouped themselves by race. American Indians, he said, cluster according to the four directions of the country: north, south, east, and west. The Latino and African American groups had the most members in Atwater. He said everyone was friendly, but he cautioned they do not get too close. Trust was a commodity reserved for one's own racial group. He and his homeboys were called the Islanders.

"You're the only deaf man out of 1,500 inmates?" I asked. "How is it here for you, a deaf man?"

"Fine. Fine. I don't get into trouble."

"Do the other prisoners hurt you?"

"Nah. I don't have any problems with the other inmates. I just keep to myself. I've always had a single room. When I first arrived, I told the warden that I needed a single room because of being deaf. They let me have it. I don't bother anyone. Nobody bothers me. Sometimes I teach my homeboys some sign language. I explain to them that with sign language, we can communicate even through the small windows on our cell doors, even when we're in lockdown. They think it's cool. Sometimes, when a guard is looking for me, one of the other inmates will let me know that he's calling my name. Most of the guards know they need to communicate with me using a pen and paper. A few are assholes, but not too many."

When Atwater USP established an honors unit, JJ was the first inmate. He said that when he first arrived, he jumped to a seat in front of one of the television sets, thereby reserving it for the other Islanders. The other inmates who came after him did the same. The Islanders claimed one of the seven televisions because their group was smaller in number.

"There are sixty-three prisoners on my honors unit," he explained. "Each television is controlled by a racial group. One goes to my homeboys. Two go to the Blacks. Two go to the Mexicans. One tv goes to the whites. One is for everyone to watch sports."

The guards always watched the groups, looking for signs of unrest and potential violence. JJ explained that sometimes the new guards had cocky attitudes. JJ imitated those guards with their bobbing, shaved heads and dark sunglasses. He said he could not show me how they walk because the rules required him to stay seated the whole time during our visit.

"The new guards act like badasses, but they soon realize that this prison is filled with murderers who are a lot more experienced in violence than they are. The new guards are like naive ducklings in a den full of wolves."

He explained that the intelligent guards know where they are and act with respect. The dumb ones, he said, learn the hard way.

JJ had known of the murders that occurred within the prison walls. He knew some specific individuals had long histories of brutal violence. Interestingly, he did not characterize himself as one of those people. Certain prisoners caused trouble for other inmates. When one inmate caused problems, like killing another inmate, the entire facility was locked down. While in lockdown, no one was allowed to leave their cell for any reason, not for showering, exercising, or eating. They sat in their rooms twenty-four hours a day, cut off from contact with anyone except the guard who slipped their meals through the metal slats of their cell doors.

In the Rivera murder, an inmate killed the guard. JJ thought the inmate was probably drunk from homemade alcohol. However, JJ said, the prisoner was a person who caused many problems within the prison. When the guard and inmate fought, the inmate used a shank and stabbed the officer. JJ said that the irony was that both the guard and the inmate were homeboys from the same racial group.

JJ explained that there were a lot of fights in prison,

usually among members of different racial groups. Some of the arguments could be very violent, though the term violence was relative in this place. Typically, altercations occurred between inmates, not between guards and prisoners. Within the prison population, there was a hierarchy among homeboy racial groups. When two rival members fought, the leader of each group would agree with who was at fault and what the consequences would be. Punishments within the group could include beatings and, in some cases, killings. Homeboys, not members of rival groups, would execute the disciplines to the person deserving the punishment. He said justice among the inmates was swift and decisive.

  JJ excused himself to go to the bathroom. He raised his hand to alert the guard behind the desk. The guard came from behind the desk and weaved between the plastic chairs and tables to unlock the inmate door. JJ walked through and prepared to be strip-searched, a process that occurred every time an inmate left or went into the visiting area.

  I looked around the room at the visitors who arrived at the same time as me. The room was filled to capacity. Everyone spoke in low tones. The African American man and his wife rested their foreheads on one another and sat silently. The white meth head and his girlfriend had their faces close together, whispering, then giggling. The Islander with the wild mane was still talking with the attorneys.

After about ten minutes, JJ came back, adjusting his belt.

"I hate going to the bathroom. When we first go back, they make us take our clothes off to search us. I guess they want to make sure that no one brings contraband into the prison. Then we go to the bathroom, and they search our bodies again. Then, finally, they let us get dressed and come back to the visitor area."

I told JJ that I also went to the bathroom while he was in the back. I noticed a sign in the bathroom that I had to ask the guard at the desk for a paper towel to dry my hands.

"Yeah, they're very careful about people bringing in things. Sometimes visitors bring drugs in their mouths. They exchange them with the prisoner when they kiss hello. There are many ways to sneak things into the prison. I don't do anything like that. It's a hassle to be strip-searched all the time."

"Do you miss your freedom?" I asked.

"No, not really. I've adjusted to my lifestyle in here.

I'm on the honors unit. I have had nine years of good behavior. No problems, no fights. I have a lot more freedom on the honors unit than the other prisoners."

I was doubtful. "You really don't miss the outside? Going shopping? Going out to eat?"

"I miss my family most of all," he explained. "Prison simplifies life for me. It takes out all of the clutter in my life. I wear plain clothes. I live within plain walls. Some other inmates wax their lockers and cell floors until they shine. I don't. All of this is government property. None of this belongs to me.

"I have three basic rules by which I live by here in prison: One. Don't go into debt with other prisoners. Two. Don't make deals with them. And three, don't lie. These things can cause a lot of trouble in prison. I follow these simple rules. My life is good."

Chapter 40

Too Quick To Be Believed

There are three types of men: One: the type that has never fought before; he has uncertainty in his eyes and lacks confidence; he can be frightened or scared easily. Two: the type that looks tough and has some experience with fighting, but also has some fear inside. And three: the type that looks tough, is an experienced fighter, and possesses no fear of anything. Ben and Eric were type one; I am type three.

—JJ

JJ's closest friend in the Atwater Penitentiary is Eti, an inmate from Somoa. Eti was serving a life term and, in 2009, was in his sixties. When JJ met him, Eti had already been imprisoned for forty years. After spending more than six hours together, JJ felt more comfortable conversing with me. He revealed that the uncle he referenced the day before was serving a life sentence for murder with a gun. He told me that another uncle completed his sentence at Atwater for murder and drug charges.

JJ explained the inner workings of the prison. "Everyone has a side business in here. Some can get raw chicken or pork from the kitchen and sell it after hours. Others give tattoos from a homemade tattoo machine. Another prisoner is an artist and draws portraits for inmates to send home. Others make homemade alcohol with fruits and sugar."

JJ seemed well-adjusted to the informal prison system. He described the roles of shot-callers, dominant prisoners who acted as bosses for their particular homeboy group. JJ explained that even within a homeboy group, there were separate sub-groups. There were even smaller divisions in the African American group, each with its shot-caller, the Crips, the Bloods, and the New Yorkers. There were the Mexicans, the Islanders, the whites, and the

Muslims. There was one shot-caller each for the American Indian groups, north, south, east, and west.

I asked about his family. He said, "My father, Joseph, retired as a chief warrant officer from the Army. He works now as a guard for the Department of Corrections in Guam."

Earlier in his sentence, JJ had asked for a transfer to the prison in Guam, but the warden denied his request. JJ did not know why. He said he felt close to his family, his mother, Grace, his older sister, Josephine, another sister, Joella, and his brother, Patrick. He said he thinks about where he was raised on a ranch on a mountaintop in an area called Yago. Living on a ranch, he had killed chickens and pigs for fresh meat.

He recalled killing his family's cats. "They'd bother me for attention. So, I killed them, kicked and stomped on them. It was around the same time, when I was ten years old, that I started to get into a lot of bad behavior. I knew I had behavior problems, but I couldn't stop myself. Then it just got worse. I stole from an MSSD student and an international student. Then I wanted a new experience. So, I killed."

"For the money or the experience?" I asked.

"Both. It just kept getting worse and worse."

"So, do you think you would have killed again after Ben?"

"I don't know. Maybe I would have killed a third person. I couldn't control my mind, but since I was caught and put in prison, all of my behavior problems have now gone away. I don't think about stealing or killing anyone. All those urges just went away."

Perhaps the prison structure or being surrounded by hardened murderers helped JJ keep his urges under control. If JJ had caused problems for the Islanders, he knew the shot-caller would discipline him.

I asked him about Melani, whether he still kept in contact. Melani had continued to write him while in the Washington, D.C. jail and continued when he transferred to Atwater USP. Then, from 2005 to 2009, she had stopped. JJ asked his mother to check on her and her family to see if everything was okay. When JJ's mother contacted Melani's mother, she learned Melani had moved in with her boyfriend after a terrible family argument.

Then in January 2009, as quickly as they had stopped, Melani started sending JJ letters, about two a week.

"Melani writes, 'I love you' fifty times in one letter. She doesn't need to say it so much. I will write a letter to her and say at the end, 'I love you' and sign it, 'Your one and only man.'

"She asks me not to write other friends because 'they're a bad influence,' she says. I tell her that I have friends from a long time ago. I want to keep in touch with them. Melani was always the jealous type. My other girlfriend was jealous too, but not as much as Melani. My heart belongs only to Melani now."

Though JJ now knew that Melani was living with her boyfriend, he was not worried. In fact, he was confident that her allegiance remained with him.

"Melani doesn't really want to marry him, but he wants to marry her. She's one hundred percent an innocent person. She's not a little naive; she's a lot naive. I'm two years older than her. We started dating when she was a junior in high school. That was the year I was suspended from Gallaudet."

"I had many, many girlfriends," JJ boasted. "I'd say about thirty when I started middle school. I lost my virginity when I was at MSSD. I was Melani's first boyfriend. She always looked to me for protection. When Melani planned to go to Gallaudet, her father made me promise I would take care of her."

Yet, Melani had indeed married her boyfriend and

had a child. I asked him what he thought about that. His face remained an impassive and impenetrable stone wall.

"I'm happy for her," he said finally. "I'm happy that she has a good life."

I pressed further and asked if he felt sad about that.

"No, I really feel happy. When I was dating Melani, we'd dream about where we'd live—New Zealand, Samoa, Hawaii. I had planned to marry Melani before everything happened, and I got arrested. This chapter in my life with MSSD and Gallaudet has ended. My current life is about now."

"So, how do you move on? How do you adapt from being free to being in prison for the rest of your life?"

"In here," he said, "I only think about myself, what's happening now and in my future. It's all about me. When my sister Joelle visited me, I felt emotional. When she left, it was even worse because I really missed my family. I will be here forever. Prison is my home now."

Feeling that JJ and I had developed a rapport by this point, I asked him to go back through the murders, specifically his black hands story. He described the murders impassively and unemotionally, as he had in his confession to police and during his trial. I wanted to know more details.

"Did you pull the fire alarm when the R.A.s found Ben?" I asked.

"No. It wasn't me."

I wondered if that was true. Could it have been a remarkable coincidence?

"Why did you choose Eric and Ben?"

"I don't know how I chose them. There was an angel on one shoulder telling me to be helpful and friendly and nice. Then there was a devil on the other shoulder, giving me a violent image. I'd try to control it, but I couldn't. During the killings," he continued, "my mind was disconnected from my behavior inside. I can't remember what I was thinking. My body seemed to act on its own."

"Did you feel some sort of excitement during the killings?" I asked.

"While I was killing them, there was some excitement that I was doing something wrong and not getting caught. But afterward, I felt guilty and ashamed."

I am not convinced. "But why? Why them?" I ask.

"Eric was weak from having cerebral palsy. He never knew what hit him. He was unconscious so fast. But with Ben? A different story. After I stabbed him the first time, he looked at me with fear in his eyes. He tried to defend himself, but he couldn't even though he was taller and thicker than me," JJ said, devoid of emotion.

JJ relayed the stories of the murders with factual detail, but in the tone of telling someone a list of groceries. It was clear to me that JJ indeed had no remorse for his actions.

"What about the black hands story?" I asked.

"It was bullshit. I made it up to try to lessen my charge. Obviously, it didn't work." He shrugged.

I asked him about specific characteristics of serial killers identified in the literature. I wanted to see if he fit many of the criteria referenced during his trial.

"I want to ask you some specific questions about the killings. Is that okay?"

"Sure," JJ answered.

I thought I knew the answer but asked JJ anyway. "Did you take a souvenir from either Eric or Ben's room?"

Surprisingly, JJ responded, "No."

"But you had taken a picture of Thomas Minch, right?"

"Yes."

"And you had taken Ben's shirt from his room, right?"

"Yes."

Perhaps JJ did not associate the picture and shirt

with souvenirs, or maybe he was a liar.

"Why did you leave the bodies in the positions you did?"

"Because that is where they died," says JJ.

Yet, I knew JJ repositioned the bodies in their dorm rooms. Was he trying to delay the discovery of the bodies? Did he want to delay their discoveries so that he could continue to "visit" them in their rooms?

"Any problems as a child with bedwetting?"

"No."

"Fire starting?"

"No."

"Head injury?"

"No, but one time my uncle and I were playing around. He choked me, and I passed out and fell on the floor," JJ says.

JJ answered the questions quickly, without elaboration or facial expression.

"Any sexual feelings before, during, or after the murder?"

"No, no, and no."

"Did you use gloves or a mask?"

JJ wiggled his fingers at me as if he were wearing a glove. With a smug look on his face, he said, "No."

I felt JJ was being evasive, his answers too quick. He was not sharing the information even though he confessed and then later testified to the details of the case. I pressed on. He did indeed meet the criteria for a serial killer, no matter what he claimed not to do or not remember. JJ would not tell the truth; he would only tell me what he wanted me to know, what he wanted me to see.

"Why can't you recall more details about the murders?"

"I was nervous during both of the murders. I knew it was a bad thing to be doing. So, I was nervous. But killing Ben was easier than Eric because I had more experience by that time."

JJ claimed he did not want to live in the past. The past was no longer relevant to him. I had one last question before I ended this visit with him.

"I am going to visit Eric Plunkett's family. Is there anything you would like them to know?"

His demeanor changed, a hint of fear, some sort of emotion.

"No, there is nothing I want them to know. I don't want to reopen anything."

I asked, "But isn't there anything that you would want to say? To help them know that he didn't suffer?

Anything?"

"No, I don't want you to say anything—nothing about it at all," his tone forceful.

"So, what if his family came directly to confront you about the death of their son. What would you tell them?"

He paused. "If they confronted me directly, I'd probably forget what I would say. But without confronting me, I'd say that I was sorry that they never had a chance to be proud that their son graduated from Gallaudet, that they'll never have a chance to see him have children and grandchildren. Ben's family too. But it wasn't a personal thing with Ben and Eric," he insisted.

I was sure that Eric and Ben's families would feel differently.

Chapter 41

My Prison World

If you want total security, go to prison. There you're fed, clothed, given medical care, and so on. The only thing lacking is freedom.

—Dwight Eisenhower, US President

JJ measured his life in discrete blocks of time: time to wake, time to eat breakfast, time to go to work, time to eat lunch, time to work again, then time to go back to the unit for the night. Each day was like the previous one. The prison world enforced rigid routines, structure, and obedience. The prison environment at Atwater is a world within a world; JJ seemed to flourish in this world.

When he joined me in the visiting area the next day, he appeared much more at ease. I could look more closely at him. He did not have wrinkles or gray hair, just a smooth olive complexion with a groomed mustache. His clothes look pressed.

JJ worked at Unicor, an electronics recycling center located on the grounds. He worked six hours a day, five days a week, and earned about $175 a month in wages. JJ's parents and Melani often put money into his account to buy items from the prison store. When he was off from work, he read books about traveling. James Patterson's novels were his favorites. He read the Bible. He used a small electronic dictionary and thesaurus to look up words he did not understand. He watched television but not rated R movies; they were prohibited. He played handball in the yard.

As usual, the interview started with food. The sandwich vending machine was broken, and most of the sodas were gone. The other machine was jammed with popcorn and cookies. JJ asked for a red Powerade, cookies, cheese crackers, and a granola bar.

"I missed breakfast because I woke up late at 7:30

a.m.," he explained.

He begins today's visit by telling me about his housekeeper.

"I pay another inmate to clean my cell. I pay him $25 a month. He mops the floor, makes my bed, cleans my toilet and sink, and washes and folds my clothes."

I noticed JJ eats his food and drinks his beverages very slowly in tiny little bites and sips throughout a six-hour visit.

I asked him more about his relationship with Melani.

He said, "I love her, but I am not in love with her. I have to remember that my real world is the prison culture here. If I fell in love, I would become emotional, and that would make me let down my guard. That's not a good thing in prison.

"When we have visitors come in, we're very happy. We smile and look forward to it. But when the visiting session is over, I shift back into my prison world."

Prisoners at Atwater USP did not share personal information. Everyone kept their lives, even the names of their loved ones, closed to others.

"After visiting hours, an inmate will ask, 'Did you have a good visit?' but that's about it. We don't ask any more than that."

The women who visited the inmates, called prison wives or girlfriends, have a type of camaraderie among themselves. They often knew each other, even if superficially, because of the structure of the visiting schedules.

On Saturdays and Sundays, there were inmate headcounts. Even if it was visiting hour, at 9:45 a.m., they stood from their seats in the visiting room and lined up against the visiting room wall to be counted. When guards called their names, the inmates yelled out their prison numbers. JJ's was 04577-007. Guards no longer called out JJ's name because he could not hear them. Inmates did not call out his number. Instead, JJ followed the others when they lined up.

JJ wanted to talk about his Chamorro culture and his home island, Guam.

"My mother's family lives on the north side in the mountains. My father's family lives on the south side of the island. When I was younger, I loved to climb coconut trees. I'd use my bare hands and feet without any ropes. I could climb all the way up and get the coconuts. I love to eat Spam too. They used to have it here at Atwater, but the prison store doesn't sell it anymore.

"I like the island girls, too. They all have a similar attitude, like mine. We just understand each other living an island life." He paused to reflect. "I accept that I will be here for the rest of my life. I have everything I need here. I just have to accept where I am."

We observe the interactions between the prisoners and their visitors for a moment. We watched the guards as they watched us. My eyes followed a female correctional officer who had her top blouse buttons unbuttoned and wore heavy makeup. My facial expression conveyed my curiosity. JJ followed my eyes to the guards.

"Female guards sometimes have sex with the prisoners," JJ replied to my unasked question. "There were three times recently when a female guard was caught, then fired. Some of the guards charge the inmates money.

"I don't feel tempted, though. One time, a female guard asked me to come to her office. When I got there, she started to ask personal questions like, 'Where are you from?' I didn't answer her because I don't want to become friends with the guards."

JJ wanted his alliances to be clear to the other inmates. He did not want to associate with guards; he was not a snitch. JJ talked again about the death of the Atwater guard killed in 2007.

"After [the inmate] killed the guard," JJ explained, "he got transferred to death row at another prison. The other prisoners were very happy to get rid of the troublemaker. After he killed the guard, Atwater was on lockdown for three months. Then after that, the Blacks were fighting the Whites, then we got another two months of lockdown. We were on lockdown for five months—no leaving our cells at all. No showering. No TV. No work."

"Do you support the death penalty?" I asked.

"Yes, I support it."

"Could you throw the switch on the electric chair?"

"No, I couldn't do that. I would look at him in the eye and murder him."

Goosebumps rose on my skin. Finally, I was getting closer to the essence that embodies JJ. His response rang true.

He continued, "If I pulled the switch, I'd be killing someone for the guards. No. With Ben and Eric, that was for me, not for anyone else, only myself."

Though JJ said he supported the death penalty, especially for inmates who keep killing others and making trouble for others, he did not wish the death penalty for himself.

"If the person is changed in prison, then I don't

think the death penalty is needed," he said.

JJ's world is controlled and absolute, without room for many options. Prison is an environment in which he seemed to thrive. The rules are clear and unchanging, swift and substantial. He no longer had to pretend to feel things he did not feel or do something for the approval of his parents or friends. He could exist in the prison world just as he was, and so could the other prisoners. Communication between prisoner to prisoner and prisoner to guard was understood. Punishment would be exacting and swift.

"Living in here is almost the same as living free, except we can't have women or drugs or alcohol. Other things, like shopping, watching movies, stuff like that, it's the same as on the outside."

On even days of the month, JJ was allowed to go outside in the yard for fresh air. It was there that he played handball. He washed laundry on the weekends, or rather, his housekeeper did it for him. Prison simplified his life for him, broke it into manageable chunks. He wears the same clothes and lives within the same walls. All the complications and complexities of life were pared down to their essentials, the basic building blocks of living: eat, sleep, work. In an environment where one was expected to feel depressed or sad, or aggrieved, JJ showed no signs of these things. He was where he belonged. He seemed to accept his fate and even embraced it.

Chapter 42

A Stable Future

Analysis begins with the crime scene, as the interaction between the offender and the victim can highlight a number of factors: the approach to the victim, the nature of the physical interaction, the nature of the sexual interaction, if any, choice of weapon, the matter of death, and the method of body disposal. All of these factors can also help determine the criminal experience and skill of the offender.

—<u>Serial Murder: Pathways for Investigations</u>

by Robert Morton, Jennifer Tillman, and Stephanie Gaines of the FBI Behavioral Analysis Unit, National Center for the Analysis of Violent Crime

I drove the now-familiar entranceway into Atwater USP. I entered the same waiting area; it looked like the walls had a fresh coat of paint. A group of visitors stood around me. There was one white woman who walked in ahead of me. There was an Asian woman with long black hair. A Latino mother with two young sons waited as well. There was a Black family, a wife with her brother and sister.

The guard behind the desk looked like a gang member. He had shoulder-length hair and wore a San Francisco Giants baseball cap with sunglasses balanced on the visor. He was wearing a Giants tee-shirt and cargo pants. Dark tattoos lined his right forearm. The guard processed and directed us to our seats.

Guards escorted the prisoners into the visiting area. JJ recognized me quickly and stepped over to our sitting area. He was signing better now and seemed comfortable. He told me his sister had recently visited.

"Joelle and Johnny-boy came to visit last Saturday and Sunday," he told me. "Joelle cried a lot, but I cried too.

I had not seen her since I left for Gallaudet in 2000. I didn't see her at my trial either. Joelle was here in the area doing some training for the Army, something about a computer entry job. She even remembered some signs and knew the ABCs."

We engaged in a few minutes of chit-chat; then, it was time to get him some food. JJ asked for a Pepsi and pepperoni pizza from the vending machines. JJ explained that the prison store sells pizza with sauce, but no cheese or pepperoni. He had to buy each one separately. He said he would buy a block of cheese and make a homemade grater with a bottle cap. He would poke holes in the top to make small spikes to grate the cheese.

I was curious about JJ's familial relationships, especially with Patrick. Though he seemed proud of his Chamorro culture, I was surprised to learn of the physical harm he inflicted on Patrick. He told me that his family stays within the Chamorro culture; his two sisters married Chamorro men, and Patrick was engaged to a Chamorro woman.

"In the trial transcript, I read that you seriously hurt Patrick a few times. What was that about?"

JJ responded, "The attorney wanted Patrick to use that to highlight my mental state. It was all about trying to help me in court. Patrick and I were very close, though. He knows I would never try to hurt him.

"When I was in the mental hospital, I tried to act mentally ill. I would talk to myself. The nurses and staff stood around watching me and laughed to themselves. They probably knew I wasn't mentally ill."

JJ's defense strategy at his trial did not work. Since his incarceration, JJ said he had not had one episode of violence. In fact, he said he was considered a model prisoner at Atwater. I asked him whether he had a prison psychologist or counselor to whom he talks.

"They have a psychologist here, but I don't need one. I am one hundred percent normal. Other inmates who see the psychologist are made fun of here. There are only a very few here who are truly mentally ill."

He told me that some of the prisoners have other types of issues. Particular inmates stood out among the group.

"Crankshaft was very hairy. He has hair on his arms, chest, neck, and back. He is hunched over. His arms are long. He has big ears. Everyone makes fun of him, but I feel sorry for him. One day Crankshaft and I were writing to each other to communicate. He used a big word that I didn't know. I didn't want to tell him I didn't know because

I would be embarrassed. He asked me why I was in here. I told him he should never ask another prisoner that. Other inmates had told me that Crankshaft was very, very smart. Later, someone got mad at him and beat him up in his cell. There was blood all over the place. I don't know why, but I've always had a soft spot in my heart for those who are different."

The irony of his statement was not lost on me. JJ had murdered two friends whom he considered different, Eric with cerebral palsy and Ben with unusual sign language and mannerisms.

"Did you feel sorry for Eric?" I ask.

"Yes, I felt sorry that he had cerebral palsy. Eric was a very happy boy. He was always smiling. He never had any troubles." JJ pauses. "If I had confided in a social worker or psychologist or Melani about my stealing problems, maybe I wouldn't have killed anyone. I was ashamed, though, to admit my problems. Stealing was like an addiction. I don't know why I did it. I had plenty of money."

I waited to see what JJ would offer next. He seemed deep in thought, but guarded.

"I can't remember what color Eric's hair was. I can't really remember any details about him at all," he says.

"But I did consider Anna, Chad, Cappy, Sara, Laney, Manda, Ben, and Eric as friends. They were my friends."

JJ changed the subject, and I went with it.

"Last night, I made chili with onions and peppers and tomatoes," he says.

This reminded me of when he was a student at Gallaudet. He and Melani often cooked food in their rooms.

"I bought the ingredients privately from someone who stole them from the kitchen," he continued. "The vegetables cost about ninety cents each. I mixed them with beans, spices, and hotdogs. The other inmates love my cooking."

JJ told me that the recreation counselor posted an advertisement in the common area asking for donations of clothes, blankets, and shoes for babies abandoned at the local hospital. JJ said that he and many inmates felt compelled to donate items to "the innocent babies."

"One inmate can crochet and knit beautiful things," he said. "It will probably cost about $80 for yarn and the inmate's time to make a blanket and pillowcase. I ordered one for him to make as my donation."

An inmate approached us. JJ had paid for two tickets to have our pictures taken, one for him, one for me. The inmate responsible for taking the picture asked us to stand against a cinder block wall painted with a tropical background. We smiled for the camera. JJ said he would mail me the picture when it was developed.

Afterward, we walked back to our seats. JJ told me he watched a movie called *Time Machine*, where people can travel through time. In the film, the husband kept going back in time to do things differently so his wife would not die. Even though the circumstances changed, the wife's death date stayed the same.

I asked, "If you could go back in time, would you change how things came about at Gallaudet?"

"I couldn't change their death date," he responded.

"But couldn't you change your involvement with their deaths?" I asked.

"Yes, I wish I could change everything from the past. I apologized to my sister, Joelle, for all the pain I caused to my family, my friends, Eric's and Ben's families. I wish I could go back and change it all. Joelle told me that the past is the past. It's important to focus on my future."

"And when you think about your future, that you will always be in prison, what do you think about?" I ask.

"I don't know. That I'll have a stable future."

He said he has thought about transferring from a maximum-security prison to a medium-security one. He explained that he meets with a team of four staff members who review his behavior, involvement with the prison programs, and restitution fees paid to the court every six months.

"I'm not ready to transfer to the medium-security prison, though. I know everyone here. I know the system. I don't know how long I'll be ready. Maybe another five or ten years. The medium-security prison will have more programs, more privileges, more freedom."

Almost two years had passed since my first visit to JJ. Melani was now married and had a baby girl. I asked JJ what he thinks about all that, now that he sees his childhood love creating the life she had once planned with him.

"I'm happy for her. I'm happy that she has a good life."

"Doesn't it make you sad?"

"No, I really feel happy. When I talked with Joelle about Melani, Joelle started to cry. She hadn't seen her in such a long time."

I asked JJ about his uncle, whom he was reluctant to discuss when we first met.

"My uncle is still here in Atwater. He's serving his forty-fourth year in prison. He stays alone in his room all day. He doesn't socialize with anyone."

JJ had crafted a different life inside his prison world. He made friends with other inmates. He explained that the Island boys now come from Vietnam, the Philippines, and Guam. He wakes up at 5:00 a.m. for work and mixes a cup of Taster's Choice instant coffee with water. He leaves his cell in a particular order, coffee in one place, the bed made without wrinkles, to see if someone had gone into his cell when he was gone. Then he starts his routine again, every day almost identical to the one before it.

We ended the day with a discussion about pets in prison. He explained prisoners had all manner of pets. Some had snakes; others had frogs; still, others had crickets.

"The inmates catch bees and flies and spiders to feed to their pets. They even make homes for them with mud and grass that they get outside. They put out little bowls of water.

"One inmate has a black widow spider. It's fascinating," he said. "The black widow uses two of its legs to spin a web and trap its prey. It bites the prey and leaves it alone. Then it comes back later to wrap it up and eat it. It's all very fascinating. When another spider is put in with it, it mates. Then she lays her eggs in one of those web cocoons. Then she kills the other spider."

Chapter 43

An Unfolding, Continuous Loop Of Time

July 16, 2011, was the last time I saw JJ face-to-face. The routine began the same way, the prison lobby full. Families entered the visiting room and found their assigned seats. Two families had young children. Their incarcerated loved ones came into the room and rushed to them. They held their children and played games with them. They helped the children open their food wrappers.

JJ walked in and sat opposite me. Unprompted, I picked up my back of quarters and asked him what he wanted to eat. Apparently, he realized this would be our last visit; he ordered a large meal.

"I'll have a pizza, burrito, Cheetos, Lays sour cream chips, and a Pepsi."

I planned to wrap up any remaining questions and push a little more to see if JJ would reveal more of himself.

"How does a person adapt to a life coming from full freedom to a maximum-security prison?" I asked.

"It's like there are two worlds. There is the prison world and the free world. When I first arrived here, I was only one percent or two percent in the prison world and ninety-nine percent in the free world. Now that I've been here for ten years, I am about forty percent in the prison world and sixty percent in the free world."

"For you, what do you consider the 'free world?'"

"In here, the prison world, I only think about myself. I think about what's happening today, now, and my future. In here, it's all about me. Sometimes when I'm at work, I will daydream about the outside world, the free world.

"One time, a new inmate threw a piece of metal at me at work just to pester me. I had to explain to him that he needs to read people's body language. If they're in another world, then let them be."

JJ shared memories of himself in the free world with his family when he was younger, before going to

Gallaudet.

"When I was younger at school, I used to be mischievous. When I was fifteen, sixteen, and seventeen, I used to do things, but really only for fun. When I went to MSSD, I would punch in the walls or kick holes. I wasn't angry. It was just for fun. It was easy to make holes and then watch the staff at MSSD fix it. MSSD would have to pay for it.

"I used to have a teacher who had really blue eyes. One day, my watch reflected the sun; I aimed at her so it would shine in her eyes. The teacher became really frustrated. I told her, 'If you want me to be a good student, then you have to give me cake.' That's what I was like.

"When I flew home to Guam, my father didn't say anything about it. Patrick said, 'Shh, come here. Someone from school called Dad and said something about a watch.' My father never said a thing to me about it.

"One time, a friend and I went into a store and had planned to steal a porn DVD. We each put a DVD into our shirts. I walked through the scanner but didn't hear the alarm. Someone from the store followed me out. I went into another store and tossed the DVD onto a shelf, but the person caught me.

"Later, my father picked me up because he was

attending some kind of training nearby. We drove onto base and parked at the store. My father said, 'Don't steal anything from the store, okay?' I obeyed him. I didn't do it.

"But something changed when I turned eighteen and nineteen. I don't know why, but things were building up inside me. Then I hurt people. It was like something else was controlling my mind. I don't know what was going on. But when I was arrested and went to jail, the thoughts of wanting to hurt people disappeared. I've never had any other thoughts about hurting anyone."

JJ had plenty of time to think about his past. Though he considered his family upstanding and strict, JJ knew he was different from them, and not just by being deaf. He had trouble following rules. He was impulsive and greedy. He enjoyed disrupting others' lives, yet he was committed to his family. He had broken rules, crossed boundaries, and annihilated trust, yet remained protected by a strong family structure. Perhaps prison life was a proxy for his family unit. It provided the discipline, both formal and informal, for infractions. It offered protection and trust to a certain degree. It was a family that JJ had not been born into, yet it was something with whom he would spend the rest of his life.

I asked, "How do you get along in here?"

"I show them that I am not soft, that I'm smart. One time I was betting on a game. I put fifteen stamps down."

"Stamps?"

"Yes, we can't have actual money here. So, we buy books of stamps and use them like money. That is how I paid for the things that I needed to buy.

"I put down fifteen stamps. I won the bet, but the inmate who collected the stamps said I only put down ten. I told him, 'Come on, I know I put down fifteen.' He knew it, and I knew it, but he kept denying it. So, from then on, I only put down a dollar's worth and made him count the stamps in front of me. I have plenty of money, so I don't make a big deal out of it. But I have to show them that I'm smart."

The prisoners played card games for money. JJ and another inmate, Rafa, often paired together to win poker, pinochle, dominoes, and spades. He had recently won $30 on a two-dollar bet.

"There are three kinds of prisoners here," JJ says. "The first kind is experienced inmates, like those who transfer from other prisons. The second kind of prisoner is the one who is excited because it's something new. The third kind is depressed. When I first came here, I was depressed. It took me a long time to learn prison culture.

On my first day here, the captain introduced me to the other Islanders. One was from Saipan, and another was from Samoa. That helped me a lot."

JJ now had a cellmate. He said his roommate was sentenced to life because of having two ounces of methamphetamine and prior arrests. His roommate wanted to get a pen pal from an online website.

The inmate with the camera approached us for the second time during my visits. JJ had purchased two more photos. We stood again in front of the wall and smiled toward the camera. When we were finished, we walked back to our chairs.

"Did anyone in your family ever ask you why you killed Eric and Ben?"

"No, they never asked."

"Really? No one? Not Joella, Fina, Patrick? Not even your parents?"

"No, we never talked about it. I apologized to them for doing all of this, but they never asked me anything more."

It seemed that JJ's experiences in his family and those in prison were eerily similar. His family never asked him why he killed Eric and Ben. The prisoners never ask each other what they did and why, their experiences suppressed somewhere deep inside. JJ said that he'd had plenty of opportunities to steal, connive, and deceive in prison. He claimed he does not, that he no longer has the compulsions or urges to do that in prison. The consequences of doing those things in this environment would be much more dangerous. His JJ's survival instincts had taken over.

JJ prided himself on his work ethic, something his father had instilled in him when he was young. He said that even though many of his coworkers fall asleep on the job, don't do their work, or go home early, he does not. He takes on the extra work without complaint.

"I'm not an ass-kisser with the guards," JJ said. "I don't flatter them or ask for special favors. I focus on myself and try to have a better life."

"If you were released from prison. Do you think whatever was inside of you would come back?" I asked.

"No. I would remember what prison is like. I'd push any urges I had to the side."

"Are those urges gone or still somewhere deep inside you?"

"I don't know. I think maybe they're gone. I will be here forever. So now, prison is my home."

JJ's life unfolded in a single, continuous loop of

time. His life in the prison world was a mock-up of what he should have created in the outside world. When it was time to end our visit, JJ thanked me for visiting and buying him food. He said he hoped he would see me again.

Though JJ speculated he would never kill again if he were to be released, I was not so sure. JJ lacked the introspection and reflection, the basic mechanisms of ordinary human functioning, to produce real change. That he did not murder any of the inmates does not translate into never murdering again. His lack of remorse, aside from disappointing his family, could not be reinstalled like a computer software program. I believe JJ was hard-wired to be who he was and continues to be.

Epilogue

On May 22, 2020, JJ sent me an unexpected email through the prison email communication system. JJ wrote he transferred to FCI Sheridan, a medium-security prison in Sheridan, Oregon. He apologized for the long delay in sending communication. He asked how Gallaudet and I had been doing. I told him we had been fine. I asked him what he had been doing at his new home. He wrote he is attending a group twice a month at the psychology department for lifers, who will remain in prison for the rest of their lives. He reported they talk about how to deal with the prison system and how to cope with life sentences. He wrote:

> *The major reason, for sure, why I am here is MONEY. It took my life. The education staff that I work for*

can't believe that I did what I did. I lower my head, not knowing how to respond to them. I wish I could have some magic to make everything turn back to the time of the murder and prior to it. I would have passed their rooms, Eric's and Ben's, and found a job instead. My crime makes no sense! Stupid mistakes. Big-time regrets. No repair.

With the email system, I did not have the luxury of prompting JJ to talk more. It seemed as though he had changed his thinking, but it is hard to know for sure with the type of person he is and where he is living. His following email gave me an indication of what prompted his first correspondence. He wanted something from me.

May 24, 2000

I hope you're enjoying the Memorial Day weekend. You're lucky that you can always find something to do when you're bored. I'm so bored. I have nothing to read. I have always wanted to order books, but I don't have enough money. Would you please help order four books for me? I don't mean to ask you - I am hoping that you don't mind. I want to stay away from being bored. Each book should cost less than $8, but I can't be sure. Please understand that I will not be able to pay you back because *my work pay is no good -- $18 a month. I need it for email and commissary.*

I read your email. You're still asking a lot of questions. Ha-ha. So, I need time to answer each question. Yesterday I was thinking -- first of all, I want to thank you for thinking of me as a friendly and caring person. Every time I think about the bad choices I made in the first place, I regret it and I am angry at myself. But, it helps me understand better why it happened. Like I said in the last email, money took my life. Money provides everything in life -- food, clothes, house, pay bills, etc. Wise people consider responsibilities for the care of their lives. I did it the other way. I was not wise. I always bought things that I never thought would mean anything in my life. I kept doing it until I was satisfied. But it was never enough. I made it a habit. As soon as I ran out of money, the habit pushed me into temptation of stealing money from people who worked very hard for themselves. :(I can feel a stab of pain in my chest when I think about this. I never meant to do them harm. I had always failed my promises that I would not do it again. I was helpless. I felt like the habit was out of control -- it controlled my life, especially mentally. It made me steal more and more. Why did I kill innocent people? I don't know! I always wish I could die for them and their families. A life sentence is something I do not deserve. Why not? They're dead and I am still alive. Is this justice fair to me and them? No.

A mistake teaches an important lesson. A regret teaches us not to do it again. Can I repair? I would say no because I will never be able to bring them back alive. It would make a big difference if I seek help from psychologists or social workers.

Teresa, it feels so good to get it off my chest. I've kept it to myself for a very long time. I will continue later, okay? Don't forget to let me know if you are okay with the book order.

JJ listed his four books, address, and instructions to send the books directly from the publishers. I never sent the books. JJ had polished his skills in manipulations, the same ones that were only developing in his youth. His next email was on May 25, 2020.

My childhood was... Horrible! I was the only person to make trouble in the family. I grew up stealing money from my relatives, grandfather, and teachers. My parents had been very upset and hurt. They begged me to stop doing it, but I couldn't help it. I think I learned it from people in school. My first steal was in elementary school... I was always bullied by some students. They took off and broke my hearing aids. I was hurt and very passive. I think that is maybe why I took it out on cats -- bullied and killed them. I didn't do it for fun. I remember after I hit and kicked one of my cats, it came back begging me to pet it. It makes me feel like I want to cry. I don't know if it knew I was bad. It knew only the good hearts of people. Cats and dogs are very good at providing love, even if they get bullied. If I go home, I want to own many pets. I want to make sure that they're taken good care of... I can only remember that Eric was funny and loved to talk, but I didn't talk much to him. Only Melani. Ben was quiet and liked to stay in his room. I'd hardly see him out. Teresa, I really don't know why I chose them as my murder victims. I didn't do it for fun. It was not because of [Eric] being crippled or something. Most of it in my confession isn't true! I talked too fast without thinking. Did I plan to kill them? No. I just happened to do it. All of the police questions. I answered YES to most of the questions because I didn't understand what those questions meant. See, I also didn't understand fully my rights. I went ahead and said that I understood. Because I was so scared, not thinking straight. You know what? I was going to appeal because I didn't understand the rights. I know I answered YES when I understood but I never knew or learned about the meaning of rights. As you can see, my English was REALLY poor at that time when I was in college. So, I know the bad choice I made -- only happened when I committed it. I'm doing the respectable time and I will not bother to appeal. Well... how's the weather in Maryland?

Subsequent emails from JJ took on a superficial tone, probably because he realized he was unsuccessful at convincing me to buy him things. He wrote about the COVID lockdown, about the quarantine, about making burritos for other inmates who would soon be released from FCI Sheridan. He stopped referring to the murders. He wrote he had received another email from Melani out of the blue. Then, on June 17, 2000, he sent another email:

Hafa adai and hello Teresa! I am sorry about the delay. I've been at work since two days ago. I feel better that I am out of the covid lockdown. I asked my boss if she can keep me at work throughout the lockdown. She will try, but can't promise. How are you doing? Good I hope. As for me, I am okay. Recently I was watching the local news on TV this morning and it's getting me disappointed and upset because there are 280 new cases in Oregon. FCI Sheridan was anticipating to return to the normal schedule in a few weeks. If you believe in God, I think He's angry at people who are disobedient and ignorant. He's given them a consequence of punishment. I am not sure if I am correct. What do you think? When do you think Gallaudet will reopen? Do you stay in touch with my old friends from Gallaudet or MSSD?

JJ was thinking about the free world. I am still in contact with his friends, but I do not tell him. The deaf world is small. We can always find each other in such a small world. I will not be a conduit for his messages to his friends. Had he asked his parents or siblings to send him books? Doubtful. Are they still keeping his prison account flush with money? Maybe not. Yet, JJ's true character is in keeping with how it has always been, but now there is seasoning, a honed set of skills. He seems to understand better that to manipulate people into doing what he wants, he needs to spend time wooing them, bringing them closer to what they want from him.

On March 19, 2021, another unexpected email arrived from JJ.

Hafa adai, Teresa. It has been almost one year since we've exchanged messages. Sorry for not getting in touch with you. I am not good at it. By the way, I am sending this message to see if your email address is still activated. I am hoping to go to other correctional facilities, maybe FCI Tucson or FCI Phoenix. A new change every 10 years is good for me. I've done almost fifteen years in USP Atwater. I hope all is well with you. :) I look forward to hearing from you soon. —JJ

His emails continued with increasing requests.

June 5, 2021

Good morning! How are you? I hope you are enjoying the weekend :) As for me, I am doing okay. Today I will go out to the rec yard and enjoy the sun. It will be 78 degrees. Later on tonight, I need to finish my Bible courses. I am a little behind because of my work schedule and because I have given my time to help teach others ASL. Oh, before I forget, I would like to write a letter to you. When I am bored, I write a letter or draw a picture. Something to do to keep myself busy. Can you please contact Christbook at [phone number] asap and see if they have ever sent my Dake's Annotated Reference Bible NKJV? I ordered it last month. I'm worried whether it was sent back for some reason or they don't have it in stock this time. That's why I'm asking for a little help in finding out for me. Hope to hear from you soon. Have a nice day :) —JJ

June 13, 2021

Can you please go to the IRS online today? Maybe you can type "where is my money?" or whatever you can do to find out about my second stimulus check of $1,800. I got the first one for $1,400. I've been waiting for the second one for nearly two months. Can you find out if it is canceled out for some reason or already printed and sent? That is all I need to know. If it's already sent off, I guess I have to wait a little more longer. My family got the second letter from the IRS for me and sent it out. They are not sure if it is a letter or check because they never opened the envelope. It should take minutes to find out. Thank you.

June 17, 2021

I would like to know if you can order a book for me before they adjust its current price? It costs only $7.99 plus postage and handling. It's Clearance Day. The order online is better and quick. If so, I will send you a money order to pay you back. Let me know. Thank you. They don't *accept any payment from Guam. I hope all is well with you.*

His final emails to me were on July 21 and July 25, 2021. He tells me that he's become a skilled craftsman after five years of being in the leather program. He writes that it helps him stay out of trouble. He worries about the Delta variant at the Tokyo Olympics. He says that last week the plumber tested positive for COVID-19. He and his inmate crew had to be quarantined for two weeks. He asks how it's going and advises me to take care and be safe. He hopes that I am enjoying the weekend.

Acknowledgments

Many people contributed to the creation of this book. Without their love, support, and assistance, the book would never have seen the light of day. My heartfelt thanks go first to my husband and children, Theodosios Margas, Selina Johnston, Diane Mason, and Alec Crowe. They encouraged me to continue forward even when I was ready to give up. They are my die-hard cheerleading troupe. I offer appreciation to my family members who were with me from the start but have since passed on to their heavenly homes: my mother, Patricia Ann Lintner, my father, Charles Robert Crowe, my belated husband, James Henry Mason, and my mother-in-law, Colene Ann Frederick. To Craig and Lois Plunkett, who allowed me to spend time with them to learn about the many wonders of Eric, thank you. To my creative team who made me look good. Thank you to my editor,

Alena Orrison, who polished my writing; my marketing specialist and mentor, Emily Moore; and my cover designer, Mary Budnitz, who brought my ideas into visual form. To the group of friends who brought this story to life, thank you: Chad, Manda, Sara, Cappy, Annalyn, and Chris. To my Gallaudet family, thank you to I. King Jordan, Jane Fernandez, Earl Parks, Tommy Farr, Mercy Coogan, and all of the former students who knew Eric Plunkett and Ben Varner.

ABOUT THE AUTHOR

Teresa Crowe has a Ph.D. in social work and is a licensed clinical social worker in Maryland and the District of Columbia. She specializes in behavioral health with deaf and hard-of-hearing adults. Since 2000, she has been a professor in the master of social work program at Gallaudet University. Dr. Crowe is fluent in American Sign Language and has been involved with the deaf community since 1987 when she learned ASL and later began working at the Maryland School for the Deaf. She has a master of fine arts degree in creative nonfiction from Goucher College. She lives with her husband and two dogs in Edgewater, Maryland, two blocks from Chesapeake Bay.

www.ingramcontent.com/pod-product-compliance
Lightning Source LLC
LaVergne TN
LVHW012245070526
838201LV00090B/130